D1633504

Daily Readings from J.C.Ryle

Volume 2

Daily Readings
from
J.C. RYLE

VOLUME 2
JOHN

Compiled by Robert Sheehan

 EVANGELICAL PRESS

EVANGELICAL PRESS
16/18 High Street, Welwyn, Hertfordshire, AL6 9EQ, England

© Evangelical Press 1985

First published 1985

Also available:

Daily Readings from J.C.Ryle
Volume 1 (Matthew, Mark and Luke)
ISBN 0 85234 164 4

Ryle, J.C.
  Daily readings from J.C.Ryle.
  Vol. 2
  1. Devotional calendars
  I. Title   II. Sheehan, Robert
  242'.2   BV4810

  ISBN 0-85234-214-4

Printed in Great Britain by The Bath Press, Avon.

Introduction

The enthusiastic reception of Volume I of *Daily Readings from J.C.Ryle* has encouraged me to produce this second volume, based on Ryle's *Expository Thoughts on St John's Gospel* and his sermon on John 21:15-17. In forming J.C.Ryle's commentaries into daily readings there has inevitably been a considerable amount of editing, but it has been my aim to bring a large proportion of the treasure from Ryle's abundant store.

On each day there are two things which are not extracted from Bishop Ryle's writings. They are the additional reading, which has been chosen because it emphasizes one of the themes in Ryle's exposition, and the closing meditation, which seeks to focus attention on one particular point for further thought throughout the day.

My thanks to the staff of Evangelical Press, who coped with a cut-and-paste manuscript, and to my wife, who always gives encouragement and to whom this volume is dedicated. They, I and Ryle will, to use his words, 'be more than repaid' if the result of this volume is 'to exalt the Lord Jesus Christ and make him beautiful and glorious in the eyes of men and to promote the increase of repentance, faith and holiness upon earth'.

Robert Sheehan

Suggestions for the use of these daily readings

1.   As Ryle is commenting on the Word of God, the Holy Scriptures, seek God's aid in prayer to understand his Word aright. Make the psalmist's prayer your own (Ps. 119:18).

2.   Remember that Ryle is commenting on God's Word. It is infallible; he is not. It must be read; his comments are aids to understanding. Resist the temptation to read his comments but not to bother to read the Bible. Where references are given, look them up.

3.   God has given the Scriptures that through them our whole lives might be changed (2 Tim. 3:15-17). Read the Scriptures and the comments with the conscious aim of reading to understand and apply what is read to your life (James 1:22-25).

4.   Avoid that state of mind that reads in order to quieten the conscience and which is satisfied with a superficial skimming of the surface of the truth. Read and think. There is a blessing promised to those who meditate on God's Word (Ps. 1:2,3).

5.   Attempt to memorize some of the Scriptures that you read. Memorized Scripture is a useful weapon in our battles with Satan (Matt. 4:1-11) and our obedience to God (Ps. 119:11).

Suggested further reading: *Colossians 1:15-18*

The Gospel of St John, which begins with these verses, is in many respects very unlike the other three Gospels. But it is enough to remember that Matthew, Mark, Luke and John wrote under the direct inspiration of God. In the general plan of their respective Gospels and in the particular details, in everything that they record and in everything that they do not record, they were all four equally and entirely guided by the Holy Ghost.

About the matters which St John was specially inspired to relate in his Gospel one general remark will suffice. The things which are peculiar to his Gospel are among the most precious possessions of the church of Christ. No one of the four Gospel writers has given us such full statements about the divinity of Christ, about justification by faith, about the offices of Christ, about the work of the Holy Ghost and about the privileges of believers as we read in the pages of St John.

The five verses now before us contain a statement of matchless sublimity concerning the divine nature of our Lord Jesus Christ. He it is, beyond all question, whom St John means when he speaks of 'the Word'. No doubt there are heights and depths in that statement which are far beyond man's understanding. And yet there are plain lessons in it which every Christian would do well to treasure up in his mind.

Our Lord Jesus Christ is eternal. St John tells us that 'In the beginning was the Word.' He did not begin to exist when the heavens and the earth were made. Much less did he begin to exist when the gospel was brought into the world. He had glory with the Father 'before the world was' (John 17:5). He was existing when matter was first created and before time began. He was 'before all things' (Col. 1:17). He was from all eternity.

For meditation: *Our Lord is the great unifying theme of all Scripture because he is not a word to us among many, but **the** Word.*

Suggested further reading: Hebrews 1:1-14

Our Lord Jesus Christ is a person distinct from God the Father
and yet one with him. St John tells us that 'The Word was with
God.' The Father and the Word, though two persons, are
joined by an ineffable union. Where God the Father was from
all eternity, there also was the Word, even God the Son — their
glory equal, their majesty co-eternal and yet their Godhead
one. This is a great mystery! Happy is he who can receive it as a
little child without attempting to explain it.

The Lord Jesus Christ is very God. St John tells us that 'The
Word was God.' He is not merely a created angel, or a being
inferior to God the Father and invested by him with power to
redeem sinners. He is nothing less than perfect God — equal to
the Father as touching his Godhead, God of the substance of
the Father, begotten before the worlds.

The Lord Jesus Christ is the Creator of all things. St John
tells us that 'By him were all things made, and without him was
not anything made that was made.' So far from being a
creature of God, as some heretics have falsely asserted, he is the
being who made the worlds and all that they contain. 'He commanded and they were created' (Ps. 148:5).

The Lord Jesus Christ is the source of all spiritual life and
light. St John tells us that 'In him was life; and the life was the
light of men.' He is the eternal fountain, from which alone the
sons of men have ever derived life. The vast majority of mankind in every age have refused to know him, have forgotten the
Fall and their own need of a Saviour. The light has been constantly shining 'in darkness'. The most have 'not comprehended the light'. But if any men and women out of the countless
millions of mankind have ever had spiritual life and light, they
have owed all to Christ.

For meditation: *Our Lord has life in himself and is light. All
life, whether physical or spiritual, and all light, all goodness and
truth, have him as their source.*

Suggested further reading: Philippians 2:5-11

These wonderful verses appear to contain much in them, without controversy, which is above our reason, but there is nothing contrary to it. There is much that we cannot explain and must be content humbly to believe. Let us, however, never forget that there are plain practical consequences flowing from the passage which we can never grasp too firmly, or know too well.

Would we know, for one thing, the exceeding sinfulness of sin? Let us often read these first five verses of St John's Gospel. Let us mark what kind of being the Redeemer of mankind must needs be, in order to provide eternal redemption for sinners. If no one less than the eternal God, the Creator and Preserver of all things, could take away the sin of the world, sin must be a far more abominable thing in the sight of God than most men suppose. The right measure of sin's sinfulness is the dignity of him who came into the world to save sinners. If Christ is so great, then sin must indeed be sinful!

Would we know, for another thing, the strength of a true Christian's foundation for hope? Let us often read these first five verses of St John's Gospel. Let us mark that the Saviour in whom the believer is bid to trust is nothing less than the eternal God, one able to save to the uttermost all that come to the Father by him. He that was 'with God' and 'was God' is also 'Emmanuel, God with us'. Let us thank God that our help is laid on one that is mighty (Ps. 89:19). In ourselves we are great sinners. But in Jesus Christ we have a great Saviour. He is a strong foundation-stone, able to bear the weight of a world's sin. He that believeth on him shall not be confounded (1 Peter 2:6).

For meditation: *Only a man could die as a substitute for men, but only God could die as a substitute for millions of men. Therefore Christ, as God and man, is the very Saviour we need.*

Suggested further reading: Acts 20:17-24

St John, after beginning his Gospel with a statement of our Lord's nature as God, proceeds to speak of his forerunner, John the Baptist. The contrast between the language used about the Saviour and that used about his forerunner ought not to be overlooked. Of Christ we are told that he was the eternal God, the Creator of all things, the source of life and light. Of John the Baptist we are told simply that 'There was a man sent from God, whose name was John.'

We see in these verses the true nature of a Christian minister's office. We have it in the description of John the Baptist. He 'came for a witness, to bear witness of the Light, that all men through him might believe'. Christian ministers are not priests, nor mediators between God and man. They are not agents into whose hands men may commit their souls and carry on their religion by deputy. They are witnesses. They are intended to bear testimony to God's truth and specially to the great truth that Christ is the only Saviour and light of the world. This was St Peter's ministry on the Day of Pentecost: 'With many other words did he *testify*' (Acts 2:40). This was the whole tenor of St Paul's ministry: '*Testifying* both to the Jews and also to the Greeks, repentance toward God, and faith toward our Lord Jesus Christ' (Acts 20:21). Unless a Christian minister bears a full testimony to Christ, he is not faithful to his office. So long as he does testify of Christ, he has done his part and will receive his reward, although his hearers may not believe his testimony. Until a minister's hearers believe on that Christ of whom they are told, they receive no benefit from the ministry. They may be pleased and interested, but they are not profited until they believe. The great end of a minister's testimony is 'that through him, men may believe'.

For meditation: *Your minister may have many faults – and is probably more aware of them than you are – but, if he preaches Christ, value him.*

Suggested further reading: John 3:16-21

We see in these verses one principal position which our Lord Jesus Christ occupies towards mankind. We have it in the words: He 'was the true light, which lighteth every man that cometh into the world'.

Christ is to the souls of men what the sun is to the world. He is the centre and source of all spiritual light, warmth, life, health, growth, beauty and fertility. Like the sun, he shines for the common benefit of all mankind — for high and for low, for rich and for poor, for Jew and for Greek. Like the sun, he is free to all. All may look at him and drink health out of his light. If millions of mankind were mad enough to dwell in caves underground, or to bandage their eyes, their darkness would be their own fault and not the fault of the sun. So, likewise, if millions of men and women love spiritual 'darkness rather than light', the blame must be laid on their blind hearts and not on Christ.

We see in these verses the desperate wickedness of man's natural heart. We have it in the words: Christ 'was in the world, and the world was made by him, and the world knew him not. He came unto his own, and his own received him not.' He came to the very people whom he had brought out from Egypt and purchased for his own. He came to the Jews, whom he had separated from other nations and to whom he had revealed himself by the prophets. He came to those very Jews who had read of him in the Old Testament Scriptures, seen him under types and figures in their temple services and professed to be waiting for his coming. And yet, when he came, those very Jews received him not. They even rejected him, despised him and slew him. Well may the natural heart be called 'desperately wicked'!

For meditation: *No statement during our Lord's earthly ministry is more tragic than his rebuke to unbelieving Jews (Matt. 23:37).*

Suggested further reading:　Galatians 3:26-4:7

We see in these verses the vast privileges of all who receive Christ and believe on him. We are told that 'As many as received him, to them gave he power to become the sons of God, even to them that believe on his name.'

Christ will never be without some servants. If the vast majority of the Jews did not receive him as the Messiah, there were, at any rate, a few who did. To them he gave the privilege of being God's children. He adopted them as members of his Father's family. He reckoned them his own brethren and sisters, bone of his bone and flesh of his flesh. He conferred on them a dignity which was ample recompense for the cross which they had to carry for his sake. He made them sons and daughters of the Lord Almighty.

Privileges like these, be it remembered, are the possession of all, in every age, who receive Christ by faith and follow him as their Saviour. They are 'children of God by faith in Christ Jesus' (Gal. 3:26). They are born again by a new and heavenly birth and adopted into the family of the King of kings. Few in number, and despised by the world as they are, they are cared for with infinite love by a Father in heaven who, for his Son's sake, is well pleased with them. In time he provides them with everything that is for their good. In eternity he will give them a crown of glory that fadeth not away. These are great things! But faith in Christ gives men an ample title to them. Good masters care for their servants and Christ cares for his.

Are we ourselves sons of God? Have we been born again? Have we the marks which always accompany the new birth — sense of sin, faith in Jesus, love of others, righteous living, separation from the world? Let us never be content till we can give a satisfactory answer to these questions.

For meditation:　*The idea of his being a child of God filled John with praise, anticipation and longings to be holy (1 John 3:1-3). What does it do for you?*

Suggested further reading: Hebrews 2:14-18

The main truth which this verse teaches is the reality of our
Lord Jesus Christ's incarnation or being made man. St John
tells us that 'The Word was made flesh, and dwelt among us.'
   The plain meaning of these words is that our divine Saviour
really took human nature upon him, in order to save sinners.
He really became a man like ourselves in all things, sin only
excepted. Like ourselves, he was born of a woman, though
born in a miraculous manner. Like ourselves, he grew from
infancy to boyhood and from boyhood to man's estate, both in
wisdom and in stature (Luke 2:52). Like ourselves, he
hungered, thirsted, ate, drank, slept, was wearied, felt pain,
wept, rejoiced, marvelled, was moved to anger and compassion. Having become flesh and taken a body, he prayed,
read the Scriptures, suffered, being tempted, and submitted his
human will to the will of God the Father. And finally, in the
same body, he really suffered and shed his blood, really died,
was really buried, really rose again and really ascended up into
heaven. And yet all this time he was God as well as man!
   This constant undivided union of two perfect natures in
Christ's person is exactly that which gives infinite value to his
mediation and qualifies him to be the very Mediator that sinners need. Our Mediator is one who can sympathize with us,
because he is very man. And yet at the same time he is one who
can deal with the Father for us on equal terms, because he is
very God. It is the same union which gives infinite value to his
righteousness, when imputed to believers. It is the righteousness of one who was God as well as man. It is the same union
which gives infinite value to the atoning blood which he shed
for sinners on the cross. It is the blood of one who was God as
well as man.

For meditation: *God the Son shares with us a common
experience of living in a fallen world. His understanding of us is
not therefore theoretical but personally experienced.*

Suggested further reading: *Ephesians 1:3-14*

Did the Word become flesh? Then he is one who can be touched with the feeling of his people's infirmities, because he has suffered himself, being tempted. He is almighty, because he is God, and yet he can feel with us, because he is man.

Did the Word become flesh? Then he can supply us with a perfect pattern and example for our daily life. Had he walked among us as an angel or a spirit, we would never have copied him. But having dwelt among us as a man, we know that the true standard of holiness is to 'walk even as he walked' (1 John 2:6). He is a perfect pattern, because he is God. But he is also a pattern exactly suited to our wants, because he is man.

It is Christ alone who supplies all the spiritual wants of all believers. It is written that 'Of his fulness have we all received, and grace for grace.'

There is an infinite fulness in Jesus Christ. As St Paul says, 'It pleased the Father that in him should all fulness dwell.' 'In him are hid all the treasures of wisdom and knowledge' (Col. 1:19; 2:3). There is laid up in him, as in a treasury, a boundless supply of all that any sinner can need, either in time or in eternity. The Spirit of life is his special gift to the church and conveys from him, as from a great root, sap and vigour to all the believing branches. He is rich in mercy, grace, wisdom, righteousness, sanctification and redemption. Out of Christ's fulness, all believers in every age of the world have been supplied. They did not clearly understand the fountain from which their supplies flowed in Old Testament times. The Old Testament saints only saw Christ afar off and not face to face. But from Abel downwards, all saved souls have received all they have had from Jesus Christ alone. Every saint in glory will at last acknowledge that he is Christ's debtor for all he is. Jesus will prove to have been all in all.

For meditation: *Every blessing that God gives may be summarized by one word – Christ. With him all things are freely given to us (Rom. 8:32).*

Suggested further reading: 2 Corinthians 3:6-11

Moses was employed by God 'as a servant', to convey to Israel the moral and ceremonial law (Heb. 3:5). As a servant, he was faithful to him who appointed him, but he was only a servant. The moral law, which he brought down from Mount Sinai, was holy and just and good. But it could not justify. It had no healing power. It could wound, but it could not bind up. It 'worked wrath' (Rom. 4:15). It pronounced a curse against any imperfect obedience. The ceremonial law, which he was commanded to impose on Israel, was full of deep meaning and typical instruction. Its ordinances and ceremonies made it an excellent schoolmaster to guide men towards Christ (Gal. 3:24). But the ceremonial law was only a schoolmaster. It could not make him that kept it perfect, as pertaining to the conscience (Heb. 9:9). It laid a grievous yoke on men's hearts, which they were not able to bear. It was a ministration of death and condemnation (2 Cor. 3:7-9). The light which men got from Moses and the law was at best only starlight compared to noonday.

    Christ, on the other hand, came into the world 'as a Son', with the keys of God's treasury of grace and truth entirely in his hands (Heb. 3:6). Grace came by him when he made fully known God's gracious plan of salvation by faith in his own blood and opened the fountain of mercy to all the world. Truth came by him when he fulfilled in his own person the types of the Old Testament and revealed himself as the true sacrifice, the true mercy-seat and the true Priest. No doubt there was much of 'grace and truth' under the law of Moses. But the whole of God's grace and the whole truth about redemption were never known until Jesus came into the world and died for sinners.

For meditation: *The requirements of the law are very demanding (Gal. 3:10), but salvation is a gift of grace (Acts 15:10,11).*

Suggested further reading: John 14:8-11

It is Christ alone who has revealed God the Father to man. It is written that 'No man hath seen God at any time; the only begotten Son, which is in the bosom of the Father, he hath declared him.'

The eye of mortal man has never beheld God the Father. No man could bear the sight. Even to Moses it was said, 'Thou canst not see my face: for there shall no man see me, and live' (Exod. 33:20). Yet all that mortal man is capable of knowing about God the Father is fully revealed to us by God the Son. He, who was in the bosom of the Father from all eternity, has been pleased to take our nature upon him and to exhibit to us, in the form of a man, all that our minds can comprehend of the Father's perfections. In Christ's words and deeds and life and death we learn as much concerning God the Father as our feeble minds can at present bear. His perfect wisdom, his almighty power, his unspeakable love to sinners, his incomparable holiness, his hatred of sin could never be represented to our eyes more clearly than we see them in Christ's life and death. In truth, 'God was manifest in the flesh,' when the Word took on him a body (1 Tim. 3:16). 'He was the brightness of the Father's glory, and the express image of his person' (Heb. 1:3). He says himself, 'I and my Father are one' (John 10:30). 'He that hath seen me hath seen the Father' (John 14:9). 'In him dwelleth all the fulness of the Godhead bodily' (Col. 2:9). These are deep and mysterious things. But they are true.

And now, after reading this passage, can we ever give too much honour to Christ? Can we ever think too highly of him? Christ is the meeting-point between the Trinity and the sinner's soul.

For meditation: *Our understanding of the character of God need not be vague and indistinct, because our Lord has lived as God with us and made him known.*

Suggested further reading: Luke 22:24-27

John the Baptist was an eminent saint of God. There are few names which stand higher than his in the Bible calendar of great and good men. The Lord Jesus himself declared that 'Among them that are born of women there hath not risen a greater than John the Baptist' (Matt. 11:11). The Lord Jesus himself declared that he was 'a burning and a shining light' (John 5:35). Yet here in this passage we see this eminent saint lowly, self-abased and full of humility. He puts away from himself the honour which the Jews from Jerusalem were ready to pay him. He declines all flattering titles. He speaks of himself as nothing more than the 'voice of one crying in the wilderness' and as one who 'baptized with water'. He proclaims loudly that there is one standing among the Jews far greater than himself, one whose shoe-latchet he is not worthy to unloose. He claims honour not for himself, but for Christ. To exalt Christ was his mission and to that mission he steadfastly adhered.

If we profess to have any real Christianity, let us strive to be of John the Baptist's spirit. Let us study humility. This is the grace with which all must begin who would be saved. We have no true religion about us until we cast away our high thoughts and feel ourselves sinners. This is the grace which all saints may follow after and which none have any excuse for neglecting. All God's children have not gifts, or money, or time to work, or a wide sphere of usefulness, but all may be humble. This is the grace, above all, which will appear most beautiful in our latter end. Never shall we feel the need of humility so deeply as when we lie on our deathbeds and stand before the judgement-seat of Christ. Our whole lives will then appear a long catalogue of imperfections, ourselves nothing and Christ all.

For meditation: *All that we become and all that we accomplish is due to the grace of God at work in us (1 Cor. 15:10). Self-congratulation is, therefore, always wrong.*

Suggested further reading: 1 Corinthians 1:18-25

We have in these verses a mournful example of the blindness of unconverted men. That example is supplied by the state of the Jews who came to question John the Baptist.

These Jews professed to be waiting for the appearance of Messiah. Like all the Pharisees, they prided themselves on being children of Abraham and possessors of the covenants. They rested in the law and made their boast of God. They professed to know God's will and to believe God's promises. They were confident that they themselves were guides of the blind and lights of them that sat in darkness (Rom. 2:17-19). And yet at this very moment their souls were utterly in the dark. 'There was standing among them,' as John the Baptist told them, 'one whom they knew not.' Christ himself, the promised Messiah, was in the midst of them, and yet they neither knew him, nor saw him, nor received him, nor acknowledged him, nor believed him. And worse than this, the vast majority of them never would know him! The words of John the Baptist are a prophetic description of a state of things which lasted during the whole of our Lord's earthly ministry. Christ 'stood among the Jews' and yet the Jews knew him not and the greater part of them died in their sins.

It is a solemn thought that John the Baptist's words in this place apply strictly to thousands in the present day. Christ is still standing among many who neither see, nor know, nor believe. Christ is passing by in many a parish and many a congregation and the vast majority have neither an eye to see him, nor an ear to hear him. The spirit of slumber seems poured out upon them. Money and pleasure and the world they know, but they know not Christ. The kingdom of God is close to them, but they sleep. Salvation is within their reach, but they sleep.

For meditation: *It is not enough to be near to Christ, to listen to him and to admire his words and works. We must believe in him (Luke 13:24-27).*

Suggested further reading: 1 Peter 1:18-21

Let us notice in this passage the peculiar name which John the Baptist gives to Christ. He calls him 'the Lamb of God'.

This name did not merely mean, as some have supposed, that Christ was meek and gentle as a lamb. This would be truth, no doubt, but only a very small portion of the truth. There are greater things here than this! It meant that Christ was the great sacrifice for sin, who was come to make atonement for transgression by his own death upon the cross. He was the true Lamb which Abraham told Isaac at Moriah God would provide (Gen. 22:8). He was the true Lamb to which every morning and evening sacrifice in the temple had daily pointed. He was the Lamb of which Isaiah had prophesied that he would be 'brought to the slaughter' (Isa. 53:7). He was the true Lamb of which the Passover lamb in Egypt had been a vivid type. In short, he was the great propitiation for sin which God had covenanted from all eternity to send into the world. He was God's Lamb.

Let us take heed that, in all our thoughts of Christ, we first think of him as John the Baptist here represents him. Let us serve him faithfully as our Master. Let us obey him loyally as our King. Let us study his teaching as our Prophet. Let us walk diligently after him as our Example. Let us look anxiously for him as our coming Redeemer of body as well as soul. But above all, let us prize him as our sacrifice and rest our whole weight on his death as an atonement for sin. Let his blood be more precious in our eyes every year we live. Whatever else we glory in about Christ, let us glory above all things in his cross. This is the corner-stone, this is the citadel, this is the rule of true Christian theology. We know nothing rightly about Christ until we see him with John the Baptist's eyes and can rejoice in him as 'the Lamb that was slain'.

For meditation: *Only where God saw the blood of the lamb did the destroyer pass over in Egypt (Exod. 12:23). Christ our Passover Lamb is sacrificed (1 Cor. 5:7), so destruction will pass us by.*

Suggested further reading: *1 Peter 2:21-25*

Let us notice in this passage the peculiar work which John the Baptist describes Christ as doing. He says that 'He taketh away the sin of the world.'

Christ is a Saviour. He did not come on earth to be a conqueror, or a philosopher, or a mere teacher of morality. He came to save sinners. He came to do that which man could never do for himself — to do that which money and learning can never obtain, to do that which is essential to man's real happiness — he came to 'take away sin'.

Christ is a complete Saviour. He 'taketh away sin'. He did not merely make vague proclamations of pardon, mercy and forgiveness. He 'took' our sins upon himself and carried them away. He allowed them to be laid upon himself and 'bore them in his own body on the tree' (1 Peter 2:24). The sins of everyone that believes on Jesus are made as though they had never been sinned at all. The Lamb of God has taken them clean away.

Christ is an almighty Saviour and a Saviour for all mankind. He 'taketh away the sin of the world'. He did not die for the Jews only, but for the Gentile as well as the Jew. The payment that he made on the cross was more than enough to make satisfaction for the debts of all. The blood that he shed was precious enough to wash away the sins of all. His atonement on the cross was sufficient for all mankind, though efficient only to them that believe. The sin that he took up and bore on the cross was the sin of the whole world.

Last, but not least, Christ is a perpetual and unwearied Saviour. He 'taketh away' sin. He is daily taking it away from everyone that believes on him — daily purging, daily cleansing, daily washing the souls of his people, daily granting and applying fresh supplies of mercy.

For meditation: *My sin – oh, the bliss of this glorious thought! –*
                      My sin, not in part, but the whole,
                      Is nailed to the cross, and I bear it no more!
                      Praise the Lord! Praise the Lord! O my soul
                                          (H.G.Spafford).

Suggested further reading: Acts 15:6-11

Let us notice in this passage the peculiar office which John the Baptist attributes to Christ. He speaks of him as him 'which baptizeth with the Holy Ghost'.

The baptism here spoken of is not the baptism of water. It does not consist either of dipping or sprinkling. It does not belong exclusively either to infants or to grown-up people. It is not a baptism which any man can give, Episcopalian or Presbyterian, Independent or Methodist, layman or minister. It is a baptism which the great Head of the church keeps exclusively in his own hands. It consists of the implanting of grace into the inward man. It is the same thing with the new birth. It is a baptism, not of the body, but of the heart. It is a baptism which the penitent thief received, though neither dipped nor sprinkled by the hand of man. It is a baptism which Ananias and Sapphira did not receive, though admitted into church communion by apostolic men.

Let it be a settled principle in our religion that the baptism of which John the Baptist speaks here is the baptism which is absolutely necessary to salvation. The baptism of water is a most blessed and profitable ordinance and cannot be neglected without great sin. But the baptism of the Holy Ghost is of far greater importance. The man who dies with his heart not baptized by Christ can never be saved.

Let us ask ourselves, as we leave this passage, whether we are baptized with the Holy Ghost and whether we have any real interest in the Lamb of God. Thousands, unhappily, are wasting their time in controversy about water baptism and neglecting the baptism of the heart. Thousands more are content with a head-knowledge of the Lamb of God, or have never sought him by faith that their own sins may be actually taken away. Let us take heed that we ourselves have new hearts and believe to the saving of our souls.

For meditation: *The Pharisees were very concerned to have clean bodies. Our Lord was concerned with clean hearts (Matt. 15:1,2,10,11,16-20). Are you more concerned with your body or your soul?*

Suggested further reading: *1 Corinthians 2:1-5*

We see, for one thing, in these verses, what good is done by continually testifying of Christ. This simple story is a pattern of the way in which good has been done to souls in every age of the Christian church.By such testimony as that before us, and by none else, men and women are converted and saved. It is by exalting Christ, not the church, Christ, not the sacraments, Christ, not the ministry — it is by this means that hearts are moved and sinners are turned to God. To the world such testimony may seem weakness and foolishness. Yet, like the ram's horns before whose blast the walls of Jericho fell down, this testimony is mighty to the pulling down of strongholds. The story of the crucified Lamb of God has proved in every age the power of God unto salvation. Those who have done most for Christ's cause in every part of the world have been men like John the Baptist. They have not cried, 'Behold me!' or 'Behold the church!' or 'Behold the ordinances!' but 'Behold the Lamb!' If souls are to be saved, men must be pointed directly to Christ.

One thing, however, must never be forgotten. There must be patient continuance in preaching and teaching the truth, if we want good to be done. Christ must be set forth again and again as the 'Lamb of God which taketh away the sin of the world'. The story of grace must be told repeatedly, line upon line and precept upon precept. It is the constant dropping which wears away the stone. The promise shall never be broken that 'God's word shall not return unto him void' (Isa. 55:11). But it is nowhere said that it shall do good the very first time that it is preached. It was not the first proclamation of John the Baptist, but the second, which made Andrew and his companion follow Jesus.

For meditation: *Persistence in the work of evangelism, and in all service to God, has a promise of ultimate blessing connected to it (Gal. 6:9).*

Suggested further reading: Mark 5:18-20

No sooner does Andrew become a disciple than he tells his
brother Simon what a discovery he has made. Like one who has
unexpectedly heard good tidings, he hastens to impart it to the
one nearest and dearest to him. And to Andrew's outspoken
testimony, under God, the great apostle Peter owed the first
beginning of light in his soul.

The fact before us is most striking and instructive. Out of the
three first members of the Christian church, one at least was
brought to Jesus by the private, quiet word of a relative. He
seems to have heard no public preaching. He saw no mighty
miracle wrought. He was not convinced by any powerful
reasoning. He only heard his brother telling him that he had
found a Saviour himself and at once the work began in his soul.
The simple testimony of a warm-hearted brother was the first
link in the chain by which Peter was drawn out of the world and
joined to Christ. The first blow in that mighty work by which
Peter was made a pillar of the church was struck by Andrew's
words: 'We have found the Christ.'

Well would it be for the church of Christ, if all believers were
more like Andrew! Well would it be for souls, if all men and
women who have been converted themselves would speak to
their friends and relatives on spiritual subjects and tell them
what they have found! How much good might be done! How
many might be led to Jesus who now live and die in unbelief!
The work of testifying to the gospel of the grace of God ought
not to be left to ministers alone. All who have received mercy
ought to find a tongue and to declare what God has done for
their souls. Thousands, humanly speaking, would listen to a
word from a friend who will not listen to a sermon. Every
believer ought to be a home missionary, a missionary to his
family, children, servants, neighbours and friends.

For meditation: *Has every member of your family heard the
gospel at least once from you? If you do not evangelize them, who
will?*

Suggested further reading:　Acts 8:26-35

Let us observe, as we read these verses, how various are the paths by which souls are led into the narrow way of life.

We are told of a man named Philip being added to the little company of Christ's disciples. He does not appear to have been moved, like Andrew and his companions, by the testimony of John the Baptist. He was not drawn, like Peter, by the outspoken declaration of a brother. He seems to have been called directly by Christ himself and the agency of man seems not to have been used in his calling. Yet in faith and life he became one with those who were disciples before him. Though led by different paths, they all entered the same road, embraced the same truths, served the same Master and at length reached the same home.

The fact before us is a deeply important one. It throws light on the history of all God's people in every age and of every tongue. There are diversities of operations in the saving of souls. All true Christians are led by one Spirit, washed in one blood, serve one Lord, lean on one Saviour, believe one truth and walk by one general rule. But all are not converted in one and the same manner. All do not pass through the same experience. In conversion, the Holy Ghost acts as a sovereign.

We must beware of making the experience of other believers the measure of our own. We must beware of denying another's grace, because he has not been led by the same way as ourselves. Has a man got the real grace of God? This is the only question that concerns us. Is he a penitent man? Is he a believer? Does he live a holy life? Provided these inquiries can be answered satisfactorily, we may well be content. It matters nothing by what path a man has been led, if he has only been led at last into the right way.

For meditation:　*In accepting fellow believers it is not race, social standing, gender, etc. that matters, but their acceptance by our Lord (Gal. 3:28; Rom. 15:7).*

Suggested further reading: *2 Timothy 2:23-26*

Let us observe in these verses the good advice which Philip gave to Nathanael. The mind of Nathanael was full of doubts about the Saviour of whom Philip told him. 'Can there any good thing,' he said, 'come out of Nazareth?' And what did Philip reply? He said, 'Come and see.'

Wiser counsel than this it would be impossible to conceive! If Philip had reproved Nathanael's unbelief, he might have driven him back for many a day and given offence. If he had reasoned with him, he might have failed to convince him, or might have confirmed him in his doubts. But by inviting him to prove the matter for himself, he showed his entire confidence in the truth of his own assertion and his willingness to have it tested and proved. And the result shows the wisdom of Philip's words. Nathanael owed his early acquaintance with Christ to that frank invitation: 'Come and see'.

If we call ourselves true Christians, let us never be afraid to deal with people about their souls as Philip dealt with Nathanael. Let us invite them boldly to make proof of our religion. Let us tell them confidently that they cannot know its real value until they have tried it. Let us assure them that vital Christianity courts every possible inquiry. It has no secrets. It has nothing to conceal. Its faith and practice are spoken against, just because they are not known. Its enemies speak evil of things with which they are not acquainted. They understand neither what they say nor whereof they affirm. Philip's mode of dealing, we may be sure, is one principal way to do good. Few are ever moved by reasoning and argument. Still fewer are frightened into repentance. The man who does most good to souls is often the simple believer who says to his friends, 'I have found a Saviour; come and see him.'

For meditation: *It sometimes gives us great satisfaction to win an argument with an unbeliever. We should, however, be more concerned to win the person.*

Suggested further reading: Luke 24:25-27, 44-48

How much of Christ there is in the Old Testament Scriptures! We read that when Philip described Christ to Nathanael, he said, 'We have found him of whom Moses in the law and the prophets did write.'

Christ is the sum and substance of the Old Testament. To him the earliest promises pointed in the days of Adam and Enoch and Noah and Abraham and Isaac and Jacob. To him every sacrifice pointed in the ceremonial worship appointed at Mount Sinai. Of him every high priest was a type and every part of the tabernacle was a shadow and every judge and deliverer of Israel was a figure. He was the Prophet like unto Moses, whom the Lord God promised to send, and the King of the house of David, who came to be David's Lord as well as Son. He was the Son of the virgin and the Lamb foretold by Isaiah, the righteous Branch mentioned by Jeremiah, the true Shepherd foreseen by Ezekiel, the Messenger of the covenant promised by Malachi and the Messiah who, according to Daniel, was to be cut off, though not for himself. The further we read in the volume of the Old Testament, the clearer do we find the testimony about Christ. The light which the inspired writers enjoyed in ancient days was, at best, but dim, compared to that of the gospel. But the coming person they all saw afar off, and on whom they all fixed their eyes, was one and the same. The Spirit, which was in them, testified of Christ (1 Peter 1:11).

Do we stumble at this saying? Do we find it hard to see Christ in the Old Testament, because we do not see his name? Let us pray for a more humble, childlike and teachable spirit. May we never rest till we can subscribe to our Lord's words about the Old Testament Scriptures: 'They are they which testify of me' (John 5:39).

For meditation: *In the earliest days of the church the Christians only had the Old Testament to prove that Jesus is the Christ. How would you have managed?*

Suggested further reading: 1 Samuel 3:2-10

Let us observe, lastly, in these verses the high character which
Jesus gives of Nathanael. He calls him 'an Israelite indeed, in
whom is no guile'.
   Nathanael, there can be no doubt, was a true child of God
and a child of God in difficult times. He was one of a very little
flock. Like Simeon and Anna and other pious Jews, he was
living by faith and waiting prayerfully for the promised
Redeemer when our Lord's ministry began. He had that which
grace alone can give — an honest heart, a heart without guile.
His knowledge was probably small. His spiritual eyesight was
dim. But he was one who had lived carefully up to his light. He
had diligently used such knowledge as he possessed. His eye
had been single, though his vision had not been strong. His
spiritual judgement had been honest, though it had not been
powerful. What he saw in Scripture, he had held firmly, in spite
of Pharisees and Sadducees and all the fashionable religion of
the day. He was an honest Old Testament believer who had
stood alone. And here was the secret of our Lord's peculiar
commendation! He declared Nathanael to be a true son of
Abraham, a Jew inwardly, possessing circumcision in the spirit
as well as in the letter, an Israelite in heart, as well as a son of
Jacob in the flesh.
   Let us pray that we may be of the same spirit as Nathanael.
An honest, unprejudiced mind, a childlike willingness to follow
the truth, wherever the truth may lead us, a simple, hearty
desire to be guided, taught and led by the Spirit, a thorough
determination to use every spark of light which we have are a
possession of priceless value. A man of this spirit may live in
the midst of much darkness and be surrounded by every possible disadvantage to his soul. But the Lord Jesus will take care
that such a man does not miss the way to heaven. 'The meek
will he guide in judgement: and the meek will he teach his way'
(Ps. 25:9).

For meditation: *How teachable are you? Or are you self-
opinionated and puffed up with your own knowledge?*

Suggested further reading: *Ephesians 5:22-33*

How honourable in the sight of Christ is the estate of matrimony! To be present at a 'marriage' was almost the first public act of our Lord's earthly ministry.

Marriage is not a sacrament, as the church of Rome asserts. It is simply a state of life ordained by God for man's benefit. But it is a state which ought never to be spoken of with levity, or regarded with disrespect. The Prayer Book service has well described it as 'an honourable estate, instituted of God in the time of man's innocency, and signifying unto us the mystical union that is betwixt Christ and his church'. Society is never in a healthy condition and true religion never flourishes in that land where the marriage tie is lightly esteemed. They who lightly esteem it have not the mind of Christ. He who 'beautified and adorned the estate of matrimony by his presence and first miracle that he wrought in Cana of Galilee' is one who is always of one mind. 'Marriage,' says the Holy Ghost by St Paul, 'is honourable in all' (Heb. 13:4).

One thing, however, ought not to be forgotten. Marriage is a step which so seriously affects the temporal happiness and spiritual welfare of two immortal souls that it ought never to be taken in hand 'unadvisedly, lightly, wantonly and without due consideration'. To be truly happy, it should be undertaken 'reverently, discreetly, soberly and in the fear of God'. Christ's blessing and presence are essential to a happy wedding. The marriage at which there is no place for Christ and his disciples is not one that can justly be expected to prosper.

We learn from these verses that there are times when it is lawful to be merry and rejoice. Our Lord himself sanctioned a wedding feast by his own presence. He did not refuse to be a guest at 'a marriage in Cana of Galilee'.

For meditation: *In days of soaring divorce rates and rampant immorality, faithfulness and purity among Christians should be guarded.*

Suggested further reading: Matthew 11:16-19

'A feast', it is written, 'is made for laughter, and wine maketh merry' (Eccles. 10:19). Our Lord, in the passage before us, countenances both the feast and the use of wine. True religion was never meant to make men melancholy. On the contrary, it was intended to increase real joy and happiness among men. The servant of Christ unquestionably ought to have nothing to do with races, balls, theatres and suchlike amusements, which tend to frivolity and dissipation, if not to sin. But he has no right to hand over innocent recreations and family gatherings to the devil and the world. The Christian who withdraws entirely from the society of his fellow men and walks the earth with a face as melancholy as if he was always attending a funeral does injury to the cause of the gospel. A cheerful, kindly spirit is a great recommendation to a believer. It is a positive misfortune to Christianity when a Christian cannot smile. A merry heart and a readiness to take part in all innocent mirth are gifts of inestimable value. They go far to soften prejudices, to take up stumbling-blocks out of the way and to make way for Christ and the gospel.

The subject, no doubt, is a difficult and delicate one. On no point of Christian practice is it so hard to hit the mean between that which is lawful and that which is unlawful, between that which is right and that which is wrong. It is very hard indeed to be both merry and wise.

One golden rule on the subject may be laid down, the use of which will save us much trouble. Let us take care that we always go to feasts in the spirit of our divine Master and that we never go where he would not have gone. Let us endeavour to bring the salt of grace into every company and to drop the word in season in every ear we address.

For meditation: _A life lived in reverent fear (1 Peter 1:17) and set on pleasing Christ and gaining his approval (2 Cor. 5:9,10) will avoid much sin._

Suggested further reading: Psalm: 27:1-6

We learn from these verses the almighty power of our Lord Jesus Christ. We are told of a miracle which he wrought at the marriage feast when the wine failed. By a mere act of will he changed water into wine and so supplied the need of all the guests.

The manner in which the miracle was worked deserves especial notice. We are not told of any outward visible action which preceded or accompanied it. It is not said that he touched the waterpots containing the water that was made wine. It is not said that he commanded the water to change its qualities, or that he prayed to his Father in heaven. He simply willed the change and it took place. We read of no prophet or apostle in the Bible who ever worked a miracle after this fashion. He who could do such a mighty work, in such a manner, was nothing less than very God.

It is a comfortable thought that the same almighty power of will which our Lord here displayed is still exercised on behalf of his believing people. They have no need of his bodily presence to maintain their cause. They have no reason to be cast down because they cannot see him with their eyes interceding for them, or touch him with their hands, that they may cling to him for safety. If he 'wills' their salvation and the daily supply of all their spiritual need, they are as safe and well provided for as if they saw him standing by them. Christ's *will* is as mighty and effectual as Christ's *deed*. The will of him who could say to the Father, 'I will that they whom thou hast given me be with me where I am' (John 17:24) is a will that has all power in heaven and earth and must prevail.

Happy are those who, like the disciples, believe on him by whom this miracle was wrought!

For meditation: *Whatever has been determined by God must happen. It is unable to be stopped and is above any legitimate criticism (Dan. 4:35).*

Suggested further reading: Ezekiel 33:30-33

How much Christ disapproves all irreverent behaviour in the house of God! We are told that he drove out of the temple those whom he found selling oxen and sheep and doves within its walls, that he poured out the changers' money and overthrew their tables and that he said to them that sold doves, 'Take these things hence; make not my Father's house an house of merchandise.' On no occasion in our Lord's earthly ministry do we find him acting so energetically and exhibiting such righteous indignation as on the occasion now before us. Nothing seems to have called from him such a marked display of holy wrath as the gross irreverence which the priests permitted in the temple, notwithstanding all their boasted zeal for God's law.

The passage is one that ought to raise deep searchings of heart in many quarters. Are there none who profess and call themselves Christians, behaving every Sunday just as badly as these Jews? Are there none who secretly bring into the house of God their money, their lands, their houses, their cattle and a whole train of worldly affairs? Are there none who bring their bodies only into the place of worship and allow their hearts to wander into the ends of the earth? Are there none who are 'almost in all evil, in the midst of the congregation'? (Prov. 5:14.) Multitudes, it may be feared, could not give a satisfactory answer. Christian churches and chapels, no doubt, are very unlike the Jewish temple. They are not built after a divine pattern. They have no altars or holy places. Their furniture has no typical meaning. But they are places where God's Word is read and where Christ is specially present. The man who professes to worship in them should surely behave with reverence and respect. The man who brings his worldly matters with him when he professes to worship is doing that which is evidently most offensive to Christ.

For meditation: *Our Lord detests that worship which is only outward and insincere (Matt. 15:7,8).*

Suggested further reading: Daniel 9:1-14

Men may remember words of religious truth long after they are spoken and may one day see a meaning in them which at first they did not see. We are told that our Lord said to the Jews, 'Destroy this temple and in three days I will raise it up.' St John informs us distinctly that 'He spake of the temple of his body,' that he referred to his own resurrection. Yet the meaning of the sentence was not understood by our Lord's disciples at the time that it was spoken. It was not till 'he was risen from the dead', three years after the events here described, that the full significance of the sentence flashed on their hearts. For three years it was a dark and useless saying to them. For three years it lay sleeping in their minds, like a seed in a tomb, and bore no fruit. But at the end of that time the darkness passed away. They saw the application of their Master's words and as they saw it were confirmed in their faith. 'They remembered that he had said this,' and as they remembered 'they believed'.

It is a comfortable and cheering thought that the same kind of thing that happened to the disciples is often going on at the present day. The sermons that are preached to apparently heedless ears in churches are not all lost and thrown away. The instruction that is given in schools and pastoral visits is not all wasted and forgotten. The texts that are taught by parents to children are not all taught in vain. There is often a resurrection of sermons and texts and instruction after an interval of many years. The good seed sometimes springs up after he that sowed it has been long dead and gone. Let preachers go on preaching and teachers go on teaching and parents go on training up children in the way they should go. Let them sow the good seed of Bible truth in faith and patience. Their labour is not in vain in the Lord.

For meditation: *In a day when everything has to be instant and readily disposable, patience in sowing God's Word is needed (Eccles. 11:1).*

Suggested further reading: *Jeremiah 17:5-10*

How perfect is our Lord Jesus Christ's knowledge of the human heart! We are told that when our Lord was at Jerusalem the first time he 'did not commit himself' to those who professed belief in him. He knew that they were not to be depended on. They were astonished at the miracles which they saw him work. They were even intellectually convinced that he was the Messiah whom they had long expected. But they were not 'disciples indeed' (John 8:31). They were not converted and true believers. Their hearts were not right in the sight of God, though their feelings were excited. Their inward man was not renewed, whatever they might profess with their lips. Our Lord knew that nearly all of them were stony-ground hearers (Luke 8:13). As soon as tribulation or persecution arose because of the Word, their so-called faith would probably wither away and come to an end. All this our Lord saw clearly, if others around him did not. Andrew and Peter and John and Philip and Nathanael perhaps wondered that their Master did not receive these seeming believers with open arms. But they could only judge things by the outward appearance. Their Master could read hearts. 'He knew what was in man.'

The truth now before us is one which ought to make hypocrites and false professors tremble. They may deceive men, but they cannot deceive Christ. They may wear a cloak of religion and appear, like whited sepulchres, beautiful in the eyes of men. But the eyes of Christ see their inward rottenness and the judgement of Christ will surely overtake them except they repent. Christ is already reading their hearts and, as he reads, he is displeased. They are known in heaven, if they are not known on earth, and they will be known at length to their shame before assembled worlds if they die unchanged. It is written: 'I know thy works, that thou hast a name that thou livest, and art dead' (Rev. 3:1).

For meditation: *There is no limit to God's knowledge of us. He sees the motives of the heart (Heb. 4:12,13).*

Suggested further reading: Matthew 12:15-21

There can be little doubt that Nicodemus acted as he did on this occasion from fear of man. He was afraid of what man would think, or say, or do, if his visit to Jesus was known. He came 'by night', because he had not faith and courage enough to come by day. And yet there was a time afterwards when this very Nicodemus took our Lord's part in open day in the council of the Jews. 'Doth our law judge any man,' he said, 'before it hear him and know what he doeth?' (John 7:51.) Nor was this all. There came a time when this very Nicodemus was one of the only two men who did honour to our Lord's dead body. He helped Joseph of Arimathea to bury Jesus, when even the apostles had forsaken their Master and fled. His last things were more than his first. Though he began ill, he ended well.

The history of Nicodemus is meant to teach us that we should never 'despise the day of small things' in religion (Zech. 4:10). We must not set down a man as having no grace, because his first steps towards God are timid and wavering and the first movements of his soul are uncertain, hesitating and stamped with much imperfection. We must remember our Lord's reception of Nicodemus. He did not 'break the bruised reed, or quench the smoking flax' which he saw before him (Matt. 12:20). Like him, let us take inquirers by the hand and deal with them gently and lovingly. In everything there must be a beginning. It is not those who make the most flaming profession of religion at first who endure the longest and prove the most steadfast. Judas Iscariot was an apostle when Nicodemus was just groping his way slowly into full light. Yet afterwards, when Nicodemus was boldly helping to bury his crucified Saviour, Judas Iscariot had betrayed him and hanged himself! This is a fact which ought not to be forgotten.

For meditation: *Even Paul dismissed the usefulness of Mark after he had deserted him in Pamphylia (Acts 15:37,38) but later recognized his value (Col. 4:10). Hasty judgements are best avoided.*

Suggested further reading: Ephesians: 2:1-10

What a mighty change our Lord declares to be needful to salvation, and what a remarkable expression he uses in describing
it! He speaks of a new birth. He says to Nicodemus, 'Except a
man be born again, he cannot see the kingdom of God.' He
announces the same truth in other words, in order to make it
more plain to his hearer's mind: 'Except a man be born of water
and of the Spirit, he cannot enter into the kingdom of God.' By
this expression he meant Nicodemus to understand that no one
could become his disciple, unless his inward man was as
thoroughly cleansed and renewed by the Spirit as the outward
man is cleansed by water. To possess the privileges of Judaism
a man only needed to be born of the seed of Abraham after the
flesh. To possess the privileges of Christ's kingdom a man must
be born again of the Holy Ghost.

The change which our Lord here declares needful to salvation is evidently no slight or superficial one. It is not merely
reformation, or amendment, or moral change, or outward
alteration of life. It is a thorough change of heart, will and
character. It is a resurrection. It is a new creation. It is a passing
from death to life. It is the implanting in our dead hearts of a
new principle from above. It is the calling into existence of a
new creature, with a new nature, new habits of life, new tastes,
new desires, new appetites, new judgements, new opinions,
new hopes and new fears. All this, and nothing less than this, is
implied when our Lord declares that we all need a 'new birth'.

Would we know what the marks of the new birth are? The
man born of God 'believes that Jesus is the Christ', 'doth not
commit sin', 'doeth righteousness', 'loves the brethren', 'over-
comes the world', 'keepeth himself from the wicked one'. This
is the man born of the Spirit!

For meditation: *It is no use dealing with sin's symptoms without
dealing with its root – the sinful heart of man.*

Suggested further reading: *Ezekiel 37:1-10*

This change of heart is rendered absolutely necessary to salvation by the corrupt condition in which we are all without exception born. 'That which is born of the flesh is flesh.' Our nature is thoroughly fallen. The carnal mind is enmity against God (Rom. 8:7). We come into the world without faith, or love, or fear towards God. We have no natural inclination to serve him or obey him and no natural pleasure in doing his will. Left to himself, no child of Adam would ever turn to God. The truest description of the change which we all need in order to make us real Christians is the expression 'new birth'.

This mighty change, it must never be forgotten, we cannot give to ourselves. The very name which our Lord gives to it is a convincing proof of this. He calls it a birth. No man is the author of his own existence and no man can quicken his own soul. We might as well expect a dead man to give himself life as expect a natural man to make himself spiritual. A power from above must be put in exercise, even that same power which created the world (2 Cor. 4:6). Man can do many things, but he cannot give life either to himself or to others. To give life is the peculiar prerogative of God. Well may our Lord declare that we need to be 'born again'!

This mighty change, we must above all remember, is a thing without which we cannot go to heaven and could not enjoy heaven if we went there. Our Lord's words on this point are distinct and express: 'Except a man be born again, he can neither see nor enter the kingdom of God.' Heaven may be reached without money, or rank, or learning. But it is clear as daylight, if words have any meaning, that nobody can enter heaven without a 'new birth'.

For meditation: *Thank God that he intervenes in the lives of men to save them from their state of spiritual stupor and death.*

Suggested further reading: 1 John 2:28-3:10

We should notice in these verses the instructive comparison which our Lord uses in explaining the new birth. He saw Nicodemus perplexed and astonished by the things he had just heard. He graciously helped his wondering mind by an illustration drawn from the wind. A more beautiful and fitting illustration of the work of the Spirit it is impossible to conceive. There is much about the wind that is mysterious and inexplicable. 'Thou canst not tell', says our Lord, 'whence it cometh and whither it goeth.' We cannot handle it with our hands, or see it with our eyes. When the wind blows, we cannot point out the exact spot where its breath first began to be felt and the exact distance to which its influence shall extend. But we do not on that account deny its presence. It is just the same with the operations of the Spirit in the new birth of man. They may be mysterious, sovereign and incomprehensible to us in many ways. But it is foolish to stumble at them because there is much about them that we cannot explain.

But whatever mystery there may be about the wind, its presence may always be known by its sound and effects. 'Thou hearest the sound thereof,' says our Lord. When our ears hear it whistling in the windows and our eyes see the clouds driving before it, we do not hesitate to say, 'There is wind.' It is just the same with the operations of the Holy Spirit in the new birth of man. Marvellous and incomprehensible as his work may be, it is work that can always be seen and known. The new birth is a thing that 'cannot be hid'. There will always be visible 'fruits of the Spirit' in everyone that is born of the Spirit.

Have we been born again? A day will come when those who are not born again will wish that they had never been born at all.

For meditation: *When there is no evidence of physical life a person is pronounced dead and is buried. A fruitless Christian is a spiritual corpse (John 15:5, 6).*

Suggested further reading: 1 Corinthians 2:6-15

What gross spiritual ignorance there may be in the mind of a great and learned man! We see a 'master of Israel' unacquainted with the first elements of saving religion. Nicodemus is told about the new birth and at once exclaims, 'How can these things be?' When such was the darkness of a Jewish teacher, what must have been the state of the Jewish people? It was indeed due time for Christ to appear! The pastors of Israel had ceased to feed the people with knowledge. The blind were leading the blind and both were falling into the ditch (Matt. 15:14).

Ignorance like that of Nicodemus is unhappily far too common in the church of Christ. We must never be surprised if we find it in quarters where we might reasonably expect knowledge. Learning and rank and high ecclesiastical office are no proof that a minister is taught by the Spirit. The successors of Nicodemus in every age are far more numerous than the successors of St Peter. On no point is religious ignorance so common as on the work of the Holy Ghost. That old stumbling-block, at which Nicodemus stumbled, is as much an offence to thousands in the present day as it was in the days of Christ. The natural man receiveth not the things of the Spirit of God' (1 Cor. 2:14). Happy is he who has been taught to prove all things by Scripture and to call no man master upon earth! (1 Thess. 5:21; Matt. 23:9.)

These verses show us the original source from which man's salvation springs. That source is the love of God the Father. Our Lord says to Nicodemus, 'God so loved the world that he gave his only begotten Son, that whosoever believeth in him should not perish, but have everlasting life.'

This wonderful verse has been justly called by Luther 'the Bible in miniature'. No part of it, perhaps, is so deeply important as the first five words: 'God so loved the world.'

For meditation: *Our salvation does not depend on the level of education we have, but on God giving us spiritual sight.*

Suggested further reading: Numbers 21:4-9

By being 'lifted up', our Lord meant nothing less than his own death upon the cross. That death, he would have us know, was appointed by God to be 'the life of the world' (John 6:51). It was ordained from all eternity to be the great propitiation and satisfaction for man's sin. It was the payment, by an almighty Substitute and Representative, of man's enormous debt to God. When Christ died upon the cross, our many sins were laid upon him. He was made 'sin' for us (2 Cor. 5:21). He was made 'a curse' for us (Gal. 3:13). By his death he purchased pardon and complete redemption for sinners.

The brazen serpent, lifted up in the camp of Israel, brought health and cure within the reach of all who were bitten by serpents. Christ crucified, in like manner, brought eternal life within reach of lost mankind. Christ has been lifted up on the cross and man looking to him by faith may be saved.

The truth before us is the very foundation-stone of the Christian religion. Christ's death is the Christian's life. Christ's cross is the Christian's title to heaven. Christ 'lifted up' and put to shame on Calvary is the ladder by which Christians 'enter into the holiest' and are at length landed in glory. It is true that we are sinners, but Christ has suffered for us. It is true that we deserve death, but Christ has died for us. It is true that we are great debtors, but Christ has paid our debts with his own blood. This is the real gospel! This is the good news! On this let us lean while we live. To this let us cling when we die. Christ has been 'lifted up' on the cross and has thrown open the gates of heaven to all believers.

For meditation: *The serpent on the pole gave life but suffered nothing. Bronze does not feel pain. Our Saviour gave a better life, but at terrible personal cost.*

Suggested further reading: Psalm 145:8-17

The love here spoken of is not that special love with which the Father regards his own elect, but that mighty pity and compassion with which he regards the whole race of mankind. Its object is not merely the little flock which he has given to Christ from all eternity, but the whole 'world' of sinners, without any exception. There is a deep sense in which God loves that world. All whom he has created he regards with pity and compassion. Their sins he cannot love, but he loves their souls. 'His tender mercies are over all his works' (Ps. 145:9).

Let us take heed that our views of the love of God are scriptural and well-defined. We must maintain firmly that God hates wickedness and that the end of all who persist in wickedness will be destruction. It is not true that God's love is 'lower than hell'. It is not true that God so loved the world that all mankind will be finally saved, but that he so loved the world that he gave his Son to be the Saviour of all who believe. His love is offered to all men freely, fully, honestly and unreservedly, but it is only through the one channel of Christ's redemption. He that rejects Christ cuts himself off from God's love and will perish everlastingly. On the other hand, we must beware of narrow and contracted opinions. We must not hesitate to tell any sinner that God loves him. It is not true that God cares for none but his own elect, or that Christ is not offered to any but those who are ordained to eternal life. There is a 'kindness and love' in God towards all mankind. It was in consequence of that love that Christ came into the world and died upon the cross. Let us not be wise above that which is written, or more systematic in our statements than Scripture itself. God has no pleasure in the death of the wicked. God is not willing that any should perish. God would have all men to be saved. God loves the world (John 6:33; Titus 3:4; 1 John 4:10; 2 Peter 3:9; 1 Tim. 2:4; Ezek. 33:11).

For meditation: *God's love to us requires more than a smile in response!*

Suggested further reading: Romans 4:1-8

These verses show us the way in which the benefits of Christ's death are made our own. That way is simply to put faith and trust in Christ. Faith is the same thing as believing. Three times our Lord repeats this glorious truth to Nicodemus. Twice he proclaims that 'Whosoever believeth shall not perish.' Once he says, 'He that believeth on the Son of God is not condemned.'

Faith in the Lord Jesus is the very key of salvation. He that has it has life and he that has it not has not life. Nothing whatever *beside* this faith is necessary to our complete justification; but nothing whatever *except* this faith will give us an interest in Christ. We may fast and mourn for sin and do many things that arc right and use religious ordinances and give all our goods to feed the poor and yet remain unpardoned and lose our souls. But if we will only come to Christ as guilty sinners and believe on him, our sins shall at once be forgiven and our iniquities shall be entirely put away. Without faith there is no salvation, but through faith in Jesus the vilest sinner may be saved.

If we would have a peaceful conscience in our religion, let us see that our views of saving faith are distinct and clear. Let us beware of supposing that justifying faith is anything more than a sinner's simple trust in a Saviour, the grasp of a drowning man on the hand held out for his relief. Let us beware of mingling anything else with faith in the matter of *justification*. Here we must always remember faith stands entirely alone. A justified man, no doubt, will always be a holy man. True believing will always be accompanied by godly living. But that which gives a man an interest in Christ is not his *living*, but his *faith*.

For meditation: *Salvation is through Christ alone, by God's grace alone, received by faith alone.*

Suggested further reading: *Ezekiel 33:1-11*

These verses show us the true cause of the loss of man's soul. Our Lord says to Nicodemus, 'This is the condemnation, that light is come into the world, and men loved darkness rather than light, because their deeds were evil.'

The words before us form a suitable conclusion to the glorious tidings which we have just been considering. They completely clear God of injustice in the condemnation of sinners. They show in simple and unmistakable terms that, although man's salvation is entirely of God, his ruin, if he is lost, will be entirely from himself. He will reap the fruit of his own sowing.

'God sent not his Son into the world to condemn the world, but that the world through him might be saved.' There is no unwillingness on God's part to receive any sinner, however great his sins. God has sent 'light' into the world and if man will not come to the light the fault is entirely on man's side. His blood will be on his own head if he makes shipwreck of his soul. The blame will be at his own door if he misses heaven. His eternal misery will be the result of his own choice. His destruction will be the work of his own hand. God loved him and was willing to save him, but he loved darkness and therefore darkness must be his everlasting portion. He would not come to Christ and therefore he could not have life (John 5:40).

The truths we have been considering are peculiarly weighty and solemn. Do we live as if we believed them? Salvation by Christ's death is close to us today. Have we embraced it by faith and made it our own? Let us never rest till we know Christ as our own Saviour. Let us look to him without delay for pardon and peace, if we have never looked before. Let us go on believing on him, if we have already believed. 'Whosoever', is his own gracious word — *'whosoever* believeth on him, shall not perish, but have eternal life.'

For meditation: *Every mouth is stopped before God. The unbeliever's condemnation is above criticism because entirely just.*

Suggested further reading: 1 Corinthians:1:10-17

We have in these verses a humbling example of the petty jealousies and party spirit which may exist among professors of religion. We are told that the disciples of John the Baptist were offended, because the ministry of Jesus began to attract more attention than that of their master. 'They came unto John, and said unto him, Rabbi, he that was with thee beyond Jordan, to whom thou barest witness, behold the same baptizeth, and all men come to him.'

The spirit exhibited in this complaint is unhappily too common in the churches of Christ. The succession of these complainers has never failed. There are never wanting religious professors who care far more for the increase of their own party than for the increase of true Christianity and who cannot rejoice in the spread of religion if it spreads anywhere except within their own pale. There is a generation which can see no good doing except in the ranks of its own congregations and which seems ready to shut men out of heaven if they will not enter therein under its banner.

The true Christian must watch and pray against the spirit here manifested by John's disciples. It is very insidious, very contagious and very injurious to the cause of religion. Nothing so defiles Christianity and gives the enemies of truth such occasion to blaspheme as jealousy and party spirit among Christians. Wherever there is real grace, we should be ready and willing to acknowledge it, even though it may be outside our own pale. We should strive to say with the apostle, 'If Christ be preached, I rejoice, yea, and will rejoice' (Phil. 1:18). If good is done, we ought to be thankful, though it even may not be done in what we think the best way. If souls are saved, we ought to be glad, whatever be the means that God may think fit to employ.

For meditation: _We must be careful to distinguish between the enemies of the gospel, whom we are to avoid (2 John 10,11), and brethren, whom we are to receive (3 John 5-8)._

Suggested further reading: Philippians 2:5-8

We have in these verses a splendid pattern of true and godly humility. We see in John the Baptist a very different spirit from that displayed by his disciples. He begins by laying down the great principle that acceptance with man is a special gift of God and that we must therefore not presume to find fault when others have more acceptance than ourselves. 'A man can receive nothing except it be given him from heaven.' He goes on to remind his followers of his repeated declaration that one greater than himself was coming: 'I said, I am not the Christ.' He tells them that his office, compared to that of Christ, is that of the bridegroom's friend, compared to the bridegroom. And, finally, he solemnly affirms that Christ must and will become greater and greater and that he himself must become less and less important until, like a star eclipsed by the rising sun, he has completely disappeared.

A frame of mind like this is the highest degree of grace to which mortal man can attain. The greatest saint in the sight of God is the man who is most thoroughly 'clothed with humility' (1 Peter 5:5). Would we know the prime secret of being men of the stamp of Abraham and Moses and Job and David and Daniel and St Paul and John the Baptist? They were all eminently humble men. Living at different ages and enjoying very different degrees of light, in this matter at least they were all agreed. In themselves they saw nothing but sin and weakness. To God they gave all the praise of what they were. Let us walk in their steps. Let us covet earnestly the best gifts, but above all let us covet humility. The way to true honour is to be humble. No man ever was so praised by Christ as the very man who says here, 'I must decrease,' the humble John the Baptist.

For meditation: *Self-effacement is a rare quality in a day of personality cults in Christendom.*

Suggested further reading: 1 John 5:9-13

John the Baptist teaches his disciples once more the true greatness of the person whose growing popularity offended them. Once more, and perhaps for the last time, he proclaims him as one worthy of all honour and praise. He uses one striking expression after another to convey a correct idea of the majesty of Christ. He speaks of him as 'the bridegroom' of the church, as 'him that cometh from above', as 'him whom God hath sent', as 'him to whom the Spirit is given without measure', as him 'whom the Father loves' and into 'whose hands all things are given', to believe in whom is life everlasting and to reject whom is eternal ruin. Each of these phrases is full of deep meaning and would supply matter for a long sermon. All show the depth and height of John's spiritual attainments. More honourable things are nowhere written concerning Jesus than these verses recorded as spoken by John the Baptist.

John the Baptist declares, 'He that believeth on the Son hath everlasting life.' He is not intended to look forward with a sick heart to a far distant privilege. He 'hath' everlasting life as soon as he believes. Pardon, peace and a complete title to heaven are an immediate possession. They become a believer's own from the very moment he puts faith in Christ. They will not be more completely his own if he lives to the age of Methuselah.

The truth before us is one of the most glorious privileges of the gospel. There are no works to be done, no conditions to be fulfilled, no price to be paid, no wearing years of probation to be passed before a sinner can be accepted with God. Let him only believe on Christ and he is at once forgiven. Salvation is close to the chief of sinners. Let him only repent and believe and this day it is his own. By Christ all that believe are at once justified from all things.

For meditation: _As our Lord is the one in whom we receive every spiritual blessing (Eph. 1:3), to have Christ is to be unspeakably rich._

Suggested further reading:　1 Corinthians 1:13-17

We read that 'Jesus himself baptized not, but his disciples.' To baptize is not the principal work for which Christian ministers are ordained. Frequently we read of our Lord preaching and praying. Once we read of his administering the Lord's Supper. But we have not a single instance recorded of his ever baptizing anyone. And here we are distinctly told that it was a subordinate work, which he left to others. Jesus 'himself baptized not, but his disciples'.

The lesson is one of peculiar importance in the present day. Baptism, as a sacrament ordained by Christ himself, is an honourable ordinance and ought never to be lightly esteemed in the churches. It cannot be neglected or despised without great sin. When rightly used, with faith and prayer, it is calculated to convey the highest blessings. But baptism was never meant to be exalted to the position which many nowadays assign to it in religion. It does not act as a charm. It does not necessarily convey the grace of the Holy Ghost. The benefit of it depends greatly on the manner in which it is used. The doctrine taught and the language employed about it in some quarters are utterly inconsistent with the fact announced in the text. If baptism was all that some say it is, we should never have been told that 'Jesus himself baptized not'.

Let it be a settled principle in our minds that the first and chief business of the church of Christ is to preach the gospel. The words of St Paul ought to be constantly remembered: 'Christ sent me not to baptize, but to preach the gospel' (1 Cor. 1:17). When the gospel of Christ is faithfully and fully preached we need not fear that the sacraments will be undervalued. Baptism and the Lord's Supper will always be most truly reverenced in those churches where the truth as it is in Jesus is most fully taught and known.

For meditation:　*The dying thief had nothing but faith in Christ, but paradise was gained (Luke 23:42,43). Christ saves, not water.*

Suggested further reading: *Hebrews 2:14-18*

Jesus was 'wearied with his journey'. We learn from this, as well as many other expressions in the Gospels, that our Lord had a body exactly like our own.

The truth before us is full of comfort for all who are true Christians. He to whom sinners are bid to come for pardon and peace is one who is man as well as God. He had a real human nature when he was upon earth. He took a real human nature with him when he ascended up into heaven. We have at the right hand of God a High Priest who can be touched with the feeling of our infirmities, because he has suffered himself, being tempted. When we cry to him in the hour of bodily pain and weakness, he knows well what we mean. When our prayers and praises are feeble through bodily weariness, he can understand our condition. He knows our frame. He has learned by experience what it is to be a man. To say that the virgin Mary, or anyone else, can feel more sympathy for us than Christ is ignorance no less than blasphemy. The man Christ Jesus can enter fully into everything that belongs to man's condition. The poor, the sick and the suffering have in heaven one who is not only an almighty Saviour, but a most feeling Friend.

Power and sympathy are marvellously combined in him who died for us on the cross. Because he is God, we may repose the weight of our souls upon him with unhesitating confidence. He is mighty to save. Because he is man, we may speak to him with freedom about the many trials to which flesh is heir. He knows the heart of a man. Here is rest for the weary! Here is good news! Our Redeemer is man as well as God and God as well as man. He that believeth on him has everything that a child of Adam can possibly require, either for safety or for peace.

For meditation: *The perfect Mediator relates to God as God and to man as man.*

Suggested further reading: *1 Corinthians 9:19-23*

The Samaritan woman shows us how our Lord dealt with an ignorant, carnal-minded woman, whose moral character was more than ordinarily bad.

We should mark the mingled tact and condescension of Christ in dealing with a careless sinner.

Our Lord was sitting by Jacob's well when a woman of Samaria came thither to draw water. At once he says to her, 'Give me to drink.' He does not wait for her to speak to him. He does not begin by reproving her sins, though he doubtless knew them. He opens communication by asking a favour. He approaches the woman's mind by the subject of 'water', which was naturally uppermost in her thoughts. Simple as this request may seem, it opened a door to spiritual conversation. It threw a bridge across the gulf which lay between her and him. It led to the conversion of her soul.

Our Lord's conduct in this place should be carefully remembered by all who want to do good to the thoughtless and spiritually ignorant. It is vain to expect that such persons will voluntarily come to us and begin to seek knowledge. We must begin with them and go down to them in the spirit of courteous and friendly aggression. It is vain to expect that such persons will be prepared for our instruction and will at once see and acknowledge the wisdom of all we are doing. We must go to work wisely. We must study the best avenues to their hearts and the most likely way of arresting their attention. There is a handle to every mind and our chief aim must be to get hold of it. Above all, we must be kind in manner and beware of showing that we feel conscious of our own superiority. If we let ignorant people fancy that we think we are doing them a great favour in talking to them about religion, there is little hope of doing good to their souls.

For meditation: *How willing are you to think carefully before you speak to others about the Lord or are you too lazy to bother whether they understand or not?*

Suggested further reading: Matthew 6:25-33

We should mark Christ's readiness to give mercies to careless sinners. He tells the Samaritan woman that if she had asked, 'he would have given her living water'.

The infinite willingness of Christ to receive sinners is a golden truth, which ought to be treasured up in our hearts and diligently impressed on others. The Lord Jesus is far more ready to hear than we are to pray and far more ready to give favours than we are to ask them. All day long he stretches out his hands to the disobedient and gainsaying. He has thoughts of pity and compassion towards the vilest of sinners, even when they have no thoughts of him. He stands waiting to bestow mercy and grace on the worst and most unworthy, if they will only cry to him. He will never draw back from that well-known promise: 'Ask and ye shall receive: seek and ye shall find.' The lost will discover at the last day that they had not because thay asked not.

We should mark the priceless excellence of Christ's gifts when compared with the things of this world. Our Lord tells the Samaritan woman, 'He that drinketh of this water shall thirst again, but he that drinketh of the water that I shall give him shall never thirst.'

The truth of the principle here laid down may be seen on every side by all who are not blinded by prejudice or love of the world. Thousands of men have every temporal good thing that heart could wish and are yet weary and dissatisfied. Riches and rank and place and power and learning and amusements are utterly unable to fill the soul. He that only drinks of these waters is sure to thirst again.

There is no heart satisfaction in this world until we believe on Christ. Jesus alone can fill up the empty places of our inward man. Jesus alone can give solid, lasting, enduring happiness. The peace that he imparts is a fountain which, once set flowing within the soul, flows on to all eternity.

For meditation: *Which is more important to you: time or eternity?*

Suggested further reading: Matthew 15:1-8

We should mark the absolute necessity of conviction of sin before a soul can be converted to God. The Samaritan woman seems to have been comparatively unmoved until our Lord exposed her breach of the seventh commandment. Those heart-searching words, 'Go, call thy husband,' appear to have pierced her conscience like an arrow. From that moment, however ignorant, she speaks like an earnest, sincere inquirer after truth. And the reason is evident. She felt that her spiritual disease was discovered. For the first time in her life she saw herself.

To bring thoughtless people to this state of mind should be the principal aim of all teachers and ministers of the gospel. They should carefully copy their Master's example in this place. Till men and women are brought to feel their sinfulness and need, no real good is ever done to their souls. Till a sinner sees himself as God sees him, he will continue careless, trifling and unmoved.

Never does a soul value the gospel medicine until it feels its disease. Never does a man see any beauty in Christ as a Saviour until he discovers that he is himself a lost and ruined sinner. Ignorance of sin is invariably attended by neglect of Christ.

We should mark the uselessness of any religion which only consists of formality. The Samaritan woman, when awakened to spiritual concern, started questions about the comparative merits of the Samaritan and Jewish modes of worshipping God. Our Lord tells her that true and acceptable worship depends not on the place in which it is offered, but on the state of the worshipper's heart. The heart is the principal thing in all our approaches to God. 'The Lord looketh on the heart' (1 Sam. 16:7). The feeblest gathering of three or four poor believers in a cottage to read the Bible and pray is a more acceptable sight to him who searches the heart than the fullest congregation which is ever gathered in St Peter's at Rome.

For meditation: *Have our consciences been convicted and cleansed and our hearts been given to the Lord?*

Suggested further reading: Luke 7:36-50

We should mark Christ's gracious willingness to reveal himself
to the chief of sinners. He concludes his conversation with the
Samaritan woman by telling her openly and unreservedly that
he is the Saviour of the world. 'I that speak to thee,' he says,
'am the Messiah.' Nowhere in all the Gospels do we find our
Lord making such a full avowal of his nature and office as he
does in this place. And this avowal, be it remembered, was
made not to learned scribes, or moral Pharisees, but to one who
up to that day had been an ignorant, thoughtless and immoral
person!

Dealings with sinners such as these form one of the grand
peculiarities of the gospel. Whatever a man's past life may have
been, there is hope and a remedy for him in Christ. If he is only
willing to hear Christ's voice and follow him, Christ is willing
to receive him at once as a friend and to bestow on him the
fullest measure of mercy and grace. The Samaritan woman, the
penitent thief, the Philippian jailor, the publican Zacchæus are
all patterns of Christ's readiness to show mercy and to confer
full and immediate pardons. It is his glory that, like a great
physician, he will undertake to cure those who are apparently
incurable and that none are too bad for him to love and heal.
Let these things sink down into our hearts. Whatever else we
doubt, let us never doubt that Christ's love to sinners passeth
knowledge and that Christ is as willing to receive as he is
almighty to save.

What are we ourselves? This is the question, after all, which
demands our attention. We may have been up to this day
careless, thoughtless, sinful as the woman whose story we have
been reading. But yet there is hope. He who talked with the
Samaritan woman at the well is yet living at God's right hand
and never changes. Let us only ask and he will 'give us living
water'.

For meditation: *The gospel is for the chief of sinners. Do we
'write off' the openly wicked or do we call them to the Saviour of
sinners?*

Suggested further reading: Luke 15:1-7

How marvellous in the eyes of man are Christ's dealings with souls! We are told that the disciples 'marvelled that he talked with the woman'. That their Master should take the trouble to talk to a woman at all, and to a Samaritan woman, and to a strange woman at a well, when he was wearied with his journey — all this was wonderful to the eleven disciples.

The feeling displayed by the disciples on this occasion does not stand alone in the Bible. When our Lord allowed publicans and sinners to draw near to him and be in his company, the Pharisees marvelled. They exclaimed, 'This man receiveth sinners and eateth with them' (Luke 15:2). When Saul came back from Damascus, a converted man and a new creature, the Christians at Jerusalem were astonished. 'They believed not that he was a disciple' (Acts 9:26). When Peter was delivered from Herod's prison by an angel and brought to the door of the house where disciples were praying for his deliverance, they were so taken by surprise that they could not believe it was Peter. 'When they saw him they were astonished' (Acts 12:16).

If there was more real faith on the earth, there would be less surprise felt at the conversion of souls. If Christians believed more, they would expect more, and if they understood Christ better, they would be less startled and astonished when he calls and saves the chief of sinners. We should consider nothing impossible and regard no sinner as beyond the reach of the grace of God. The astonishment expressed at conversions is a proof of the weak faith and ignorance of these latter days. The thing that ought to fill us with surprise is the obstinate unbelief of the ungodly and their determined perseverance in the way to ruin. This was the mind of Christ. It is written that he thanked the Father for conversions. But he marvelled at unbelief (Matt. 11:25; Mark 6:6).

For meditation: *Have we the Father's heart for the returning prodigal (Luke 15:20-24) or a cold, repulsive look of disapproval?*

Suggested further reading: Matthew 13:44-46

How absorbing is the influence of grace when it first comes into a believer's heart! We are told that after our Lord had told the woman he was the Messiah, 'She left her waterpot and went her way into the city, and saith to the men, Come, see a man which told me all things that ever I did.' She had left her home for the express purpose of drawing water. She had carried a large vessel to the well, intending to bring it back filled. But she found at the well a new heart and new objects of interest. She became a new creature. Old things passed away. All things became new. At once everything else was forgotten for the time. She could think of nothing but the truths she had heard and the Saviour she had found. In the fulness of her heart she 'left her waterpot' and hastened away to express her feelings to others.

Conduct like that here described is doubtless uncommon in the present day. Rarely do we see a person so entirely taken up with spiritual matters that attention to this world's affairs is made a secondary matter or postponed. And why is it so? Simply because true conversions to God are uncommon. Few really feel their sins and flee to Christ by faith. Few really pass from death to life and become new creatures. Yet these few are the real Christians of the world. These are the people whose religion, like the Samaritan woman's, tells on others. Happy are they who know something by experience of this woman's feelings and can say with Paul, 'I count all things but loss for the excellency of the knowledge of Christ' (Phil. 3:8). Happy are they who have given up everything for Christ's sake, or at any rate have altered the relative importance of all things in their minds! 'If thine eye be single thy whole body shall be fulll of light' (Matt. 6:22).

For meditation: *Is your relationship with Christ a polite interest or a healthy obsession?*

Suggested further reading: *Acts 9:15-22*

How zealous a truly converted person is to do good to others!
We are told that the Samaritan woman 'went into the city, and
said to the men, Come, see a man which told me all things that
ever I did: is not this the Christ?' In the day of her conversion
she became a missionary. She felt so deeply the amazing benefit
she had received from Christ that she could not hold her peace
about him. Just as Andrew told his brother Peter about Jesus,
and Philip told Nathanael that he had found Messiah, and Saul
when converted straightway preached Christ, so, in the same
way, the Samaritan woman said, 'Come and see Christ.' She
used no abstruse arguments. She attempted no deep reasoning
about our Lord's claim to be the Messiah. She only said, 'Come
and see.' Out of the abundance of her heart her mouth spoke.

That which the Samaritan woman here did, all true
Christians ought to do likewise. The church needs it. The state
of the world demands it. Common sense points out that it is
right. Everyone who has received the grace of God and tasted
that Christ is gracious ought to find words to testify of Christ to
others. Where is our faith, if we believe that souls around us are
perishing and that Christ alone can save them and yet hold our
peace? Where is our charity if we can see others going down to
hell and yet say nothing to them about Christ and salvation?
We may well doubt our own love to Christ if our hearts are
never moved to speak of him. We may well doubt the safety of
our own souls if we feel no concern about the souls of others.

Do we ever talk to others about God and Christ and eternity
and the soul and heaven and hell? If not, what is the value of
our faith? Where is the reality of our Christianity?

For meditation: *Are you more talkative about the weather,
your family and your hobbies than about your Saviour?*

Suggested further reading: Acts 20:17-35

We have in these verses an instructive pattern of zeal for the good of others. We read that our Lord Jesus Christ declares, 'My meat is to do the will of him that sent me, and to finish his work.' To do good was not merely duty and pleasure to him. He counted it as his food, meat and drink. Job, one of the holiest Old Testament saints, could say that he esteemed God's Word 'more than his necessary food' (Job 23:12). The great Head of the New Testament church went even further. He could say the same of God's work.

Do we do any work for God? Do we try, however feebly, to set forward his cause on earth, to check that which is evil, to promote that which is good? If we do, let us never be ashamed of doing it with all our heart and soul and mind and strength. Whatsoever our hand finds to do for the souls of others, let us do it with our might (Eccles. 9:10). The world may mock and sneer and call us enthusiasts. The world can admire zeal in any service but that of God and can praise enthusiasm on any subject but that of religion. Let us work on unmoved. Whatever men may say and think, we are walking in the steps of our Lord Jesus Christ.

Let us, beside this, take comfort in the thought that Jesus Christ never changes. He that sat by the well of Samaria and found it 'meat and drink' to do good to an ignorant soul is always in one mind. High in heaven at God's right hand, he still delights to save sinners and still approves zeal and labour in the cause of God. The work of the missionary and the evangelist may be despised and ridiculed in many quarters. But while man is mocking, Christ is well pleased. Thanks be to God, Jesus is the same yesterday and today and for ever.

For meditation: *What are you doing in the service of the Lord, for the good of others and the glory of God?*

Suggested further reading: Psalm 126

Work for the souls of men is undoubtedly attended by great discouragements. The heart of natural man is very hard and unbelieving. The blindness of most men to their own lost condition and peril of ruin is something past description. 'The carnal mind is enmity against God' (Rom. 8:7). No one can have any just idea of the desperate hardness of men and women until he has tried to do good. No one can have any conception of the small number of those who repent and believe until he has personally endeavoured to 'save some' (1 Cor. 9:22). To suppose that everybody who is told about Christ and entreated to believe will become a true Christian is mere childish ignorance. 'Few there be that find the narrow way!' The labourer for Christ will find the majority of those among whom he labours unbelieving and impenitent, in spite of all that he can do. 'The many' will not turn to Christ. These are discouraging facts. But they are facts and facts that ought to be known.

The true antidote against despondency in God's work is an abiding recollection of such promises as that before us. There are 'wages' laid up for faithful reapers. They shall receive a reward at the last day, far exceeding anything they have done for Christ — a reward proportioned not to their success, but to the quantity of their work. They are gathering 'fruit' which shall endure when this world has passed away — fruit in some souls saved, if many will not believe, and fruit in evidences of their own faithfulness, to be brought out before assembled worlds. Do our hands ever hang down and our knees wax faint? Do we feel disposed to say, 'My labour is in vain and my words without profit'? Let us lean back at such seasons on this glorious promise. There are 'wages' yet to be paid. One single soul saved shall outlive and outweigh all the kingdoms of the world.

For meditation: *Christ has promised to bring all his chosen sheep into the flock. He cannot fail. Therefore evangelism cannot be in vain (John 10:16).*

Suggested further reading: Matthew 10:1-4

We have in these verses a most teaching instance of the variety of ways by which men are led to believe Christ. We read that 'Many of the Samaritans believed on Christ for the saying of the woman.' But this is not all. We read again, 'Many more believed because of Christ's own word.' In short, some were converted through the means of the woman's testimony and some were converted by hearing Christ himself.

The words of St Paul should never be forgotten: 'There are diversities of operations, but it is the same God which worketh all in all' (1 Cor. 12:6). The way in which the Spirit leads all God's people is always one and the same. But the paths by which they are severally brought into that road are often widely different. There are some in whom the work of conversion is sudden and instantaneous. There are others in whom it goes on slowly, quietly and by imperceptible degrees. Some have their hearts gently opened, like Lydia. Others are aroused by violent alarm, like the jailor at Philippi. All are finally brought to repentance towards God, faith towards our Lord Jesus Christ and holiness of conversation. But all do not begin with the same experience. The weapon which carries conviction to one believer's soul is not the one which first pierces another. The arrows of the Holy Ghost are all drawn from the same quiver. But he uses sometimes one and sometimes another, according to his own sovereign will.

Are we converted ourselves? This is the one point to which our attention ought to be directed. Our experience may not tally with that of other believers. But that is not the question. Do we feel sin, hate it and flee from it? Do we love Christ and rest solely on him for salvation? Are we bringing forth fruits of the Spirit in righteousness and true holiness? If these things are so, we may thank God and take courage.

For meditation: *The twelve disciples were of diverse backgrounds. The church consists of a variety of people bound together by the one thing that matters: a common faith in Christ (Gal. 3:26-28).*

Suggested further reading: Romans 8:18-25

The rich have afflictions as well as the poor. We read of a nobleman in deep anxiety because his son was sick. We need not doubt that every means of restoration was used that money could procure. But money is not almighty. The sickness increased and the nobleman's son lay at the point of death.

The lesson is one which needs to be constantly impressed on the minds of men. There is no more common or more mischievous error than to suppose that the rich have no cares. The rich are as liable to sickness as the poor and have a hundred anxieties beside, of which the poor know nothing at all.

Let the servant of Christ beware of desiring riches. They are certain cares and uncertain comforts. Let him pray for the rich and not envy them. How hardly shall a rich men enter the kingdom of God! Above all, let him learn to be content with such things as he has. He only is truly rich who has treasure in heaven.

Sickness and death come to the young as well as to the old. We read of a son sick unto death and a father in trouble about him. We see the natural order of things inverted. The elder is obliged to minister to the younger and not the younger to the elder. The child draws nigh to the grave before the parent and not the parent before the child.

He that is wise will never reckon confidently on long life. We never know what a day may bring forth. The strongest and fairest are often cut down and hurried away in a few hours, while the old and feeble linger on for many years. The only true wisdom is to be always prepared to meet God, to put nothing off which concerns eternity and to live like men ready to depart at any moment. So living, it matters little whether we die young or old. Joined to the Lord Jesus, we are safe in any event.

For meditation: *Freedom from sickness and death are future blessings for the Christian (Rev. 21:3,4). While we stay in this world we are subject to the effects of the Fall.*

Suggested further reading: *Hebrews 12:4-13*

What benefits affliction can confer on the soul! We read that anxiety about a son led the nobleman to Christ, in order to obtain help in time of need. Once brought into Christ's company, he learned a lesson of priceless value. In the end, 'He believed, and his whole house.' All this, be it remembered, hinged upon the son's sickness. If the nobleman's son had never been ill, his father might have lived and died in his sins.

Affliction is one of God's medicines. By it he often teaches lessons which would be learned in no other way. By it he often draws souls away from sin and the world, which would otherwise have perished everlastingly.

Let us beware of murmuring in the time of trouble. Let us settle it firmly in our minds that there is a meaning, a needs-be and a message from God in every sorrow that falls upon us. There are no lessons so useful as those learned in the school of affliction.

Christ's word is as good as Christ's presence. We read that Jesus did not come down to Capernaum to see the sick young man, but only spoke the word: 'Thy son liveth.' Almighty power went with that little sentence. That very hour the patient began to amend. Christ only spoke and the cure was done. Christ only commanded and the deadly disease stood fast.

The fact before us is singularly full of comfort. It gives enormous value to every promise of mercy, grace and peace which ever fell from Christ's lips. He that by faith has laid hold on some word of Christ has got his feet upon a rock. What Christ has said, he is able to do, and what he has undertaken, he will never fail to make good. The sinner who has really reposed his soul on the word of the Lord Jesus is safe to all eternity. He could not be safer, if he saw the book of life and his own name written in it.

For meditation: *It is better to be sick and have Christ than to be well and on a road to hell.*

Suggested further reading: *Genesis 3:13-19*

We read of a man who had been ill for no less than thirty-eight years! For eight-and-thirty weary summers and winters he had endured pain and infirmity. He had seen others healed at the waters of Bethesda and going to their homes rejoicing. But for him there had been no healing.

When we read of cases of sickness like this, we should remember how deeply we ought to hate sin! Sin was the original root and cause and fountain of every disease in the world. God did not create man to be full of aches and pains and infirmities. These things are the fruits of the Fall. There would have been no sickness if there had been no sin.

No greater proof can be shown of man's inbred unbelief than his carelessness about sin. 'Fools', says the wise man, 'make a mock at sin' (Prov. 14:9). Thousands delight in things which are positively evil and run greedily after that which is downright poison. They love that which God abhors and dislike that which God loves. They are like the madman who loves his enemies and hates his friends. Their eyes are blinded. Surely if men would only look at hospitals and infirmaries and think what havoc sin has made on this earth, they would never take pleasure in sin as they do.

Well may we be told to pray for the coming of God's kingdom! Well may we be told to long for the second advent of Jesus Christ! Then, and not till then, shall there be no more curse on the earth, no more suffering, no more sorrow and no more sin. Tears shall be wiped from the faces of all who love Christ's appearing, when their Master returns. Weakness and infirmity shall all pass away. Hope deferred shall no longer make hearts sick. There will be no chronic invalids and incurable cases, when Christ has renewed this earth.

For meditation: *Christ promises his people a glorious body like his own (Phil. 3:20,21), a body transformed by his power.*

Suggested further reading: *Psalm 119:65-71*

How great are the mercy and compassion of Christ! He 'saw' the poor sufferer lying in the crowd. Neglected, overlooked and forgotten in the great multitude, he was observed by the all-seeing eye of Christ. 'He knew' full well, by his divine knowledge, how long he had been 'in that case' and pitied him. He spoke to him unexpectedly, with words of gracious sympathy. He healed him by miraculous power, at once and without tedious delay, and sent him home rejoicing.

This is just one among many examples of our Lord Jesus Christ's kindness and compassion. He is full of undeserved, unexpected, abounding love towards man. 'He delighteth in mercy' (Micah 7:18). He is far more ready to save than man is to be saved, far more willing to do good than man is to receive it.

We are taught the lesson that recovery from sickness ought to impress upon us. That lesson is contained in the solemn words which our Saviour addressed to the man he had cured: 'Sin no more, lest a worse thing come unto thee.'

Every sickness and sorrow is the voice of God speaking to us. Each has its peculiar message. Happy are they who have an eye to see God's hand and an ear to hear his voice in all that happens to them. Nothing in this world happens by chance.

And as it is with sickness, so it is with recovery. Renewed health should send us back to our post in the world with a deeper hatred of sin, a more thorough watchfulness over our own ways and a more constant purpose of mind to live to God. Far too often the excitement and novelty of returning health tempt us to forget the vows and intentions of the sick-room. There are spiritual dangers attending a recovery! Well would it be for us all after illness to grave these words on our hearts: 'Let me sin no more, lest a worse thing come unto me.'

For meditation: *Are we making the most of God's kindnesses towards us or building up wrath? (Rom. 2:5.)*

Suggested further reading: Mark 3:1-6

These verses begin one of the most deep and solemn passages in the four Gospels. They show us the Lord Jesus asserting his own divine nature, his unity with God the Father and the high dignity of his office. Nowhere does our Lord dwell so fully on these subjects as in the chapter before us. And nowhere, we must confess, do we find out so thoroughly the weakness of man's understanding! There is much, we must all feel, that is far beyond our comprehension in our Lord's account of himself. Such knowledge, in short, is too wonderful for us. 'It is high: we cannot attain unto it' (Ps. 139:6). How often men say that they want clear explanations of such doctrines as the Trinity! Yet here we have our Lord handling the subject of his own person and, behold, we cannot follow him! We seem only to touch his meaning with the tip of our fingers.

There are some works which it is lawful to do on the sabbath day. The Jews, as on many other occasions, found fault because Jesus healed a man who had been ill for thirty-eight years on the sabbath. They charged our Lord with a breach of the fourth commandment.

Our Lord's reply to the Jews is very remarkable. 'My Father,' he says, 'worketh hitherto, and I also work.' It is as though he said, 'Though my Father rested on the seventh day from his work of creation, he has never rested for a moment from his providential government of the world and from his merciful work of supplying the daily wants of all his creatures. Were he to rest from such work, the whole frame of nature would stand still. And I also work works of mercy on the sabbath day. I do not break the fourth commandment when I heal the sick, any more than my Father breaks it when he causes the sun to rise and the grass to grow on the sabbath.'

For meditation: *Those who are too busy to spend time worshipping God must not be surprised to find God absent from them.*

Suggested further reading: *John 14:8-11*

The errors of Christians on the sabbath in these latter days are of a very different kind from those of the Jews. There is little danger of men keeping the sabbath too strictly. The thing to be feared is the disposition to keep it loosely and partially, or not to keep it at all. The tendency of the age is not to exaggerate the fourth commandment, but to cut it out of the Decalogue and throw it aside altogether. Against this tendency it becomes us all to be on our guard.

We learn from these verses the dignity and greatness of our Lord Jesus Christ. The Jews, we are told, sought to kill Jesus because he said 'that God was his Father, making himself equal with God'. Our Lord, in reply, on this special occasion enters very fully into the question of his own divine nature. In reading his words, we must all feel that we are reading mysterious things and treading on very holy ground. But we must feel a deep conviction, however little we may understand, that the things he says could never have been said by one who was only man. The speaker is nothing less than 'God manifest in the flesh' (1 Tim. 3:16).

He asserts his own unity with God the Father. No other reasonable meaning can be put on the expressions: 'The Son can do nothing of himself, but what he seeth the Father do: for what things soever he doeth, these also doeth the Son likewise . . . The Father loveth the Son, and showeth him all things that himself doeth.' Such language, however deep and high, appears to mean that in operation and knowledge and heart and will the Father and the Son are one — two persons, but one God. Truths such as these are, of course, beyond man's power to explain particularly. Enough for us to believe and rest upon them.

For meditation: *Christ must be given equal honour with his Father, or neither can be honoured (John 5:23).*

Suggested further reading: Colossians 1:15-18

Life is the highest and greatest gift that can be bestowed. It is precisely that thing that man, with all his cleverness, can neither give to the work of his hands, nor restore when taken away. But life, we are told, is in the hands of the Lord Jesus, to bestow and give at his discretion. Dead bodies and dead souls are both alike under his dominion. He has the keys of death and hell. In him is life. He is the life (John 1:4; Rev. 1:18).

He asserts his own authority to judge the world. 'The Father', we are told, 'has committed all judgement unto the Son.' All power and authority over the world is committed to Christ's hands. He is the King and the Judge of mankind. Before him every knee shall bow and every tongue shall confess that he is Lord. He that was once despised and rejected of man, condemned and crucified as a malefactor, shall one day hold a great assize and judge all the world. 'God shall judge the secrets of man by Jesus Christ' (Rom. 2:16).

Is it possible to make too much of Christ in our religion? If we have ever thought so, let us cast aside the thought for ever. Both in his own nature as God, and in his office as commissioned Mediator, he is worthy of all honour. He that is one with the Father, the Giver of life, the King of kings, the coming Judge can never be too much exalted. 'He that honoureth not the Son, honoureth not the Father that sent him.'

If we desire salvation, let us lean our whole weight on this mighty Saviour. So leaning, we never need be afraid. Christ is the rock of ages and he that builds on him shall never be confounded — neither in sickness, nor in death, nor in the judgement day. The hand that was nailed to the cross is almighty. The Saviour of sinners is 'mighty to save' (Isa. 63:1).

For meditation: *As the Father intends his Son to have supremacy in all things we should not be slow to fulfil his will.*

Suggested further reading: Matthew 7:24-27

The salvation of our souls depends on hearing Christ. It is the man, we are told, who 'hears Christ's word' and believes that God the Father sent him to save sinners who 'has everlasting life'. Such 'hearing', of course, is something more than mere listening. It is hearing as a humble scholar, hearing as an obedient disciple, hearing with faith and love, hearing with a heart ready to do Christ's will — this is the hearing that saves. It is the very hearing of which God spoke in the famous prediction of a 'prophet like unto Moses': 'Unto him shall ye hearken . . . Whosoever will not hearken unto my words which he shall speak in my name, I will require it of him' (Deut. 18:15-19).

To 'hear' Christ in this way, we must never forget, is just as needful now as it was nineteen hundred years ago. It is not enough to hear sermons and run after preachers, though some people seem to think this makes up the whole of religion. We must go much further than this: we must 'hear Christ'. To submit our hearts to Christ's teaching, to sit humbly at his feet by faith and learn of him, to enter his school as penitents and become his believing scholars, to hear his voice and follow him — this is the way to heaven. Till we know something experimentally of these things, there is no life in us.

How rich and full are the privileges of the true hearer and believer! Such a man enjoys a present salvation. Even now, at this present time, he 'hath everlasting life'. Such a man is completely justified and forgiven. There remains no more condemnation for him. His sins are put away. 'He shall not come into condemnation.' Such a man is in an entirely new position before God. He is like one who has moved from one side of a gulf to another: 'He is passed from death unto life.'

For meditation: *We can have assurance of salvation now – in the same way as Paul (2 Tim. 1:12).*

Suggested further reading: 1 Corinthians 15:51-58

Our Lord tells us that 'The hour is coming, and now is, when the dead shall hear the voice of the Son of God: and they that hear shall live.' It seems most unlikely that these words were meant to be confined to the rising of men's bodies and were fulfilled by such miracles as that of raising Lazarus from the grave. It appears far more probable that what our Lord had in view was the quickening of souls, the resurrection of conversion (Eph. 2:1; Col. 2:13). Whenever any men or women among ourselves awaken to a sense of their souls' value and become alive to God, the words are made good before our eyes. It is Christ who has spoken to their hearts by his Spirit. It is the dead hearing Christ's voice and living.

Our Lord tells us that 'The hour is coming when all that are in the grave shall hear his voice, and shall come forth; they that have done good to the resurrection of life, and they that have done evil to the resurrection of damnation.'

The passage is one of those that ought to sink down very deeply into our hearts and never be forgotten. All is not over when men die. Whether they like it or not, they will have to come forth from their graves at the last day and to stand at Christ's bar. None can escape his summons. When his voice calls them before him, all must obey. When men rise again, they will not all rise in the same condition. There will be two classes, two parties, two bodies. Not all will go to heaven. Not all will be saved. Some will rise again to inherit eternal life, but some will rise again only to be condemned. These are terrible things! But the words of Christ are plain and unmistakable. Thus it is written and thus it must be.

For meditation: _Your resurrection is a certainty – but where will you spend eternity afterwards?_

Suggested further reading: Hebrews 6:7-12

In these verses we see the proof of our Lord Jesus Christ being the promised Messiah set forth before the Jews in one view. Four different witnesses are brought forward. Four kinds of evidence are offered. His Father in heaven, his forerunner, John the Baptist, the miraculous works he had done, the Scriptures, which the Jews professed to honour — each and all are named by our Lord as testifying that he was the Christ, the Son of God. Hard must those hearts have been which could hear such testimony and yet remain unmoved! But it only proves the truth of the old saying that unbelief does not arise so much from want of evidence as from want of will to believe.

What honour Christ puts on his faithful servants! See how he speaks of John the Baptist: 'He bare witness of the truth . . . he was a burning and a shining light.' John had probably passed away from his earthly labours when these words were spoken. He had been persecuted, imprisoned and put to death by Herod, none interfering, none trying to prevent his murder. But this murdered disciple was not forgotten by his divine Master. If no one else remembered him, Jesus did. He had honoured Christ and Christ honoured him.

There things ought not to be overlooked. They are written to teach us that Christ cares for all his believing people and never forgets them. Forgotten and despised by the world, perhaps, they are never forgotten by their Saviour. He knows where they dwell and what their trials are. A book of remembrance is written for them. Their 'tears are all in his bottle' (Ps. 56:8). Their names are graven on the palms of his hands. He notices all they do for him in this evil world, though they think it not worth notice, and he will confess it one day publicly before his Father and the holy angels. He that bore witness to John the Baptist never changes. Let believers remember this. In their worst estate they may boldly say with David, 'I am poor and needy; yet the Lord thinketh upon me' (Ps. 40:17).

For meditation: *'He will not forget' (Heb. 6:10). He will 'never forsake' his own people (Heb. 13:5).*

Suggested further reading: John 14:8-14

Let us observe for another thing the honour Christ puts upon miracles, as an evidence of his being the Messiah. He says, 'The works which the Father hath given me to finish, the same works that I do, bear witness of me that the Father hath sent me.'

The miracles of the Lord receive far less attention in the present day as proofs of his divine mission than they ought to do. Too many regard them with a silent incredulity as things which, not having seen, they cannot be expected to care for. Not a few openly avow that they do not believe in the possibility of such things as miracles and would fain strike them out of the Bible as weak stories, which, like burdensome lumber, should be cast overboard to lighten the ship.

But, after all, there is no getting over the fact that in the days when our Lord was upon earth, his miracles produced an immense effect on the minds of men. They aroused attention to him that worked them. They excited inquiry, if they did not convert. They were so many, so public and so incapable of being explained away that our Lord's enemies could only say that they were done by satanic agency. That they were done they could not deny. 'This man,' they said, 'doeth many miracles' (John 11:47). The facts which wise men pretend to deny now no one pretended to deny nineteen hundred years ago.

Let the enemies of the Bible take our Lord's last and greatest miracle, his own resurrection from the dead, and disprove it if they can. When they have done that, it will be time to consider what they say about miracles in general. They have never answered the evidence of it yet and they never will. Let the friends of the Bible not be moved by objections against miracles until that one miracle has been fairly disposed of.

For meditation: *The only sort of person who has problems with the miracles of the Bible is the person who does not know the God of the Bible.*

Suggested further reading: Isaiah 53

Let us observe in these verses the honour that Christ puts upon the Scriptures. He refers to them in concluding his list of evidences as the great witnesses to him. 'Search the Scriptures,' he says, 'they are they which testify of me.'

The 'Scriptures' of which our Lord speaks are, of course, the Old Testament. And his words show the important truth which too many are apt to overlook — that every part of our Bibles is meant to teach us about Christ. Christ is not merely in the Gospels and epistles. Christ is to be found directly and indirectly in the Law, the Psalms and the Prophets. In the promises to Adam, Abraham, Moses and David, in the types and emblems of the ceremonial law, in the predictions of Isaiah and the other prophets, Jesus, the Messiah, is everywhere to be found in the Old Testament.

How is it that men see these things so little? The answer is plain. They do not 'search the Scriptures'. They do not dig into that wondrous mine of wisdom and knowledge and seek to become acquainted with its contents. Simple, regular reading of our Bibles is the grand secret of establishment in the faith. Ignorance of the Scriptures is the root of all error.

What a plain duty it is to read the Scriptures! Men have no right to expect spiritual light if they neglect the great treasury of all light. If even of the Old Testament our Lord said, 'Search . . . it testifies of me,' how much more is it a duty to search the whole Bible!

And now what will men believe, if they do not believe the divine mission of Christ? Great indeed is the obstinacy of infidelity. A cloud of witnesses testify that Jesus was the Son of God. To talk of wanting evidence is childish folly. The plain truth is that the chief seat of unbelief is the heart. Many do not wish to believe and therefore remain unbelievers.

For meditation: _The Scriptures make us wise unto salvation – they teach about Christ – but only faith in Christ saves (2 Tim. 3:15)._

Suggested further reading: 2 Peter 3:8-14

The Lord Jesus says to the unbelieving Jews, 'Ye will not come to me that ye might have life.'

It is want of will to come to Christ for salvation that will be found, at last, to have shut the many out of heaven. It is not men's sins. All manner of sin may be forgiven. It is not any decree of God. We are not told in the Bible of any whom God has only created to be destroyed. It is not any limit in Christ's work of redemption. He has paid a price sufficient for all mankind. It is something far more than this. It is man's own innate unwillingness to come to Christ, repent and believe. Either from pride, or laziness, or love of sin, or love of the world, the many have no mind, or wish, or heart, or desire to seek life in Christ. 'God has given to us eternal life, and this life is in his Son' (1 John 5:11). But men stand still and will not stir hand or foot to get life. And this is the whole reason why many of the lost are not saved.

This is a painful and solemn truth, but one that we can never know too well. It contains a first principle in Christian theology. Thousands, in every age, are constantly labouring to shift the blame of their condition from off themselves. They talk of their inability to change. They tell you complacently that they cannot help being what they are! They know that they are wrong, but they cannot be different! It will not do. Such talk will not stand the test of the Word of Christ before us. The unconverted are what they are because they have no will to be better. 'Light is come into the world, and men love darkness rather than light' (John 3:19). The words of the Lord Jesus will silence many: 'I would have gathered you, and ye would not be gathered' (Matt. 23:37).

For meditation: *Condemnation comes to those who have not believed the truth but have delighted in wickedness (2 Thess. 2:12). Is that a description of you?*

Suggested further reading: John 12:37-43

We are all by nature dead in trespasses and sins. Spiritual life is laid up for sinners in Christ alone. To receive benefit from Christ men must come to him by faith. The real reason why men do not come to Christ, and consequently die in their sins, is their want of will to come.

Let us mark in this passage one principal cause of unbelief. The Lord Jesus says to the Jews, 'How can ye believe which receive honour one of another, and seek not the honour that cometh of God only?' He meant by that saying that they were not honest in their religion. With all their apparent desire to hear and learn, they cared more in reality for pleasing man than God. In this state of mind they were never likely to believe.

A deep principle is contained in this saying of our Lord's and one that deserves special attention. True faith does not depend merely on the state of man's head and understanding, but on the state of his heart. His mind may be convinced. His conscience may be pricked. But so long as there is anything the man is secretly loving more than God, there will be no true faith. The man himself may be puzzled and wonder why he does not believe. He does not see that he is like a child sitting on the lid of his box and wishing to open it, but not considering that his own weight keeps it shut. Let a man make sure that he honestly and really desires first the praise of God. It is the want of an honest heart which makes many stick fast in their religion all their days and die at length without peace. Those who complain that they hear and approve and assent, but make no progress and cannot get any hold on Christ, should ask themselves this simple question: 'Am I honest? Am I sincere? Do I really desire first the praise of God?'

For meditation: *Which is more important to you – the praise of your friends or the approval of God?*

Suggested further reading:　2 Timothy 3:12-4:4

That there really was such a person as Moses, that he really was the author of the writings commonly ascribed to him — on both these points our Lord's testimony is distinct: 'He wrote of me.' Can we suppose for a moment that our Lord was only accommodating himself to the prejudices and traditions of his hearers and that he spoke of Moses as a writer though he knew in his heart that Moses never wrote at all? Such an idea is profane. It would make out our Lord to have been dishonest. Can we suppose for a moment that our Lord was ignorant about Moses and did not know the wonderful discoveries which learned men, falsely so called, have made in the twentieth century? Such an idea is ridiculous blasphemy. To imagine the Lord Jesus speaking ignorantly in such a chapter as the one before us is to strike at the root of all Christianity. There is but one conclusion about the matter. There was such a person as Moses. The writings commonly ascribed to him were written by him. The facts recorded in them are worthy of all credit. Our Lord's testimony is an unanswerable argument. The sceptical writers against Moses and the Pentateuch have greatly erred.

Let us beware of handling the Old Testament irreverently and allowing our minds to doubt the truth of any part of it because of alleged difficulties. The simple fact that writers of the New Testament continually refer to the Old Testament and speak even of the most miraculous events recorded in it as undoubtedly true should silence our doubts. Is it at all likely, probable or credible, that men of the twentieth century are better informed about Moses than Jesus and his apostles? God forbid that we should think so! Then let us stand fast and not doubt that every word in the Old Testament, as well as in the New, was given by inspiration of God.

For meditation: *Anti-biblical theologians and theology still dominate the academic world and professing church, but they have never saved one soul by their lies.*

Suggested further reading: *Romans 4:18-25*

These verses describe one of our Lord's most remarkable miracles. Of all the great works that he did, none was done so publicly as this and before so many witnesses. Of all the miracles related in the Gospels, this is the only one which all the four Gospel writers alike record. This fact alone (like the four times repeated account of the crucifixion and resurrection) is enough to show that it is a miracle demanding special attention.

We have, for one thing, in this miracle a lesson about Christ's almighty power. We see our Lord feeding five thousand men with 'five barley loaves and two small fishes'. We see clear proof that a miraculous event took place in the 'twelve baskets of fragments' that remained after all had eaten. Creative power was manifestly exercised. Food was called into existence that did not exist before. In healing the sick and raising the dead something was amended or restored that had already existed. In feeding five thousand men with five loaves something must have been created which before had no existence.

Such a history as this ought to be specially instructive and encouraging to all who endeavour to do good to souls. It shows us the Lord Jesus 'able to save to the uttermost'. He is one who has all power over dead hearts. Not only can he mend that which is broken, build up that which is ruined, heal that which is sick, strengthen that which is weak; he can do even greater things than these. He can call into being that which was not before and call it out of nothing. We must never despair of anyone being saved. So long as there is life there is hope. Reason and sense may say that some poor sinner is too hardened, or too old to be converted. Faith will reply, 'Our Master can create as well as renew. With a Saviour who, by his Spirit, can create a new heart, nothing is impossible.'

For meditation: *Is anything too hard for the Lord? (Gen. 18:14.)*

Suggested further reading: *2 Kings 4:1-7*

We see the Lord Jesus supplying the hunger of a huge multitude of five thousand men. The provision seemed, at first sight, utterly inadequate for the occasion. To satisfy so many craving mouths with such scanty fare, in such a wilderness, seemed impossible. But the event showed that there was enough and to spare. There was not one who could complain that he was not filled.

There can be no doubt that this was meant to teach the adequacy of Christ's gospel to supply the necessities of the whole world. Weak and feeble and foolish as it may seem to man, the simple story of the cross is enough for all the children of Adam in every part of the globe. The tidings of Christ's death for sinners and the atonement made by that death is able to meet the hearts and satisfy the consciences of all nations and peoples and kindreds and tongues. Carried by faithful messengers, it feeds and supplies all ranks and classes. 'The preaching of the cross is to them that perish foolishness, but to us who are saved it is the power of God' (1 Cor. 1:18). Five barley loaves and two small fishes seemed scanty provision for a hungry crowd. But blessed by Christ and distributed by his disciples, they were more than sufficient.

Let us never doubt for a moment that the preaching of Christ crucified — the old story of his blood and righteousness and substitution — is enough for all the spiritual necessities of all mankind. It is not worn out. It is not obsolete. It has not lost its power. We want nothing new, nothing more broad and kind, nothing more intellectual, nothing more efficacious. We want nothing but the true bread of life which Christ bestows, distributed faithfully among starving souls. Let men sneer or ridicule as they will. Nothing else can do good in this sinful world. No other teaching can fill hungry consciences and give them peace.

For meditation: *The provision of God is always adequate for the need that arises.*

Suggested further reading: *Luke 22:24-27*

We are told that, after feeding the multitude, he 'perceived that they would come and take him by force to make him a king'. At once he departed and left them. He wanted no such honours as these. He had come, 'not to be ministered unto, but to minister and to give his life a ransom for many' (Matt. 20:28).

We see the same spirit and frame of mind all through our Lord's earthly ministry. From his cradle to his grave he was 'clothed with humility' (1 Peter 5:5). He was born of a poor woman and spent the first thirty years of his life in a carpenter's house at Nazareth. He was followed by poor companions, many of them no better than fishermen. He was poor in his manner of living: 'The foxes had holes, and the birds of the air their nests: but the Son of man had not where to lay his head'(Matt. 8:20). When he went on the Sea of Galilee, it was in a borrowed boat. When he rode into Jerusalem, it was on a borrowed ass. When he was buried, it was in a borrowed tomb. 'Though he was rich, yet for our sakes he became poor' (2 Cor. 8:9).

The example is one which ought to be far more remembered than it is. How common are pride and ambition and high-mindedness! How rare are humility and lowly-mindedness! How few ever refuse greatness when offered to them! How many are continually seeking great things for themselves and forgetting the injunction: 'Seek them not!' (Jer. 45:5.)

Our Lord, after washing the disciples' feet, said, 'I have given you an example that ye should do as I have done' (John 13:15). There is little, it may be feared, of that feet-washing spirit among Christians.

'Tell me,' it has been said, 'how much humility a man has, and I will tell you how much religion he has.'

For meditation: *We are to be ambitious to please Christ, not to promote self (2 Cor. 5:9).*

Suggested further reading: *Job 23 1-10*

We should notice in these verses the trials through which
Christ's disciples had to pass. We are told that they were sent
over the lake by themselves, while their Master tarried behind.
And then we see them alone in a dark night, tossed about by a
great wind on stormy waters and, worst of all, Christ not with
them. It was a strange transition. From witnessing a mighty
miracle and helping it instrumentally, amidst an admiring
crowd, to solitude, darkness, winds, waves, storm, anxiety and
danger, the change was very great! But Christ knew it and
Christ appointed it and it was working for their good.

Trial, we must distinctly understand, is part of the diet which
all true Christians must expect. It is one of the means by which
their grace is proved and by which they find out what there is in
themselves. Winter as well as summer, cold as well as heat,
clouds as well as sunshine are all necessary to bring the fruit of
the Spirit to ripeness and maturity. We do not naturally like
this. We would rather cross the lake with calm weather and
favourable winds, with Christ always by our side and the sun
shining down on our faces. But it may not be. It is not in this
way that God's children are made 'partakers of his holiness'
(Heb. 12:10).

The Lord Jesus came to his disciples as they were rowing on
the stormy lake, 'walking on' the waters. He walked on them as
easily as we walk on dry land. They bore him as firmly as the
pavement of the temple, or the hills around Nazareth. That
which is contrary to all natural reason was perfectly possible to
Christ.

It was just as easy for him to walk on the sea as to form the
sea at the beginning, just as easy to suspend the common laws
of nature, as they are called, as to impose those laws at the first.

For meditation: *He who created and sustains this world can
keep his people secure through its trials and snares.*

Suggested further reading: Revelation 2:18-29

What knowledge of man's heart our Lord Jesus Christ possesses! We see him exposing the false motives of those who followed him for the sake of the loaves and fishes. They had followed him across the Lake of Galilee. They seemed at first sight ready to believe in him and do him honour. But he knew the inward springs of their conduct and was not deceived. 'Ye seek me,' he said, 'not because ye saw the miracles, but because ye did eat of the loaves and were filled.'

The Lord Jesus, we should never forget, is still the same. He never changes. He reads the secret motives of all who profess and call themselves Christians. He knows exactly why they do all they do in their religion.

Let us be real, true and sincere in our religion, whatever else we are. The sinfulness of hypocrisy is very great, but its folly is greater still. It is not hard to deceive ministers, relatives and friends. A little decent outward profession will often go a long way. But it is impossible to deceive Christ. 'His eyes are as a flame of fire' (Rev. 1:14). He sees us through and through. Happy are those who can say, 'Thou, Lord, who knowest all things, knowest that we love thee' (John 21:17).

Our Lord told the crowds who followed him so diligently for the loaves and fishes, 'not to labour for the meat that perisheth'.

What our Lord did mean to rebuke was that excessive attention to labour for the body, while the soul is neglected, which prevails everywhere in the world. What he reproved was the common habit of labouring only for the things of time and letting alone the things of eternity, of minding only the life that now is and disregarding the life to come. Against this habit he delivers a solemn warning. Happy are those who learn the respective value of soul and body and give the first and best place in their thoughts to salvation.

For meditation: *No one will be more pathetic and tragic on the Day of Judgement than the unmasked hypocrite who looked good but lacked life.*

Suggested further reading: Luke 13:22-27

Christ tells us to 'labour for the meat that endureth to ever-lasting life'. He would have us take pains to find food and satis-faction for our souls. That food is provided in rich abundance in him. But he that would have it must diligently seek it.

How are we to labour? There is but one answer. We must labour in the use of all appointed means. We must read our Bibles like men digging for hidden treasure. We must wrestle earnestly in prayer like men contending with a deadly enemy for life. We must take our whole heart to the house of God and worship and hear like those who listen to the reading of a will. We must fight daily against sin, the world and the devil like those who fight for liberty and must conquer or be slaves. These are the ways we must walk in if we would find Christ and be found of him. This is 'labouring'. This is the secret of getting on about our souls.

Labour like this no doubt is very uncommon. In carrying it on we shall have little encouragement from man and shall often be told that we are 'extreme' and go too far. Strange and absurd as it is, the natural man is always fancying that we may take too much thought about religion and refusing to see that we are far more likely to take too much thought about the world. But whatever man may say, the soul will never get spiritual food without labour. We must 'strive', we must 'run', we must 'fight', we must throw our whole heart into our soul's affairs. It is 'the violent' who take the kingdom (Matt. 11:12).

Never let us rest till we have eaten of the meat which Christ alone can give. They that are content with any other spiritual food will sooner or later 'lie down in sorrow' (Isa. 50:11).

For meditation: *Half-heartedness does not find God, but earnest seeking is always rewarded (Heb. 11:6).*

Suggested further reading: Ephesians 2:1-10

If any two things are put in strong contrast in the New Testament, they are faith and works. Not working, but believing, not of works, but through faith, are words familiar to all careful Bible-readers. Yet here the great Head of the church declares that believing on him is the highest and greatest of all 'works'! It is 'the work of God'.

Doubtless our Lord did not mean that there is anything meritorious in believing. Man's faith, at the very best, is feeble and defective. Regarded as a 'work', it cannot stand the severity of God's judgement, deserve pardon or purchase heaven. But our Lord did mean that faith in himself, as the only Saviour, is the first act of the soul which God requires at a sinner's hands. Till a man believes on Jesus and rests on Jesus as a lost sinner, he is nothing. Our Lord did mean that faith in himself is that act of the soul which specially pleases God. When the Father sees a sinner casting aside his own righteousness and simply trusting in his dear Son, he is well pleased. Without such faith it is impossible to please God. Our Lord did mean that faith in himself is the root of all saving religion. There is no life in a man till he believes. Above all, our Lord did mean that faith in himself is the hardest of all spiritual acts to the natural man. Did the Jews want something to do in religion? Let them know that the greatest thing they had to do was to cast aside their pride, confess their guilt and need and humbly believe.

Let all who know anything of true faith thank God and rejoice. Blessed are they that believe! It is an attainment which many of the wise of this world have never yet reached. We may feel ourselves poor, weak sinners. But do we believe? We may fail and come short in many things. But do we believe?

For meditation: *Receiving a free gift involves activity but it does not imply merit in the recipient.*

Suggested further reading: *Mark 6:1-6*

When our Lord bade his hearers 'labour for the meat which endureth to eternal life', they immediately began to think of works to be done and a goodness of their own to be established. 'What shall we do that we might work the works of God?' Doing, doing, doing was their only idea of the way to heaven. Again, when our Lord spoke of himself as one sent of God and the need of believing on him at once, they turn round with the question: 'What sign showest thou? What dost thou work?' Fresh from the mighty miracle of the loaves and fishes, one might have thought they had had a sign sufficient to convince them. Taught by our Lord Jesus Christ himself, one might have expected a greater readiness to believe. But, alas! there are no limits to man's dullness, prejudice and unbelief in spiritual matters. It is a striking fact that the only thing which our Lord is said to have 'marvelled' at during his earthly ministry was man's 'unbelief' (Mark 6:6).

We shall do well to remember this, if we ever try to do good to others in the matter of religion. We must not be cast down because our words are not believed and our efforts seem thrown away. We must not complain of it as a strange thing and suppose that the people we have to deal with are peculiarly stubborn and hard. We must recollect that this is the very cup of which our Lord had to drink and like him we must patiently work on. If even he, so perfect and so plain a Teacher, was not believed, what right have we to wonder if men do not believe us? Happy are the ministers and missionaries and teachers who keep these things in mind! It will save them much bitter disappointment. In working for God, it is of first importance to understand what we must expect in man. Few things are so little realized as the extent of human unbelief.

For meditation: *Let us not be amazed at unbelief, but let us not be discouraged by it either. All the chosen sheep shall hear the voice of Christ (John 10:16,27).*

Suggested further reading: Acts 4:8-12

Our Lord would have us know that he himself is the appointed food of man's soul. The soul of every man is naturally starving and famishing through sin. Christ is given by God the Father to be the satisfier, the reliever and the physician of man's spiritual need. In him and his mediatorial office, in him and his atoning death, in him and his priesthood, in him and his grace, love and power — in him alone will empty souls find their wants supplied. In him there is life. He is 'the bread of life'.

With what divine and perfect wisdom this name is chosen! Bread is necessary food. We can manage tolerably well without many things on our table, but not without bread. So is it with Christ. We must have Christ, or die in our own sins. Bread is food that suits all. Some cannot eat meat and some cannot eat vegetables. But all like bread. It is food both for the queen and for the pauper. So is it with Christ. He is just the Saviour that meets the wants of every class. Bread is food that we need daily. Other kinds of food we take, perhaps, only occasionally. But we want bread every morning and evening in our lives. So is it with Christ. There is no day in our lives but we need his blood, his righteousness, his intercession and his grace. Well may he be called, 'The bread of life'!

Do we know anything of spiritual hunger? Do we feel anything of craving and emptiness in conscience, heart and affections? Let us distinctly understand that Christ alone can relieve and supply us and that it is his office to relieve. We must come to him by faith. We must believe on him and commit our souls into his hands. So coming, he pledges his royal word we shall find lasting satisfaction for both time and eternity. It is written: 'He that cometh unto me shall never hunger, and he that believeth on me shall never thirst.'

For meditation: _Our Lord is not a spiritual delicacy to decorate the plate of a gourmet but necessary food for the spiritually starving._

Suggested further reading: Romans 8:28-39

What does 'coming' mean? It means that movement of the soul which takes place when a man, feeling his sins and finding out that he cannot save himself, hears of Christ, applies to Christ, trusts in Christ, lays hold on Christ and leans all his weight on Christ for salvation. When this happens a man is said, in Scripture language, to 'come' to Christ.

What did our Lord mean by saying, 'I will in no wise cast him out'? He meant that he will not refuse to save anyone who comes to him, no matter what he may have been. His past sins may have been very great. His present weakness and infirmity may be very great. But does he come to Christ by faith? Then Christ will receive him graciously, pardon him freely, place him in the number of his dear children and give him everlasting life.

We are taught in verse 40 that Christ has brought into the world a salvation open and free to everyone. Our Lord draws a picture of it from the story of the brazen serpent, by which bitten Israelites in the wilderness were healed. Everyone that chose to 'look' at the brazen serpent might live. Just in the same way, everyone who desires eternal life may 'look' at Christ by faith and have it freely. There is no barrier, no limit, no restriction. The terms of the gospel are wide and simple. Everyone may 'look and live'.

We are taught in verse 39 that Christ will never allow any soul that is committed to him to be lost and cast away. He will keep it safe, from grace to glory, in spite of the world, the flesh and the devil. Not one bone of his mystical body shall ever be broken. Not one lamb of his flock shall ever be left behind in the wilderness. He will raise to glory, in the last day, the whole flock entrusted to his charge and not one shall be found missing.

For meditation: *With such a clear invitation to come to Christ and such great promises made to those who come, the foolishness and sinfulness of not coming is surely clear.*

Suggested further reading: Romans 8:1-11

Christ's lowly condition, when he was upon earth, is a
stumbling-block to the natural man. We read that 'The Jews
murmured, because Jesus said, I am the bread that came down
from heaven. And they said, Is not this Jesus, the son of
Joseph, whose father and mother we know? How is it then that
he saith, I came down from heaven?' Had our Lord come as a
conquering king, with wealth and honours to bestow on his followers and mighty armies in his train, they would have been
willing enough to receive him. But a poor and lowly and suffering Messiah was an offence to them. Their pride refused to
believe that such a one was sent from God.

There is nothing that need surprise us in this. It is human
nature showing itself in its true colours. We see the same thing
in the days of the apostles. Christ crucified was 'to the Jews a
stumbling-block, and to the Greeks foolishness' (1 Cor. 1:23).
The cross was an offence to many wherever the gospel was
preached.

The salvation of a believer is a present thing. Our Lord Jesus
Christ says, 'Verily, verily, I say unto you, he that believeth on
me hath everlasting life.' How many seem to think that forgiveness and acceptance with God are things which we cannot
attain in this life, that they are things which are to be earned by
a long course of repentance and faith and holiness — things
which we may receive at the bar of God at last, but must never
pretend to touch while we are in this world! It is a complete
mistake to think so. The very moment a sinner believes on
Christ he is justified and accepted. There is no condemnation
for him. He has peace with God and that immediately and
without delay. His name is in the book of life, however little he
may be aware of it. He has a title to heaven, which death and
hell and Satan cannot overthrow. Happy are they that know
this truth! It is an essential part of the good news of the gospel.

For meditation: *True joy in the Lord can only exist where
certainty rather than doubt reigns.*

Suggested further reading: Isaiah 65:1-7

We find our Lord saying, 'No man can come unto me, except the Father which hath sent me draw him.' Until the Father draws the heart of man by his grace, man will not believe.

The solemn truth contained in these words is one that needs careful weighing. It is vain to deny that without the grace of God no one ever can become a true Christian. We are spiritually dead and have no power to give ourselves life. We need a new principle put in us from above. Facts prove it. Preachers see it.

But after all, of what does this inability of man consist? In what part of our inward nature does this impotence reside? Here is a point on which many mistakes arise. For ever let us remember that the *will* of man is the part of him which is in fault. His inability is not physical, but moral. It would not be true to say that a man has a real wish and desire to come to Christ, but no power to come. It would be far more true to say that a man has no power to come because he has no desire or wish. It is not true that he would come if he could. It is true that he could come if he would. The corrupt will, the secret disinclination, the want of heart are the real causes of unbelief. It is here the mischief lies. The power that we want is a new will. It is precisely at this point that we need the 'drawing' of the Father.

These things, no doubt, are deep and mysterious. By truths like these God proves the faith and patience of his people. Can they believe him? Can they wait for a fuller explanation at the last day? What they see not now, they shall see hereafter. One thing at any rate is abundantly clear and that is man's responsibility for his own soul. His inability to come to Christ does not make an end of his accountableness. Both things are equally true. If lost at last, it will prove to have been his own fault. His blood will be on his own head.

For meditation: *Are you described in Proverbs 29:1 or Acts 22:10?*

Suggested further reading: Luke 23:39-43

The 'eating and drinking' of which Christ speaks do not mean any literal eating and drinking. Above all, the words were not spoken with any reference to the sacrament of the Lord's Supper. For one thing, a literal 'eating and drinking' of Christ's body and blood would have been an idea utterly revolting to all Jews and flatly contradictory to an often-repeated precept of their law.

For another thing, to take a literal view of 'eating and drinking' is to interpose a bodily act between the soul of man and salvation. This is a thing for which there is no precedent in Scripture. The only things without which we cannot be saved are repentance and faith.

Last, but not least, to take a literal view of 'eating and drinking' would involve most blasphemous and profane consequences. It would shut out of heaven the penitent thief. He died long after these words were spoken, without any literal eating and drinking. Will any dare to say he had 'no life' in him? It would admit to heaven thousands of ignorant, godless communicants in the present day. They literally eat and drink, no doubt! But they have no eternal life and will not be raised to glory at the last day. Let these reasons be carefully pondered.

The plain truth is there is a morbid anxiety in fallen man to put a carnal sense on scriptural expressions, wherever he possibly can. He struggles hard to make religion a matter of forms and ceremonies, of doing and performing, of sacraments and ordinances, of sense and sight. He secretly dislikes that system of Christianity which makes the state of heart the principal thing and labours to keep sacraments and ordinances in the second place. Happy is that Christian who remembers these things and stands on his guard!

For meditation: *Many of the Jews expected acceptance with God because of their outward ordinances – yet they perished (1 Cor. 10:1-5).*

Suggested further reading: Hebrews 9:11-14

Few passages of Scripture have been so painfully wrested and perverted as that which we have now read. The Jews are not the only people who have striven about its meaning. A sense has been put upon it which it was never intended to bear. Fallen man, in interpreting the Bible, has an unhappy aptitude for turning meat into poison. The things that were written for his benefit, he often makes an occasion for falling.

Let us consider carefully what these verses do mean. The expressions thay contain are, no doubt, very remarkable. Let us try to get some clear notion of their meaning.

The 'flesh and blood of the Son of man' mean that sacrifice of his own body, which Christ offered up on the cross, when he died for sinners. The atonement made by his death, the satisfaction made by his sufferings as our Substitute, the redemption effected by his enduring the penalty of our sins in his own body on the tree — this seems to be the true idea that we should set before our minds.

The 'eating and drinking', without which there is no life in us, means that reception of Christ's sacrifice which takes place when a man believes on Christ crucified for salvation. It is an inward and spiritual act of the heart and has nothing to do with the body. Whenever a man, feeling his own guilt and sinfulness, lays hold on Christ and trusts in the atonement made for him by Christ's death, at once he 'eats the flesh of the Son of man, and drinks his blood'. His soul feeds on Christ's sacrifice by faith just as his body would feed on bread. Believing, he is said to 'eat'. Believing, he is said to 'drink'. And the special thing that he eats and drinks and gets benefit from is the atonement made for his sins by Christ's death for him on Calvary.

For meditation: *Food left on a plate is of no benefit to the body. When Christ is not received by faith he is of no benefit to the soul.*

Suggested further reading: Exodus 12:1-13

The practical lessons which may be gathered from the whole passage are weighty and important. The point being once settled that 'the flesh and blood' in these verses mean Christ's atonement and the 'eating and drinking' mean faith, we may find in these verses great principles of truth which lie at the very root of Christianity.

We may learn that faith in Christ's atonement is a thing of absolute necessity to salvation. Just as there was no safety for the Israelite in Egypt who did not eat the Passover lamb, in the night when the first-born were slain, so there is no life for the sinner who does not eat the flesh of Christ and drink his blood.

We may learn that faith in Christ's atonement unites us by the closest possible bonds to our Saviour and entitles us to the highest privileges. Our souls shall find full satisfaction for all their wants: 'His flesh is meat indeed, and his blood is drink indeed.' All things are secured to us that we can need for time and eternity: 'Whoso eateth my flesh and drinketh my blood hath eternal life, and I will raise him up at the last day.'

Last, but not least, we may learn that faith in Christ's atonement is a personal act, a daily act and an act that can be felt. No one can eat and drink for us and no one, in like manner, can believe for us. We need food every day, and not once a week or once a month, and, in like manner, we need to employ faith every day. We feel benefit when we have eaten and drunk, we feel strengthened, nourished and refreshed, and, in like manner, if we believe truly, we shall feel the better for it, by sensible hope and peace in our inward man.

For meditation: *It is because Christ died at Calvary that salvation is freely offered to us in the gospel. It is by faith that salvation is freely received by us to our eternal benefit.*

Suggested further reading: 1 Corinthians 1:18-25

The true antidote to wrong views of baptism and the Lord's Supper is a right understanding of the third and sixth chapters of St John's Gospel and the whole of St John's First Epistle. While he altogether omits to describe the institution of the Lord's Supper, and says little or nothing about baptism in the Gospel, he dwells at the same time most strongly on these two mighty truths, which he foresaw were in danger of being forgotten — *viz*, the new birth and faith in the atonement. Surely it is possible to honour baptism and the Lord's Supper without thrusting them in everywhere in our interpretation of Scripture.

We are told that 'many' who had followed our Lord for a season were offended when he spoke of 'eating his flesh and drinking his blood'. They murmured and said, 'This is an hard saying; who can hear it?' Murmurs and complaints of this kind are very common. It must never surprise us to hear them. They have been, they are, they will be as long as the world stands. To some Christ's sayings appear hard to understand. To others, as in the present case, they appear hard to believe and harder still to obey. It is just one of the many ways in which the natural corruption of man shows itself. So long as the heart is naturally proud, worldly, unbelieving and fond of self-indulgence, if not of sin, so long there will never be wanting people who will say of Christian doctrines and precepts, 'These are hard sayings; who can hear them?'

Humility is the frame of mind which we should labour and pray for, if we would not be offended. If we find any of Christ's sayings hard to understand, we should humbly remember our present ignorance and believe that we shall know more by and by. If we find any of his sayings difficult to obey, we should humbly recollect that he will never require of us impossibilities and that, what he bids us do, he will give us grace to perform.

For meditation: *Salvation by works is always popular because it exalts the efforts of men. Salvation through the blood of Christ is repugnant to many because it exalts the efforts of another in the light of the inadequacy of self.*

Suggested further reading: Ezekiel 37:1-10

Our Lord says, 'It is the Spirit that quickeneth.' By this he means that it is the Holy Ghost who is the special author of spiritual life in man's soul. By his agency it is first imparted and afterwards sustained and kept up. If the Jews thought he meant that men could have spiritual life by bodily eating or drinking, they were greatly mistaken.

Our Lord says, 'The flesh profiteth nothing.' By this he means that neither his flesh nor any other flesh, literally eaten, can do good to the soul. Spiritual benefit is not to be had through the mouth,but through the heart. The soul is not a material thing and cannot therefore be nourished by material food.

Our Lord says, 'The words that I speak unto you, they are spirit and they are life.' By this he signifies that his words and teachings, applied to the heart by the Holy Ghost, are the true means of producing spiritual influence and conveying spiritual life. By words thoughts are begotten and aroused. By words mind and conscience are stirred. And Christ's words especially are spirit-stirring and life-giving.

The principle contained in this verse, however faintly we may grasp its full meaning, deserves peculiar attention in these times. There is a tendency in many minds to attach an excessive importance to the outward and visible or 'doing' part of religion. They seem to think that the sum and substance of Christianity consists in baptism and the supper of the Lord, in public ceremonies and forms, in appeals to the eye and ear and bodily excitement. Surely they forget that it is 'the Spirit that quickeneth' and that the 'flesh profiteth nothing'. It is not so much by noisy public demonstrations as by the still quiet work of the Holy Ghost on hearts that God's cause prospers. It is Christ's words entering into consciences which 'are spirit and life'.

For meditation: *Truth and life come by God's Word and God's Spirit. Never separate the two.*

Suggested further reading: Psalm 139:1-6

Christ has a perfect knowledge of the hearts of men. We read that 'He knew from the beginning who they were that believed not, and who should betray him.'

Sentences like this are found so frequently in the Gospels that we are apt to underrate their importance. Yet there are few truths which we shall find it so good for our souls to remember as that which is contained in the sentence before us. The Saviour with whom we have to do is one who knows all things!

What light this throws on the marvellous patience of the Lord Jesus in the days of his earthly ministry! He knew the sorrow and humiliation before him and the manner of his death. He knew the unbelief and treachery of some who professed to be his familiar friends, allowing one whom he knew to be about to betray him to be one of his apostles. It was doubtless meant to teach us that false profession must be expected everywhere and must not surprise us. How much we ought to tolerate and put up with, if our Lord tolerated Judas near him! But 'for the joy that was set before him' he endured it all (Heb. 12:2).

What light this throws on the folly of hypocrisy and false profession in religion! Let those who are guilty of it recollect that they cannot deceive Christ. He sees them, knows them and will expose them at the last day, except they repent. Whatever we are as Christians and however weak, let us be real, true and sincere.

Finally, what light this throws on the daily pilgrimage of all true Christians! Let them take comfort in the thought that their Master knows them. However much unknown and misunderstood by the world, their Master knows their hearts and will comfort them at the last day. Happy is he who, in spite of many infirmities, can say with Peter, 'Lord, thou knowest all things; thou knowest that I love thee' (John 21:17).

For meditation: *Nothing goes unnoticed. The smallest good shall receive its reward (Matt. 10:42).*

Suggested further reading: Matthew 13:18-23

What an old sin backsliding is! We read that when our Lord had explained what he meant by 'eating and drinking his flesh and blood', 'from that time many went back and walked no more with him'. The true grace of God no doubt is an everlasting possession. From this men never fall away entirely when they have once received it. 'The foundation of God standeth sure' (2 Tim. 2:19). 'My sheep shall never perish' (John 10:28). But there is counterfeit grace and unreal religion in the church, wherever there is true, and from counterfeit grace thousands may and do fall away. Like the stony-ground hearers in the parable of the sower, many 'have no root in themselves, and so in time of temptation fall away'. All is not gold that glitters. All blossoms do not come to fruit. All are not Israel which are called Israel. Men may have feelings, desires, convictions, resolutions, hopes, joys, sorrows in religion and yet never have the grace of God. They may run well for a season and bid fair to reach heaven and yet break down entirely after a time, go back to the world and end like Demas, Judas Iscariot and Lot's wife.

It must never surprise us to see and hear of such cases in our own days. If it happened in our Lord's time and under our Lord's teaching, much more may we expect it to happen now. Above all, it must never shake our faith and discourage us in our course. On the contrary, we must make up our minds that there will be backsliders in the church as long as the world stands. The sneering infidel who defends his unbelief by pointing at them must find some better argument than their example. He forgets that there will always be counterfeit coin where there is true money.

For meditation: *Machines that are never serviced prove ineffi-cient and break down. Christians that neglect their relationship with God decline and grow cold.*

Suggested further reading: Matthew 16:13-20

Our Lord had said to the twelve, when many went back, 'Will ye also go away?' At once Peter replied, with characteristic zeal and fervour, 'Lord, to whom shall we go? Thou hast the words of eternal life. And we believe and are sure that thou art that Christ, the Son of the living God.'

The confession contained in these words is a very remarkable one. Living in a professedly Christian land and surrounded by Christian privileges, we can hardly form an adequate idea of its real value. For a humble Jew to say of one whom scribes and Pharisees and Sadducees agreed in rejecting, 'Thou hast the words of eternal life; thou art the Christ,' was an act of mighty faith. No wonder that our Lord said in another place, 'Blessed art thou, Simon Bar-jona: for flesh and blood hath not revealed it unto thee, but my Father which is in heaven' (Matt. 16:18).

But the question with which Peter begins is just as remarkable as his confession. 'To whom shall we go?' said the noble-hearted apostle. 'Whom shall we follow? To what teacher shall we take ourselves? Where shall we find any guide to heaven to compare with thee? What shall we gain by forsaking thee?'

The question is one which every true Chrsitian may boldly ask when urged and tempted to give up his religion and go back to the world. It is easy for those who hate religion to pick holes in our conduct, to make objections to our doctrines, to find fault with our practices. It may be hard sometimes to give them any answer. But after all, 'To whom shall we go,' if we give up our religion? Where shall we find such peace and hope and solid comfort as in serving Christ, however poorly we serve him? Can we better ourselves by turning our back on Christ and going back to our old ways? We cannot. Then let us hold on our way and persevere.

For meditation: *Our Lord is not a way, a truth and a life amongst many others, but* **the** *way,* **the** *truth,* **the** *life (John 14:6).*

Suggested further reading: Matthew 19:16-22

What little benefit some men get from religious privileges! We read that our Lord said, 'Have not I chosen you twelve, and one of you is a devil?' And it goes on, 'He spake of Judas Iscariot, the son of Simon.'

If ever there was a man who had great privileges and opportunities, that man was Judas Iscariot. A chosen disciple, a constant companion of Christ, a witness of his miracles, a hearer of his sermons, a commissioned preacher of his kingdom, a fellow and friend of Peter, James and John — it would be impossible to imagine a more favourable position for a man's soul. Yet if anyone ever fell hopelessly into hell and made shipwreck at last for eternity, that man was Judas Iscariot. The character of that man must have been black indeed, of whom our Lord could say he is 'a devil'.

Let us settle it firmly in our minds that the possession of religious privileges alone is not enough to save our souls. It is neither place, nor light, nor company, nor opportunities, but grace that man needs to make him a Christian. With grace we may serve God in the most difficult position — like Daniel in Babylon, Obadiah in Ahab's court and the saints in Nero's household. Without grace we may live in the full sunshine of Christ's countenance and yet, like Judas, be miserably cast away. Then let us never rest till we have grace reigning in our souls. Grace is to be had for the asking. There is one sitting at the right hand of God who has said, 'Ask, and it shall be given you' (Matt. 7:7). The Lord Jesus is more willing to give grace than man is to seek it. If men have it not, it is because they do not ask it.

For meditation: *Those who are so near to Christ yet so far from him will have an eternity of irreversible regret.*

Suggested further reading: 1 Kings 22:1-8

The chapter we now begin is divided from the preceding one by a wide interval of time. The many miracles which our Lord wrought while he 'walked in Galilee' are passed over by St John in comparative silence. The events which he was specially inspired to record are those which took place in or near Jerusalem.

We are told that even our Lord's 'brethren did not believe in him'. Holy and harmless and blameless as he was in life, some of his nearest relatives according to the flesh did not receive him as the Messiah. It was bad enough that his own people, 'the Jews sought to kill him'. But it was even worse that 'his brethren did not believe'.

Verse 7 reveals one of those secret principles which influence men in their treatment of religion. They help to explain that deadly enmity with which many during our Lord's earthly ministry regarded him and his gospel. It was not so much the high doctrines which he preached as the high standard of practice which he proclaimed which gave offence. It was not even his claim to be the Messiah which men disliked so much as his witness against the wickedness of their lives. In short, they could have tolerated his opinions if he would only have spared their sins.

The principle, we may be sure, is one of universal application. It is at work now just as much as it was nineteen hundred years ago. The real cause of many people's dislike to the gospel is the holiness of living which it demands. Teach abstract doctrines only and few will find any fault. Denounce the fashionable sins of the day and call on men to repent and walk consistently with God and thousands at once will be offended. The true reason why many profess to be infidels and abuse Christianity is the witness that Christianity bears against their own bad lives. Like Ahab, they hate it, 'because it does not prophesy good concerning them, but evil' (1 Kings 22:8).

For meditation: *Does a lack of opposition suggest a lack of godliness? (2 Tim. 3:12.)*

Suggested further reading: *2 Timothy 4:9-18*

That great scriptural doctrine, man's need of preventing and converting grace, stands out here, as if written with a sunbeam. It becomes all who question that doctrine to look at this passage and consider. Let them observe that seeing Christ's miracles, hearing Christ's teaching, living in Christ's own company were not enough to make men believers. The mere possession of spiritual privileges never yet made anyone a Christian. All is useless without the effectual and applying work of God the Holy Ghost. No wonder that our Lord said in another place, 'No man can come to me, except the Father which hath sent me draw him' (John 6:44).

The true servants of Christ in every age will do well to remember this. They are often surprised and troubled to find that in religion they stand alone. They are apt to fancy that it must be their own fault that all around them are not converted like themselves. They are ready to blame themselves because their families remain worldly and unbelieving. But let them look at the verse before us. In our Lord Jesus Christ there was no fault either in temper, word, or deed. Yet even Christ's own 'brethren did not believe in him'.

Our blessed Master has truly learned by experience how to sympathize with all his people who stand alone. This is a thought 'full of sweet, pleasant and unspeakable comfort'. He knows the heart of every isolated believer and can be touched with the feeling of his trials. He has drunk this bitter cup. He has passed through this fire. Let all who are fainting and cast down, because brothers and sisters despise their religion, turn to Christ for comfort and pour out their hearts before him. He 'has suffered himself being tempted' in this way and he can help as well as feel (Heb. 2:18).

For meditation: *Never has anyone known desertion as our Lord knew it (Matt. 27:46). He is uniquely suited to sympathize with the lonely.*

Suggested further reading: Matthew 10:34-39

We are told that 'There was much murmuring among the people concerning him: for some said, He is a good man: others said, Nay; but he deceiveth the people.' The words which old Simeon had spoken thirty years before were here accomplished in a striking manner. He had said to our Lord's mother, 'This child is set for the fall and rising again of many in Israel: and for a sign which shall be spoken against . . . that the thoughts of many hearts may be revealed' (Luke 2:34,35). In the diversities of opinion about our Lord which arose among the Jews, we see the good old man's saying fulfilled.

In the face of such a passage as this, the endless differences and divisions about religion, which we see on all sides in the present day, ought never to surprise us. The open hatred of some towards Christ, the carping, fault-finding, prejudiced spirit of others, the bold confession of the few faithful ones, the timid, man-fearing temper of the many faithless ones, the unceasing war of words and strife of tongues with which the churches of Christ are so sadly familiar are only modern symptoms of an old disease. Such is the corruption of human nature that Christ is the cause of division among men wherever he is preached. So long as the world stands, some when they hear of him will love and some will hate; some will believe and some will believe not. That deep, prophetical saying of his will be continually verified: 'Think not that I come to send peace on earth; I came not to send peace, but a sword' (Matt. 10:34).

What think we of Christ ourselves? This is the one question with which we have to do. Let us never be ashamed to be of that little number who believe on him, hear his voice, follow him and confess him before men. While others waste their time in vain jangling and unprofitable controversy, let us take up the cross and give all diligence to make our calling and election sure.

For meditation: *Many divisions are unnecessary in this world and ought to be avoided, but divisions over Christ are essential and eternal.*

Suggested further reading: Acts 18:24-28

The difficulty of finding out 'what is truth' in religion is a common subject of complaint among men. They point to the many differences which prevail among Christians on matters of doctrine and profess to be unable to decide who is right. In thousands of cases this professed inability to find out truth becomes an excuse for living without any religion at all.

The saying of our Lord before us is one that demands the serious attention of persons in this state of mind. It supplies an argument whose edge and point they will find it hard to evade. It teaches that one secret of getting the key of knowledge is to practise honestly what we know, and that if we conscientiously use the light that we now have, we shall soon find more light coming down into our minds. In short, there is a sense in which it is true that by doing we shall come to knowing.

There is a mine of truth in this principle. Well would it be for men if they would act upon it. Instead of saying, as some do, 'I must first know everything clearly, and then I will act,' we should say, 'I will diligently use such knowledge as I possess and believe that in the using fresh knowledge will be given to me.' How many mysteries this simple plan would solve! How many hard things would soon become plain if men would honestly live up to their light and 'follow on to know the Lord'! (Hosea 6:3.)

It should never be forgotten that God deals with us as moral beings and not as beasts or stones. He loves to encourage us to self-exertion and diligent use of such means as we have in our hands. The plain things in religion are undeniably very many. Let a man honestly attend to them and he shall be taught the deep things of God. Let him humbly use what little knowledge he has got and God will soon give him more.

For meditation: *Because Apollos told others what he knew, he learned more of what he needed to know. When we use the little we have, we gain more.*

Suggested further reading: *2 Corinthians 4:1-6*

A self-exalting spirit in ministers of religion is entirely opposed to the mind of Christ. Our Lord says, 'He that speaketh of himself seeketh his own glory; but he that seeketh his glory that sent him, the same is true, and no unrighteousness is in him.' The wisdom and truth of this sentence will be evident at once to any reflecting mind. The minister truly called of God will be deeply sensible of his Master's majesty and his own infirmity and will see in himself nothing but unworthiness. He, on the other hand, who knows that he is not 'inwardly moved by the Holy Ghost' will try to cover over his defects by magnifying himself and his office. The very desire to exalt ourselves is a bad symptom. It is a sure sign of something wrong within.

Does anyone ask illustrations of the truth before us? He will find them, on the one side, in the scribes and Pharisees of our Lord's times. If one thing more than another distinguished these unhappy men, it was their desire to get praise for themselves. He will find them, on the other side, in the character of the apostle St Paul. The keynote that runs through all his epistles is personal humility and zeal for Christ's glory: 'I am less than the least of all saints (Eph. 3:8). 'I am not meet to be called an apostle'(1 Cor. 15:9). 'I am chief of sinners' (1 Tim. 1:15). 'We preach not ourselves but Christ Jesus the Lord, and ourselves your servants for Jesus' sake' (2 Cor. 4:5).

Does anyone ask for a test by which he may discern the real man of God from the false shepherd in the present day? Let him remember our Lord's weighty words and notice carefully what is the main object that a minister loves to exalt. Not he who is ever crying, 'Behold the church! Behold the sacraments! Behold the ministry!' but he who says, 'Behold the Lamb!' is the pastor after God's own heart.

For meditation: *Many modern ministers and evangelists parade self rather than exalting Christ. So do many non-ministers!*

Suggested further reading: Matthew 7:21-23

We learn in this passage the danger of forming a hasty judgement. The Jews at Jerusalem were ready to condemn our Lord
as a sinner against the law of Moses, because he had done a
miracle of healing on the sabbath day. They forgot in their
blind enmity that the fourth commandment was not meant to
prevent works of necessity or works of mercy. And hence they
drew down on themselves the rebuke: 'Judge not according to
the appearance, but judge righteous judgement.'

The practical value of the lesson before us is very great. We
shall do well to remember it as we travel through life and to correct our estimate of people and things by the light which it
supplies.

We are often too ready to be deceived by an appearance of
good. We are in danger of rating some men as very good
Christians because of a little outward profession of religion
and a decent Sunday formality — because, in short, they talk
the language of Canaan and wear the garb of pilgrims. We
forget that all is not good that appears good, even as all is not
gold that glitters, and that daily practice, choice, tastes, habits,
conduct, private character are the true evidence of what a man
is. In a word, we forget our Lord's saying: 'Judge not according
to the appearance.'

We are too ready, on the other hand, to be deceived by the
appearance of evil. We must remember that the best of men are
but men at their very best and that the most eminent saints may
be overtaken by temptation and yet be saints at heart after all.
We must not hastily suppose that all is evil where there is an
occasional appearance of evil. The holiest man may fall sadly
for a time and yet the grace within him may finally get a victory.
Is a man's general character godly? Then let us suspend our
judgement when he falls and hope on. Let us 'judge righteous
judgement'.

For meditation: *The failing saint is to be treated differently to
the brazenly rebellious (Gal. 6:1; 1:8).*

Suggested further reading: James 2:14-20

We are told that some of our Lord's hearers knew clearly where Christ was to be born. They referred to Scripture, like men familiar with its contents. And yet the eyes of their understanding were not enlightened. Their own Messiah stood before them and they neither received, nor believed, nor obeyed him.

A certain degree of religious knowledge, beyond doubt, is of vast importance. Ignorance is certainly not the mother of true devotion and helps nobody towards heaven. An 'unknown God' can never be the object of a reasonable worship. Happy indeed would it be for Christians if they all knew the Scriptures as well as the Jews seem to have done when our Lord was on earth!

But while we value religious knowledge, we must take care that we do not overvalue it. We must not think it enough to know the facts and doctrines of our faith, unless our hearts and lives are thoroughly influenced by what we know. The very devils know the creed intellectually and 'believe and tremble', but remain devils still (James 2:19). It is quite possible to be familiar with the letter of Scripture and to be able to quote texts appropriately and reason about the theory of Christianity and yet to remain dead in trespasses and sins. Like many of the generation to which our Lord preached, we may know the Bible well and yet remain faithless and unconverted.

Heart-knowledge, we must always remember, is the one thing needful. It is something which schools and universities cannot confer. It is the gift of God. To find out the plague of our own hearts and hate sin, to become familiar with the throne of grace and the fountain of Christ's blood, to sit daily at the feet of Jesus and humbly learn of him — this is the highest degree of knowledge to which mortal man can attain. Let anyone thank God who knows anything of these things.

For meditation: *What is more awful than to be always learning but never coming to a knowledge of the truth? (2 Tim. 3:7.)*

Suggested further reading: Luke 1:1-4

We see in these verses the obstinate blindness of the unbelieving Jews. We find them defending their denial of our Lord's Messiahship by saying, 'We know this man whence he is: but when Christ cometh no man knoweth whence he is.' And yet in both these assertions they were wrong!

They were wrong in saying that they 'knew whence our Lord came'. They meant no doubt to say that he was born at Nazareth and belonged to Nazareth and was therefore a Galilean. Yet the fact was that our Lord was born at Bethlehem. It is incredible to suppose that the Jews could not have found this out, if they had honestly searched and inquired. It is notorious that pedigrees, genealogies and family histories were most carefully kept by the Jewish nation. Their ignorance was without excuse.

They were wrong again in saying that no man was to know whence Christ came. There was a well-known prophecy, with which their whole nation was familiar, that Christ was to come out of the town of Bethlehem (Micah 5:2; Matt. 2:5; John 7:42). It is absurd to suppose that they had forgotten this prophecy. But apparently they found it inconvenient to remember it on this occasion.

Men's memories are often sadly dependent on their wills. They shut their eyes against the plainest facts and doctrines of Christianity. They pretend to say that they do not understand and cannot therefore believe the things that we press on their attention as needful to salvation. But, alas, in nineteen cases out of twenty it is a wilful ignorance! They do not believe what they do not like to believe. They will neither read, nor listen, nor search, nor think, nor inquire honestly after truth. Can anyone wonder if such persons are ignorant? Faithful and true is that old proverb: 'There are none so blind as those who will not see.'

For meditation: *Luke searched out the facts to give Theophilus certainty. The unbelieving Jews guessed and were wrong. Are you studious or lazy in the things of God?*

Suggested further reading:　Matthew 25:1-13

We see in these verses the miserable end to which unbelievers may one day come. We find our Lord saying to his enemies, 'Ye shall seek me, and shall not find me; and where I am thither ye cannot come.'

We can hardly doubt that these words were meant to have a prophetical sense. Whether our Lord had in view individual cases of unbelief among his hearers, or whether he looked forward to the national remorse which many would feel too late in the final siege of Jerusalem, are points which we cannot perhaps decide. But that many Jews did remember Christ's sayings long after he had ascended into heaven and did in a way seek him and wish for him when it was too late, we may be very sure.

It is far too much forgotten that there is such a thing as finding out truth too late. There may be convictions of sin, discoveries of our own folly, desires after peace, anxieties about heaven, fears of hell — but all too late. The teaching of Scripture on this point is clear and express. It is written in Proverbs: 'Then shall they call upon me, but I will not answer; they shall seek me early, but they shall not find me' (Prov. 1:28). It is written of the foolish virgins in the parable that when they found the door shut they knocked in vain, saying, 'Lord, Lord, open to us' (Matt. 25:11). Awful as it may seem, it is possible, by continually resisting light and warnings, to sin away our own souls. It sounds terrible, but it is true.

Let us take heed to ourselves lest we sin after the example of the unbelieving Jews and never seek the Lord Jesus as a Saviour till it is too late. The door of mercy is still open. The throne of grace is still waiting for us. Let us give diligence to make sure our interest in Christ, while it is called today. Better never have been born that hear the Son of God say at last, 'Where I am, thither ye cannot come.'

For meditation: *When we are tempted to put off what God requires us to do today, let us remember the wise saying: 'Tomorrow never comes.'*

Suggested further reading: Isaiah 55:1-7

We have in these verses a case supposed. The Lord Jesus says, 'If any man thirst.' These words no doubt were meant to have a spiritual meaning. The thirst before us is of a purely spiritual kind. It means anxiety of soul, conviction of sin, desire of pardon, longing after peace of conscience. When a man feels his sins and wants forgiveness, is deeply sensible of his soul's need and earnestly desires help and relief, then he is in that state of mind which our Lord had in view when he said, 'If any man thirst.' The Jews who heard Peter preach on the Day of Pentecost and were 'pricked in their hearts', the Philippian jailer who cried to Paul and Silas, 'What must I do to be saved?' are both examples of what the expression means. In both cases there was a 'thirst'.

Such thirst as this, unhappily, is known by few. All ought to feel it and all would feel it if they were wise. Sinful, mortal, dying creatures as we all are, with souls that will one day be judged and spend eternity in heaven or hell, there lives not the man or woman on earth who ought not to 'thirst' after salvation. And yet the many thirst after everything almost except salvation. Money, pleasure, honour, rank, self-indulgence — these are the things which they desire. There is no clearer proof of the fall of man and the utter corruption of human nature than the careless indifference of most people about their souls.

Happy are those who know something by experience of spiritual 'thirst'. The beginning of all true Christianity is to discover that we are guilty, empty, needy sinners. Till we know that we are lost, we are not in the way to be saved. The very first step towards heaven is to be thoroughly convinced that we deserve hell.

'Blessed indeed are they which do hunger and thirst after righteousness, for they shall be filled' (Matt. 5:6).

For meditation: *With such a clear invitation to come and drink, shall we stay thirsty and die?*

Suggested further reading: Ephesians 2:1-10

We have in these verses a remedy proposed. The Lord Jesus says, 'If any man thirst, let him come unto me and drink.' He declares that he is the true fountain of life, the supplier of all spiritual necessities, the reliever of all spiritual wants. He invites all who feel the burden of sin heavy to apply to him and proclaims himself their helper.

Those words, 'Let him come unto me,' are few and very simple. But they settle a mighty question which all the wisdom of Greek and Roman philosophers could never settle: they show how man can have peace with God. They show that peace is to be had in Christ by trusting in him as our Mediator and Substitute — in one word, by believing. To 'come' to Christ is to believe on him and to 'believe' on him is to come. The remedy may seem a very simple one, too simple to be true. But there is no other remedy than this and all the wisdom of the world can never find a flaw in it, or devise a better.

To use this grand prescription of Christ is the secret of all saving Christianity. The saints of God in every age have been men and women who drank of this fountain by faith and were relieved. They felt their guilt and emptiness and thirsted for deliverance. They heard of a full supply of pardon, mercy and grace in Christ crucified for all penitent believers. They believed the good news and rested upon it. They cast aside all confidence in their own goodness and worthiness and came to Christ by faith as sinners. So coming they found relief. So coming daily they lived. So coming they died. Really to feel the sinfulness of sin and to thirst and really to come to Christ and believe are the two steps which lead to heaven. But they are mighty steps. Thousands are too proud and careless to take them. Few, alas, think, and still fewer believe!

For meditation:
> *None but Jesus, none but Jesus*
> *Can do helpless sinners good*
> (Joseph Hart).

Suggested further reading: *John 4:10-14*

We have in these verses a promise held out. The Lord Jesus says, 'He that believeth on me, out of his belly shall flow rivers of living water.' These words, of course, were meant to have a figurative sense. They have a double application. They teach, for one thing, that all who come to Christ by faith shall find in him abundant satisfaction. They teach, for another thing, that believers shall not only have enough for the wants of their own souls, but shall also become fountains of blessings to others.

The fulfilment of the first part of the promise could be testified by thousands of living Christians in the present day. They would say, if their evidence could be collected, that when they came to Christ by faith, they found in him more than they expected. They have tasted peace and hope and comfort since they first believed, which, with all their doubts and fears, they would not exchange for anything in this world. They have found grace according to their need and strength according to their days. In themselves and their own hearts they have often been disappointed, but they have never been disappointed in Christ.

The fulfilment of the other half of the promise will never be fully known until the judgement day. That day alone shall reveal the amount of good that every believer is made the instrument of doing to others, from the very day of his conversion. Some do good while they live, by their tongues, like the apostles and first preachers of the gospel. Some do good when they are dying, like Stephen and the penitent thief and our own martyred Reformers at the stake. Some do good long after they are dead by their writings, like Baxter and Bunyan and M'Cheyne. But in one way or another, probably, almost all believers will be found to have been fountains of blessings. They know it not now, but they will find at last that it is true.

For meditation: *What is promised here is not a special blessing for the spiritual élite but a fulness of blessing for every believer.*

Suggested further reading: Daniel 3:8-18

We see, for another thing, in these verses the overruling hand of God over all his enemies. We find that the unbelieving Jews 'sought to take' our Lord, 'but no man laid hands on him, because his hour was not yet come'. They had the will to hurt him, but by an invisible restraint from above, they had not the power.

There is a mine of deep truth in the words before us which deserves close attention. They show us plainly that all our Lord's sufferings were undergone voluntarily and of his own free will. He did not go to the cross because he could not help it. He did not die because he could not prevent his death. Neither Jew nor Gentile, Pharisee nor Sadducee, Annas nor Caiaphas, Herod nor Pontius Pilate, could have injured our Lord, except power had been given them from above. All that they did was done under control and by permission. The crucifixion was part of the eternal counsels of the Trinity. The passion of our Lord could not begin until the very hour which God had appointed. This is a great mystery. But it is a truth.

The servants of Christ in every age should treasure up the doctrine before us and remember it in time of need. It is full of sweet, pleasant and unspeakable comfort to godly persons. Let such never forget that they live in a world where God overrules all times and events and where nothing can happen but by God's permission. The very hairs of their heads are all numbered. Sorrow and sickness and poverty and persecution can never touch them unless God sees fit. They may boldly say to every cross, 'Thou couldst have no power against me, except it were given thee from above.' Then let them work on confidently. They are immortal till their work is done. Let them suffer patiently, if needs be that they suffer. Their 'times are in God's hand' (Ps. 31:15). That hand guides and governs all things here below and makes no mistakes.

For meditation: *The joy of the martyr in death is a joy in the Lord who reigns over all and in all.*

Suggested further reading: Jeremiah 1:4-10

How eminent must have been our Lord's gifts as a public Teacher of religion! We are told that even the officers of the chief priests, who were sent to take him, were struck and amazed. Of the *manner* of our Lord's public speaking, we can of necessity form little idea. It was probably something very unlike what the Jewish officers were accustomed to hear. There is much in what is said in another place: 'He taught them as one having authority, and not as the scribes' (Matt. 7:29).

Of the *matter* of our Lord's public speaking, we may form some conception from the discourses which are recorded in the four Gospels. The leading features of these discourses are plain and unmistakable. The world has never seen anything like them, since the gift of speech was given to man. They often contain deep truths, which we have no line to fathom. But they often contain simple things, which even a child can understand. They are bold and outspoken in denouncing national and ecclesiastical sins and yet they are wise and discreet in never giving needless offence. They are faithful and direct in their warnings and yet loving and tender in their invitations. For a combination of power and simplicity, of courage and prudence, of faithfulness and tenderness, we may well say, 'Never man spake like this man!'

It would be well for the church of Christ if ministers and teachers of religion would strive more to speak after their Lord's pattern. Let them remember that fine bombastic language and a sensational, theatrical style of address are utterly unlike their Master. Let them realize that an eloquent simplicity is the highest attainment of public speaking. Of this their Master left them a glorious example. Surely they need never be ashamed of walking in his steps.

For meditation: *One difference between a man who preaches as a hobby and a preacher sent by God is that only the latter speaks with authority.*

Suggested further reading: Mark 8:22-26

How slowly and gradually the work of grace goes on in some hearts! We are told that Nicodemus stood up in the council of our Lord's enemies and mildly pleaded that he deserved fair dealing.

This very Nicodemus, we must remember, is the man who eighteen months before had come to our Lord by night as an ignorant inquirer. He evidently knew little then and dared not come to Christ in open day. But now, after eighteen months, he has got on so far that he dares to say something on our Lord's side. It was but little that he said, no doubt, but it was better than nothing at all. And a day was yet to come when he would go further still. He was to help Joseph of Arimathæa in doing honour to our Lord's dead body when even his chosen apostles had forsaken him and fled.

The case of Nicodemus is full of useful instruction. It teaches us that there are diversities in the operation of the Holy Spirit. All are undoubtedly led to the same Saviour, but all are not led precisely in the same way. It teaches us that the work of the Spirit does not always go forward with the same speed in the hearts of men. In some cases it may go forward very slowly indeed and yet may be real and true.

We shall do well to remember these things in forming our opinion of other Christians. We are often ready to condemn some as graceless, because their experience does not exactly tally with our own, or to set them down as not in the narrow way at all, because they cannot run as fast as ourselves. We must beware of hasty judgements. It is not always the fastest runner that wins the race. It is not always those who begin suddenly in religion and profess themselves rejoicing Christians who continue steadfast to the end. Slow work is sometimes the surest and most enduring. Nicodemus stood firm when Judas Iscariot fell away.

For meditation: *In the hard grind of pioneer missionary work William Carey's claim was 'I can plod'. To 'plod' and arrive is better than to run and fall asleep.*

Suggested further reading: Matthew 7:1-5

To suppose, as some have thought, that the narrative before us palliates the sin of adultery and exhibits our Lord as making light of the seventh commandment is surely a great mistake. There is nothing in the passage to justify such an assertion. There is not a sentence in it to warrant our saying anything of the kind. Of all whose words are recorded in the Bible there is none who has spoken so strongly about the breach of the seventh commandment as our divine Master. It is he who has taught that it may be broken by a look or a thought, as well as by an open act (Matt. 5:28). It is he who has spoken more strongly than any about the sanctity of the marriage relation (Matt. 19:5). In all that is recorded here, we see nothing inconsistent with the rest of his teaching. He simply refused to usurp the office of the judge and to pronounce condemnation on a guilty woman for the gratification of his deadly enemies.

He refused to be a 'judge' and lawgiver among them and specially in a case which their own law had already decided. He gave them at first no answer at all. But 'when they continued asking', our Lord silenced them with a withering and heart-searching reply: 'He that is without sin among you,' he said, 'let him first cast a stone at her.' He did not say that the woman had not sinned, or that her sin was a trifling and venial one. But he reminded her accusers that they at any rate were not the persons to bring a charge against her. Their own motives and lives were far from pure. They themselves did not come into the case with clean hands. What they really desired was not to vindicate the purity of God's law and punish a sinner, but to wreak their malice on himself.

For meditation: *We are to condemn sin in order to lead others to repentance, not so that we feel 'smug' and self-righteous.*

Suggested further reading: 2 Samuel 12:1-15

We learn, for one thing, the power of conscience. We read of the woman's accusers that, when they heard our Lord's appeal, 'being convicted by their own conscience, they went out one by one, beginning at the eldest, even unto the last'. Wicked and hardened as they were, they had something within which made them cowards. Fallen as human nature is, God has taken care to leave within every man a witness that will be heard.

Conscience is a most important part of our inward man and plays a most prominent part in our spiritual history. It cannot save us. It never yet led anyone to Christ. It is blind and liable to be misled. It is lame and powerless and cannot guide us to heaven. Yet conscience is not to be despised.

Happy is he who never stifles his conscience, but strives to keep it tender! Still happier is he who prays to have it enlightened by the Holy Ghost and sprinkled with Christ's blood.

We learn, for another thing, the nature of true repentance. When our Lord had said to the sinful woman, 'Neither do I condemn thee,' he dismissed her with the solemn words: 'Go and sin no more.' He did not merely say, 'Go home and repent.' He pointed out the chief thing which her case required — the necessity of immediate breaking off from her sin.

Let us never forget this lesson. It is the very essence of genuine repentance, as the church catechism well teaches, to 'forsake sin'. That repentance which consists in nothing more than feeling, talking, professing, wishing, meaning, hoping and resolving is worthless in God's sight. Action is the very life of 'repentance unto salvation not to be repented of'. Till a man ceases to do evil and turns from his sins, he does not really repent.

For meditation: *Only the blood of Christ can cleanse the conscience; only it is adequate to deal with the guilt of sin.*

Suggested further reading: Isaiah 8:19-9:2

Let us notice, for one thing, in these verses, what the Lord Jesus says of himself. He proclaims, 'I am the light of the world.'
  These words imply that the world needs light and is naturally in a dark condition. It is so in a moral and spiritual point of view and it has been so for nearly 6 000 years. In ancient Egypt, Greece and Rome, in modern England, France and Germany, the same report is true. The vast majority of men neither see nor understand the value of their souls, the true nature of God, nor the reality of a world to come! Notwithstanding all the discoveries of art and science, 'Darkness still covers the earth, and gross darkness the people' (Isa. 60:2).
  For this state of things, the Lord Jesus Christ declares himself to be the only remedy. He has risen, like the sun, to diffuse light and life and peace and salvation in the midst of a dark world. He invites all who want spiritual help and guidance to turn to him and take him for their leader. What the sun is to the whole solar system — the centre of light and heat and life and fertility — that he has come into the world to be to sinners.
  Let this saying sink down into our hearts. It is weighty and full of meaning. False lights on every side invite man's attention in the present day. Reason, philosophy, earnestness, liberalism, conscience and the voice of the church are all, in their various ways, crying loudly that they have got 'the light' to show us. Their advocates know not what they say. Wretched are those who believe their high professions! He only is the true light who came into the world to save sinners, who died as our Substitute on the cross and sits at God's right hand to be our Friend. 'In his light we shall see light' (Ps. 36:9).

For meditation: *Christ is our sunrise, who sheds light on our way and dispels our gloom (Luke 1:78, 79).*

Suggested further reading: 1 John 1:5 to 2:2

Let us notice in these verses what the Lord Jesus says of those that follow him. He promises, 'He that followeth me shall not walk in darkness, but shall have the light of life.'

To follow Christ is to commit ouselves wholly and entirely to him as our only Leader and Saviour and to submit ourselves to him in every matter, both of doctrine and practice. 'Following' is only another word for 'believing'. It is the same act of soul, only seen from a different point of view. As Israel followed the pillar of cloud and fire in all their journeyings — moving whenever it moved, stopping whenever it tarried, asking no questions, marching on in faith — so must a man deal with Christ. He must 'follow the Lamb whithersoever he goeth' (Rev. 14:4).

He that so follows Christ shall 'not walk in darkness'. He shall not be left in ignorance, like the many around him. He shall not grope in doubt and uncertainty, but shall see the way to heaven and know where he is going. He 'shall have the light of life'. He shall feel within him the light of God's countenance shining on him. He shall find in his conscience and understanding a living light which nothing can altogether quench. The lights with which many please themselves shall go out in the valley of the shadow of death and prove worse than useless. But the light that Christ gives to everyone that follows him shall never fail.

And now, where are we ourselves? Do we know? Many are living and dying in a kind of fog. Where are we going? Can we give a satisfactory answer? Hundreds go out of existence in utter uncertainty. Let us leave nothing uncertain that concerns our everlasting salvation.

For meditation: *There can be no better leader and teacher than he who is the truth and the way to God (John 14:6).*

Suggested further reading: John 17:1-8

Let us notice in these verses what the Lord Jesus says of his enemies. He tells the Pharisees that, with all their pretended wisdom, they were ignorant of God. 'Ye neither know me nor my Father: if ye had known me, ye should have known my Father also.'

Ignorance like this is only too common. There are thousands who are conversant with many branches of human learning and can even argue and reason about religion and yet know nothing really about God. That there is such a being as God they fully admit. But his character and attributes revealed in Scripture — his holiness, his purity, his justice, his perfect knowledge, his unchangeableness — are things with which they are little acquainted. In fact, the subject of God's nature and character makes them uncomfortable and they do not like to dwell upon it.

The grand secret of knowing God is to draw near to him through Jesus Christ. Approached from this side, there is nothing that need make us afraid. Viewed from this standpoint, God is the sinner's friend. God, out of Christ, may well fill us with alarm. How shall we dare to look at so high and holy a being? God in Christ is full of mercy, grace and peace. His law's demands are satisfied. His holiness need not make us afraid. Christ, in one word, is the way and door, by which we must ever draw nigh to the Father. If we know Christ, we shall know the Father. It is his own word: 'No man cometh unto the Father but by me' (John 14:6). Ignorance of Christ is the root of ignorance of God. Wrong at the starting-point, the whole sum of a man's religion is full of error. Christ, the light of the world, is for us as well as for others, if we humbly follow him, cast our souls on him and become his disciples.

For meditation: *Biographies are rarely as revealing as autobiographies. Christ is the autobiography of God – his supreme self-revelation (John 1:18; Col. 1:15).*

Suggested further reading:　*Proverbs 1:20-33*

It is possible to seek Christ in vain. Our Lord says to the unbelieving Jews, 'Ye shall seek me, and shall die in your sins.' He meant, by these words, that the Jews would one day seek him in vain.

The lesson before us is a very painful one. That such a Saviour as the Lord Jesus, so full of love, so willing to save, should ever be sought 'in vain' is a sorrowful thought. Yet so it is! A man may have many religious feelings about Christ, without any saving religion. Sickness, sudden affliction, the fear of death, the failure of usual sources of comfort — all these causes may draw out of a man a good deal of 'religiousness'. Under the immediate pressure of these he may say his prayers fervently, exhibit strong spiritual feelings and profess for a season to 'seek Christ' and be a different man. And yet all this time his heart may never be touched at all! Take away the peculiar circumstances that affected him and he may possibly return at once to his old ways. He sought Christ 'in vain', because he sought him from false motives and not with his whole heart.

Unhappily this is not all. There is such a thing as a settled habit of resisting light and knowledge, until we seek Christ 'in vain'. Scripture and experience alike prove that men may reject God until God rejects them and will not hear their prayer. They may go on stifling their convictions, quenching the light of conscience, fighting against their own better knowledge, until God is provoked to give them over and let them alone. It is not for nothing that these words are written: 'Then shall they call upon me, but I will not answer; they shall seek me early, but they shall not find me: for that they hated knowledge, and did not choose the fear of the Lord' (Prov. 1:28,29).

There is no safety but in seeking Christ while he may be found and calling on him while he is near, seeking him with a true heart and calling on him with an honest spirit.

For meditation:　*Salvation is not eternally available. There is an accepted time and it is now (2 Cor. 6:2).*

Suggested further reading: John 17:9-19

We learn how wide is the difference between Christ and the ungodly. Our Lord says to the unbelieving Jews, 'Ye are from beneath, I am from above: ye are of this world, I am not of this world.'

These words, no doubt, have a special application to our Lord Jesus Christ himself. In the highest and most literal sense, there never was but one who could truly say, 'I am from above . . . I am not of this world.' That one is he who came forth from the Father and was before the world — even the Son of God.

But there is a lower sense, in which these words are applicable to all Christ's living members. Compared to the thoughtless multitude around them, they are 'from above' and 'not of this world', like their Master. The thoughts of the ungodly are about things beneath; the true Christian's affections are set on things above. The ungodly man is full of this world — its cares and pleasures and profits absorb his whole attention. The true Christian, though in the world, is not of it; his citizenship is in heaven and his best things are yet to come.

The true Christian will do well never to forget this line of demarcation. If he loves his soul and desires to serve God, he must be content to find himself separated from many around him by a gulf that cannot be passed. He may not like to seem peculiar and unlike others, but it is the certain consequence of grace reigning within him. He may find it brings on him hatred, ridicule and hard speeches, but it is the cup which his Master drank and of which his Master forewarned all his disciples: 'If ye were of the world, the world would love his own: but because ye are not of the world, but I have chosen you out of the world, therefore the world hateth you' (John 15:19). Then let the Christian never be ashamed to stand alone and show his colours.

For meditation: *Being a Christian is two-sided. It involves God's knowledge of us and our departure from sin (2 Tim. 2:19).*

Suggested further reading: Luke 16:19-31

Our Lord says to his enemies, 'If ye believe not that I am he, ye shall die in your sins.'

These solemn words are invested with peculiar solemnity when we consider from whose lips they came. Who is this that speaks of men dying 'in their sins', unpardoned, unforgiven, unfit to meet God, of men going into another world with all their sins upon them? He that says this is no other than the Saviour of mankind, who laid down his life for his sheep — the loving, gracious, merciful, compassionate Friend of sinners. It is Christ himself! Let this simple fact not be overlooked.

They are greatly mistaken who suppose that it is harsh and unkind to speak of hell and future punishment. How can such persons get over such language as that which is before us? How can they account for many a like expression which our Lord used and specially for such passages as those in which he speaks of the 'worm that dieth not and the fire that is not quenched'? (Mark 9:46.) They cannot answer these questions. Misled by a false charity and a morbid amiability, they are condemning the plain teaching of the Scripture and are wise above that which is written.

Let us settle it in our minds, as one of the great foundation truths of our faith, that there is a hell. Just as we believe firmly that there is an eternal heaven for the godly, so let us believe firmly that there is an eternal hell for the wicked. Let us never suppose that there is any want of love in speaking of hell. Let us rather maintain that it is the highest love to warn men plainly of danger and to beseech them to 'flee from the wrath to come'. It was Satan, the deceiver, murderer and liar, who said to Eve in the beginning, 'Ye shall not die' (Gen. 3:4). To shrink from telling men that except they believe they will 'die in their sins' may please the devil, but surely it cannot please God.

For meditation: *Denying reality does not change it. Mocking reality does not transform it. Disliking reality does not destroy it. Face reality and flee from wrath to come.*

Suggested further reading: *Matthew 13:18-23*

These verses show us the importance of steady perseverance in Christ's service. There were many, it seems, at this particular period, who professed to believe on our Lord and expressed a desire to become his disciples. There is nothing to show that they had true faith. They appear to have acted under the influence of temporary excitement, without considering what they were doing. And to them our Lord addresses this instructive warning: 'If ye continue in my word, then are ye my disciples indeed.'

This sentence contains a mine of wisdom. To make a beginning in religious life is comparatively easy. Not a few mixed motives assist us. The love of novelty, the praise of well-meaning but indiscreet professors, the secret self-satisfaction of feeling 'how good I am', the universal excitement attending a new position — all these things combine to aid the young beginner. Aided by them he begins to run the race that leads to heaven, lays aside many bad habits, takes up many good ones, has many comfortable frames and feelings and gets on swimmingly for a time. But when the newness of his position is past and gone, when the freshness of his feelings is rubbed off and lost, when the world and the devil begin to pull hard at him, when the weakness of his own heart begins to appear — then it is that he finds out the real difficulties of vital Christianity. Then it is that he discovers the deep wisdom of our Lord's saying now before us. It is not beginning, but 'continuing' a religious profession that is the test of true grace.

We should remember these things in forming our estimate of other people's religion. No doubt we ought to be thankful when we see anyone ceasing to do evil and learning to do well. We must not 'despise the day of small things' (Zech. 4:10). But we must not forget that to begin is one thing and to go on is quite another.

For meditation: *No athlete receives a medal for beginning a race with a sprint and then dropping out. The Christian continues to the end.*

Suggested further reading: *2 Timothy 2:22-26*

These verses show us the nature of true slavery. The Jews were
fond of boasting, though without any just cause, that they were
politically free and were not in bondage to any foreign power.
Our Lord reminds them that there was another bondage to
which they were giving no heed, although enslaved by it. 'He
that committeth sin is the servant of sin.'

How true that is! How many on every side are thorough
slaves, although they do not acknowledge it! They are led captive by their besetting corruptions and infirmities and seem to
have no power to get free. Ambition, the love of money, the
passion for drink, the craving for pleasure and excitement,
gambling, gluttony, illicit connections — all these are so many
tyrants among men. Each and all have crowds of unhappy
prisoners bound hand and foot in their chains. The wretched
prisoners will not allow their bondage. They will even boast
sometimes that they are eminently *free*. But many of them
know better. There are times when the iron enters into their
souls and they feel bitterly that they are slaves.

There is no slavery like this. Sin is indeed the hardest of all
task-masters. Misery and disappointment by the way, despair
and hell in the end — these are the only wages that sin pays to
its servants. To deliver men from this bondage is the grand
object of the gospel. To awaken people to a sense of their degra-
dation, to show them their chains, to make them arise and
struggle to be free — this is the great end for which Christ sent
forth his ministers. Happy is he who has opened his eyes and
found out his danger. To know that we are being led captive is
the very first step towards deliverance.

For meditation: *One mark of certain types of illness is that the
sufferers totally refuse to accept that they are ill and therefore
avoid treatment. So it is with the sinner.*

Suggested further reading: *Romans 6:1-11*

These verses show us, lastly, the nature of true liberty. Our Lord declares this to the Jews in one comprehensive sentence. He says, 'If the Son shall make you free, ye shall be free indeed.'

Liberty, most Englishmen know, is rightly esteemed one of the highest temporal blessings. Freedom from foreign dominion, a free constitution, free trade, a free press, civil and religious liberty — what a world of meaning lies beneath these phrases! How many would sacrifice life and fortune to maintain the things which they represent! Yet, after all our boasting, there are many so-called freemen who are nothing better than slaves. There are many who are totally ignorant of the highest, purest form of liberty. The noblest liberty is that which is the property of the true Christian. Those only are perfectly free people whom the Son of God 'makes free'. All else will sooner or later be found slaves.

Wherein does the liberty of true Christians consist? Of what is their freedom made up? They are freed from the guilt and consequences of sin by the blood of Christ. Justified, pardoned, forgiven, they can look forward boldly to the Day of Judgement, and cry, 'Who shall lay anything to our charge? Who is he that condemneth?' They are freed from the power of sin by the grace of Christ's Spirit. Sin has no longer dominion over them. Renewed, converted, sanctified, they mortify and tread down sin and are no longer led captive by it. Liberty like this is the portion of all true Christians in the day that they flee to Christ by faith and commit their souls to him. That day they become free men. Liberty like this is their portion for evermore. Death cannot stop it. The grave cannot even hold their bodies for more than a little season. Those whom Christ makes free are free to all eternity.

For meditation: *John Knox as a slave on a galley ship was freer as a Christian than John Newton as a slave-trader without Christ.*

Suggested further reading: Romans 2:17-29

We are taught, for one thing, the ignorant self-righteousness of the natural man. We find the Jews pluming themselves on their natural descent from Abraham, as if that must needs cover all deficiencies: 'Abraham is our father.' We find them going even further than this and claiming to be God's special favourites and God's own family: 'We have one Father, even God.' They forgot that fleshly relationship to Abraham was useless unless they shared Abraham's grace. They forgot that God's choice of their father to be head of a favoured nation was never meant to carry salvation to the children, unless they walked in their father's footsteps. All this in their blind self-conceit they refused to see. 'We are Jews. We are God's children. We are the true church. We are in the covenant. We must be all right.' This was their whole argument!

Strange as it may seem, there are multitudes of so-called Christians who are exactly like these Jews. Their whole religion consists of a few notions neither wiser nor better than those propounded by the enemies of our Lord. They will tell you that they 'are regular church people', they 'have been baptized', they 'go to the Lord's table', but they can tell you no more. Of all the essential doctrines of the gospel they are totally ignorant. Of faith and grace and repentance and holiness and spiritual-mindedness they know nothing at all. But, forsooth! they are churchmen and so they hope to go to heaven! There are myriads in this condition. It sounds sad, but unhappily it is only too true.

Let us settle firmly in our minds that connection with a good church and good ancestors is no proof whatever that we ourselves are in a way to be saved. We need something more than this. We must be joined to Christ himself by a living faith. We must know something experimentally of the work of the Spirit in our hearts.

For meditation: *The very best religious pedigree and connections do not make up for the lack of salvation in Christ.*

Suggested further reading: Galatians 3:26-4:7

We are taught the true marks of spiritual sonship. Our Lord makes this point most plain by two mighty sayings. Did the Jews say, 'We have Abraham to our father'? He replies, 'If ye were Abraham's children, ye would do the works of Abraham.' Did the Jews say, 'We have one Father, even God'? He replies, 'If God were your Father, ye would love me.'

Let these two sayings of Christ sink down into our hearts. They supply an answer to two of the most mischievous, yet most common, errors of the present day. What more common, on one side, than vague talk about the universal fatherhood of God? 'All men,' we are told, 'are God's children, whatever be their creed or religion; all are finally to have a place in the Father's house, where there are many mansions.' What more common, on another side, than high-sounding statements about the effect of baptism and the privileges of church-membership? 'By baptism,' we are confidently told, 'all baptized people are made children of God; all members of the church, without distinction, have a right to be addressed as sons and daughters of the Lord Almighty.'

Statements like these can never be reconciled with the plain language of our Lord in the passage before us. If words mean anything, no man is really a child of God, who does not love Jesus Christ. The charitable judgement of a baptismal service or the hopeful estimate of a catechism may call him by the name of a son and reckon him among God's children. But the reality of sonship to God and all its blessings, no one possesses who does not love the Lord Jesus Christ in sincerity (Eph. 6:24). In matters like these we need not be shaken by mere assertions. We may well afford to despise the charge of under-valuing the sacraments. We have only to ask one question: 'What is written? What saith the Lord? And with this saying before us, we can only come to one conclusion: 'Where there is no love to Christ, there is no sonship to God.'

For meditation: *The right to call God 'Father' belongs to those who have Christ as Saviour.*

Suggested further reading: *Ephesians 6:10-20*

We are taught in these verses the reality and character of the devil. Our Lord speaks of him as one whose personality and existence are beyond dispute. In solemn words of stern rebuke he says to his unbelieving enemies, 'Ye are of your father the devil,' led by him, doing his will and showing unhappily that you are like him. And then he paints his picture in dark colours, describing him as a 'murderer' from the beginning, as a 'liar' and the father of lies.

There is a devil! We have a mighty invisible enemy always near us, one who never slumbers and never sleeps, one who is about our path and about our bed and spies out all our ways and will never leave us till we die. He is a murderer! His great aim and object is to ruin us for ever and kill our souls. To destroy, to rob us of eternal life, to bring us down to the second death in hell are the things for which he is unceasingly working. He is ever going about, seeking whom he may devour. He is a liar! He is continually trying to deceive us by false representations, just as he deceived Eve at the beginning. He is always telling us that good is evil and evil good, truth is falsehood and falsehood truth, the broad way good and the narrow way bad. Millions are led captive by his deceit and follow him, both rich and poor, both high and low, both learned and unlearned. Lies are his chosen weapons. By lies he slays many.

These are awful things, but they are true. Let us live as if we believed them. Let us not be like many who mock and sneer and scoff and deny the existence of the very being who is invisibly leading them to hell. Let us believe there is a devil and watch and pray and fight hard against his temptations. Strong as he is, there is one stronger than he who said to Peter, 'I have prayed for thee, that thy faith fail not' (Luke 22:32) and who still intercedes at God's right hand. Let us commit our souls to him. With such a being as the devil going to and fro in the world, we never need wonder to see evil abounding. But with Christ on our side, we need not be afraid.

For meditation: *The devil deceives men into denying his existence and thereby disarms them.*

Suggested further reading: *Matthew 5:10-12*

Silenced in argument, these wicked men resorted to personal abuse. To lose temper and call names is a common sign of a defeated cause.

Nicknames, insulting epithets and violent language are favourite weapons with the devil. When other means of carrying on his warfare fail, he stirs up his servants to smite with the tongue. Grievous indeed are the sufferings which the saints of God have had to endure from the tongue in every age.

The true Christian in the present day must never be surprised to find that he has constant trials to endure from this quarter. Human nature never changes. So long as he serves the world and walks in the broad way, little perhaps will be said against him. Once let him take up the cross and follow Christ and there is no lie too monstrous and no story too absurd for some to tell against him and for others to believe. But let him take comfort in the thought that he is only drinking the cup which his blessed Master drank before him. The lies of his enemies do him no injury in heaven, whatever they may on earth. Let him bear them patiently and not fret or lose his temper. When Christ was reviled, 'he reviled not again' (1 Peter 2:23). Let the Christian do likewise.

We should observe what glorious encouragement our Lord holds out to his believing people. We read that he said, 'Verily, verily, I say unto you, if a man keep my saying, he shall never see death.'

Of course, these words do not mean that true Christians shall never die. But the words do mean that they shall not be hurt by the second death, that final ruin of the whole man in hell of which the first death is only a faint type or figure (Rev. 21:8). And they do mean that the sting of the first death shall be removed from the true Christian. His flesh may fail and his bones may be racked with strong pain, but the bitter sense of unpardoned sins shall not crush him down. This is the worst part of death and in this he shall have the 'victory through our Lord Jesus Christ' (1 Cor. 15:57).

For meditation: *Romans 8:18.*

Suggested further reading:　Isaiah 53:1-12

Abraham had been dead and buried at least 1850 years and yet he is said to have seen our Lord's day! How wonderful that sounds! Yet it was quite true. Not only did Abraham 'see' our Lord and talk to him when he 'appeared unto him in the plains of Mamre' the night before Sodom was destroyed (Gen. 18:1), but by faith he looked forward to the day of our Lord's incarnation yet to come and, as he looked, he 'was glad'. That he saw many things through a glass darkly we need not doubt. That he could have explained fully the whole manner and circumstances of our Lord's sacrifice on Calvary we are not obliged to suppose. But we need not shrink from believing that he saw in the far distance a Redeemer whose advent would finally make all the earth rejoice. And as he saw it, he 'was glad'.

The plain truth is that we are too apt to forget that there never was but one way of salvation, one Saviour and one hope for sinners and that Abraham and all the Old Testament saints looked to the same Christ that we look to ourselves.

How distinctly our Lord declares his own pre-existence! We read that he said to the Jews, 'Before Abraham was, I am.' Without a controversy, these remarkable words are a great deep. They contain things which we have no eyes to see through, or mind to fathom. But if language means anything, they teach us that our Lord Jesus Christ existed long before he came into the world. Before man was created, he was. In short, they teach us that the Lord Jesus was no mere man like Moses or David. He was one whose goings forth were from everlasting, the same yesterday, today and for ever, very and eternal God.

He to whom the gospel bids us come with our sins and believe for pardon and peace is no mere man. He is nothing less than very God and therefore 'able to save to the uttermost' all who come to him.

For meditation:　*There is one divine Saviour for all God's people.*

Suggested further reading: Psalm 90:1-12

We are told of a man 'who was blind from his birth'. A more serious affliction can hardly be conceived. Of all the bodily crosses that can be laid on man, without taking away life, none perhaps is greater than the loss of sight. It cuts us off from some of the greatest enjoyments of life. It shuts us up within a narrow world of our own. It makes us painfully helpless and dependent on others. In fact, until men lose their eyesight, they never fully realize its value.

Now blindness, like every other bodily infirmity, is one of the fruits of sin. If Adam had never fallen, we cannot doubt that people would never have been blind, or deaf, or dumb. The many ills that flesh is heir to, the countless pains and diseases and physical defects to which we are all liable came in when the curse came upon the earth. 'By one man sin entered into the world, and death by sin' (Rom. 5:12).

Let us learn to hate sin with a godly hatred, as the root of more than half of our cares and sorrows. Let us fight against it, mortify it, crucify it and abhor it both in ourselves and in others.

What a solemn lesson Christ gives us about the use of opportunities! He says to the disciples who asked him about the blind man, 'I must work while it is called today: the night cometh, when no man can work.'

That saying was eminently true when applied to our Lord himself. He knew well that his own earthly ministry would only last three years altogether and, knowing this, he diligently redeemed the time. He let slip no opportunity of doing works of mercy and attending to his Father's business. Morning, noon and night, he was always carrying on the work which the Father gave him to do.

The life that we now live in the flesh is our day. Let us take care that we use it well, for the glory of God and the good of our souls.

For meditation: *Our time is very short. Our daylight will soon be gone. Opportunities once lost can never be retrieved. A second lease of life is granted to no man.*

Suggested further reading: *Matthew 28:18-20*

What different means Christ used in working miracles on different occasions! In healing the blind man he might, if he had thought fit, have merely touched him with his finger, or given command with his tongue. But he did not rest content with doing so. We are told that 'He spat on the ground, and made clay of the spittle, and he anointed the eyes of the blind man with the clay.'

The Lord of heaven and earth will not be tied down to the use of any one means or instrumentality. In conferring blessings on man, he will work in his own way and will allow no one to prescribe to him.

We should observe in this passage the almighty power that Christ holds in his hands. We see him doing that which in itself was impossible. Without medicines he cures an incurable case. He actually gives eyesight to one that was born blind.

Such a miracle as this is meant to teach an old truth, which we can never know too well. It shows us that Jesus, the Saviour of sinners, 'has all power in heaven and earth'. Such mighty works could never have been done by one that was merely man. In the cure of this blind man we see nothing less than the finger of God.

Such a miracle, above all, is meant to make us hopeful about our own souls and the souls of others. Why should we despair of salvation while we have such a Saviour? Where is the spiritual disease that he cannot take away? He can open the eyes of the most sinful and ignorant and make them see things they never saw before. He can send light into the darkest heart and cause blindness and prejudice to pass away.

Surely, if we are not saved, the fault will be all our own. There lives at God's right hand one who can heal us if we apply to him. Let us take heed lest those solemn words are found true of us: 'Light is come into the world: but men loved darkness rather than light, because their deeds were evil' (John 3:19). 'Ye will not come to me, that ye might have life' (John 5:40).

For meditation: *Christ has all power in the whole universe. He is Lord of all.*

Suggested further reading: *Hebrews 10:19-25*

These verses show us how little the Jews of our Lord's time understood the right use of the sabbath day. We read that some of the Pharisees found fault because a blind man was miraculously healed on the sabbath. They said, 'This man is not of God, because he keepeth not the sabbath day.' A good work had manifestly been done to a helpless fellow creature. A heavy bodily infirmity had been removed. A mighty act of mercy had been performed. But the blind-hearted enemies of Christ could see no beauty in the act. They called it a breach of the fourth commandment!

These would-be wise men completely mistook the intention of the sabbath. They did not see that it was 'made for man' and meant for the good of man's body, mind and soul. It was a day to be set apart from others, no doubt, and to be carefully sanctified and kept holy. But its sanctification was never intended to prevent works of necessity and acts of mercy. To heal a sick man was no breach of the sabbath day. In finding fault with our Lord for so doing, the Jews only exposed their ignorance of their own law. They had forgotten that it is as great a sin to add to a commandment as to take it away.

Here, as in other places, we must take care that we do not put a wrong meaning on our Lord's conduct. We must not for a moment suppose that the sabbath is no longer binding on Christians and that they have nothing to do with the fourth commandment. This is a great mistake and the root of great evil. Not one of the Ten Commandments has ever been repealed or put aside. Our Lord never meant the sabbath to become a day of pleasure, or a day of business, or a day of travelling and idle dissipation. He meant it to be 'kept holy' as long as the world stands. It is one thing to employ the sabbath in works of mercy, in ministering to the sick and doing good to the distressed. By the sabbath may be found out whether we love communion with God.

For meditation: *If giving God time now is a bore, why should we expect to enjoy eternity with him?*

Suggested further reading: Acts 26:9-24

We read that 'The Jews . . . agreed . . . that if any man did confess that Jesus was Christ, he should be put out of the synagogue.' They were determined not to believe. They were resolved that no evidence should change their minds and no proofs influence their will. They were like men who shut their eyes and tie a bandage over them and refuse to have it untied. Just as in after times they stopped their ears when Stephen preached and refused to listen when Paul made his defence, so they behaved at this period of our Lord's ministry.

The state of mind we should always desire to possess is that of the noble-minded Bereans. When they first heard the apostle Paul preach, they listened with attention. They received the Word 'with all readiness of mind'. They 'searched the Scriptures' and compared what they heard with God's Word. 'And therefore,' we are told, 'many of them believed.' Happy are they that go and do likewise! (Acts 17:11,12.)

Nothing convinces a man so thoroughly as his own senses and feelings. We read that the unbelieving Jews tried in vain to persuade the blind man whom Jesus healed that nothing had been done for him. They only got from him one plain answer: 'One thing I know, that whereas I was blind, now I see.' How the miracle had been worked, he did not pretend to explain. Whether the person who had healed him was a sinner, he did not profess to know. But that something had been done for him he stoutly maintained. He was not to be reasoned out of his senses. Whatever the Jews might think, there were two distinct facts of which he was conscious: 'I was blind; now I see.'

There is no kind of evidence so satisfactory as this to the heart of a real Christian. His knowledge may be small. His faith may be feeble. His doctrinal views may be at present confused and indistinct. But if Christ has really wrought a work of grace in his heart by his Spirit, he feels within him something that you cannot overthrow.

For meditation: *When men know God in their experience, theoretical denials of his existence count for nothing.*

Suggested further reading: Romans 8:31-39

We see in these verses how much wiser the poor sometimes are than the rich. The man whom our Lord healed of his blindness was evidently a person of very humble condition. It is written that he was one who 'sat and begged' (see v.8). Yet he saw things which the proud rulers of the Jews could not see and would not receive. He saw in our Lord's miracle an unanswerable proof of our Lord's divine commission. 'If this man were not of God,' he cries, 'he could do nothing.' In fact, from the day of his cure his position was completely altered. He had eyes and the Pharisees were blind.

We see secondly in these verses how cruelly and unjustly unconverted men will sometimes treat those who disagree with them. When the Pharisees could not frighten the blind man who had been cured, they expelled him from the Jewish church. Because he manfully refused to deny the evidence of his own senses, they excommunicated him and put him to an open shame. They cast him out 'as a heathen man and a publican'.

The temporal injury that such treatment did to a poor Jew was very great indeed. It cut him off from the outward privileges of the Jewish church. It made him an object of scorn and suspicion among all true Israelites. But it could do no harm to his soul. That which wicked men bind on earth is not bound in heaven. 'The curse causeless shall not come' (Prov. 26:2).

The children of God in every age have only too frequently met with like treatment. Excommunication, persecution and imprisonment have generally been favourite weapons with ecclesiastical tyrants. Unable, like the Pharisees, to answer arguments, they have resorted to violence and injustice. Let the child of God console himself with the thought that there is a true church out of which no man can cast him and a church membership which no earthly power can take away. He only is blessed whom Christ calls blessed and he only is accursed whom Christ shall pronounce accursed at the last day.

For meditation: *When a man has done his worst he has failed to destroy a single child of God (John 10:28, 29).*

Suggested further reading:　Psalm 3

We see in these verses how great is the kindness and condescension of Christ. No sooner was this poor blind man cast out of the Jewish church than Jesus finds him and speaks words of comfort. He knew full well how heavy an affliction excommunication was to an Israelite and at once cheered him with kind words. He now revealed himself more fully to this man than he did to anyone except the Samaritan woman. In reply to the question, 'Who is the Son of God?' he says plainly, 'Thou hast both seen him, and it is he that talketh with thee.'

We have here one among many beautiful illustrations of the mind of Christ. He sees all that his people go through for his sake and feels for all, from the highest to the lowest. He keeps account of all their losses, crosses and persecutions. 'Are they not all written in his book?' (Ps. 56:8.) He knows how to come to their hearts with consolation in their time of need and to speak peace to them when all men seem to hate them.

We see in these verses how dangerous it is to possess knowledge, if we do not make a good use of it. The rulers of the Jews were fully persuaded that they knew all religious truth. They were indignant at the very idea of being ignorant and devoid of spiritual eyesight. 'Are we blind also?' they cried. And then came the mighty sentence: 'If ye were blind, ye should have no sin: but now ye say, We see; therefore your sin remaineth.'

When knowledge only sticks in a man's head and has no influence over his heart and life, it becomes a most perilous possession. And when, in addition to this, its possessor is self-conceited and self-satisfied and fancies he knows everything, the result is one of the worst states of soul into which man can fall. There is far more hope about him who says, 'I am a poor blind sinner and want God to teach me,' than about him who is ever saying, 'I know it, I know it, I am not ignorant,' and yet cleaves to his sins. The sin of that man 'remaineth'.

For meditation:　*God requires dependence and humility, not self-sufficiency and pride.*

Suggested further reading: Philippians 1:12-18

We have, for one thing, in these verses a vivid picture of a false teacher of religion. Our Lord says that he is one who 'enters not by the door into the sheepfold, but climbs up some other way'. The 'door', in this sentence, must evidently mean something far more than outward calling and commission. The Jewish teachers, at any rate, were not deficient in this point: they could probably trace up their orders in direct succession to Aaron himself. Ordination is no proof whatever that a man is fit to show others the way to heaven.

The true sense of the 'door' must be sought in our Lord's own interpretation. It is Christ himself who is 'the door'. The true shepherd of souls is he who enters the ministry with a single eye to Christ, desiring to glorify Christ, doing all in the strength of Christ, preaching Christ's doctrine, walking in Christ's steps and labouring to bring men and women to Christ. The false shepherd of souls is he who enters the ministerial office with little or no thought about Christ, from worldly and self-exalting motives, but from no desire to exalt Jesus and the great salvation that is in him. Christ, in one word, is the grand touchstone of the minister of religion. The man who makes much of Christ is a pastor after God's own heart, whom God delights to honour. The minister who makes little of Christ is one whom God regards as an impostor, as one who has climbed up to his holy office not by the door, but by 'some other way'.

Thousands of ordained men in the present day know nothing whatever about Christ, except his name. They have not entered 'the door' themselves and they are unable to show it to others.

Unconverted ministers are the dry-rot of the church. 'When the blind lead the blind' both must fall into the ditch. If we would know the value of a man's ministry, we must never fail to ask, 'Where is the Lamb? Where is the Door? Does he bring forward Christ and give him his rightful place?'

For meditation: *Your minister may have many faults (so have you!) but if he preaches Christ and loves him, treasure him.*

Suggested further reading: 1 John 4:1-6

We have, for one thing, in these verses, a peculiar picture of true Christians. Our Lord describes them as sheep who 'hear the voice of a true Shepherd, and know his voice', and as 'sheep who will not follow a stranger, but will flee from him, for they know not the voice of strangers'.

The thing taught in these words is a very curious one and may seem 'foolishness' to the world. There is a spiritual instinct in most true believers, which generally enables them to distinguish between true and false teaching. When they hear unsound religious instruction, there is something within them which says, 'This is wrong.' When they hear the real truth as it is in Jesus, there is something in their hearts which responds, 'This is right.' The careless man of the world may see no difference whatever between minister and minister, sermon and sermon. The poorest sheep of Christ, as a general rule, will 'distinguish things that differ', though he may sometimes be unable to explain why.

Let us beware of despising this spiritual instinct. Whatever a sneering world may please to say, it is one of the peculiar marks of the indwelling of the Holy Ghost. As such, it is specially mentioned by St John, when he says, 'Ye have an unction from the Holy One, and ye know all things' (1 John 2:20). Let us rather pray for it daily, in order that we may be kept from the influence of false shepherds. To lose all power of distinguishing between bitter and sweet is one of the worst symptoms of bodily disease. To be unable to see any difference between law and gospel, truth and error, Protestantism and popery, the doctrine of Christ and the doctrine of man is a sure proof that we are yet dead in heart and need conversion.

For meditation: *The gospel in which the Christian rejoices is the very thing that others scorn and find offensive (1 Cor. 1:23,24).*

Suggested further reading: Hebrews 10:19-25

We have in these verses a most instructive picture of Christ himself. He utters one of those golden sayings which ought to be dear to all true Christians. They apply to people as well as to ministers. 'I am the door: by me if any man enter in, he shall be saved, and shall go in and out, and find pasture.'

We are all by nature separate and far off from God. Sin, like a great barrier wall, rises between us and our Maker. The sense of guilt makes us afraid of him. The sense of his holiness keeps us at a distance from him. Born with a heart at enmity with God, we become more and more alienated from him by practice the longer we live. The very first questions in religion that must be answered are these: 'How can I draw near to God? How can I be justified? How can a sinner like me be reconciled to my Maker?'

The Lord Jesus Christ has provided an answer to these mighty questions. By his sacrifice for us on the cross, he has opened a way through the great barrier and provided pardon and peace for sinners. He has 'suffered for sin, the just for the unjust, to bring us to God'. He has opened a way into the holiest, through his blood, by which we may draw near to God with boldness and approach God without fear. And now he is able to save to the uttermost all who come unto God by him. In the highest sense he is 'the door'. No one 'can come to the Father' but by him.

Let us take heed that we use this door and do not merely stand outside looking at it. It is a door free and open to the chief of sinners: 'If any man enter in by it he shall be saved.' It is a door within which we shall find a full and constant supply for every want of our souls. We shall find that we can 'go in and out' and enjoy liberty and peace. The day comes when this door will be shut for ever and men shall strive to enter in, but not be able. Then let us make sure work of our own salvation. Let us not stand tarrying without and halting between two opinions. Let us enter in and be saved.

For meditation: *The door to heaven is still wide open. Have you yet entered in?*

Suggested further reading: *2 Timothy 1:8-12*

These verses show us, for one thing, the great object for which Christ came into the world. He says, 'I am come that [men] might have life, and that they might have it more abundantly.' The truth contained in these words is of vast importance. They supply an antidote to many crude and unsound notions which are abroad in the world. Christ did not come to be only a teacher of new morality, or an example of holiness and self-denial, or a founder of new ceremonies, as some have vainly asserted. He left heaven and dwelt for thirty-three years on earth for far higher ends than these. He came to procure eternal life for man by the price of his own vicarious death. He came to be a mighty fountain of spiritual life for all mankind, to which sinners coming by faith might drink and, drinking, might live for evermore. By Moses came laws, rules, ordinances, ceremonies. By Christ came grace, truth and eternal life.

Important as this doctrine is, it requires to be fenced with one word of caution. We must not overstrain the meaning of our Lord Jesus Christ's words. We must not suppose that eternal life was a thing entirely unknown until Christ came, or that the Old Testament saints were in utter darkness about the world to come. The way of life by faith in a Saviour was a way well known to Abraham and Moses and David. A Redeemer and a sacrifice was the hope of all God's children from Abel down to John the Baptist, but their vision of these things was necessarily imperfect. They saw them afar off and not distinctly. They saw them in outline only and not completely. It was the coming of Christ which made all things plain and caused the shadows to pass away. Life and immortality were brought into full light by the gospel. In short, to use our Lord's own words, even those who had life had it 'more abundantly' when Christ came into the world.

For meditation: *The life that our Lord brings transforms our present life on earth and opens up a new life for ever.*

Suggested further reading: Psalm 23

These verses show us one of the principal offices which Jesus Christ fills for true Christians. Twice over our Lord uses an expression which, to an Eastern hearer, would be singularly full of meaning. Twice over he says emphatically, 'I am the Good Shepherd.' It is a saying rich in consolation and instruction.

Like a good shepherd, Christ knows all his believing people. Their names, their families, their dwelling-places, their circumstances, their private history, their experience, their trials — with all these things Jesus is perfectly acquainted. There is not a thing about the least and lowest of them with which he is not familiar. The children of this world may not know Christians and may count their lives folly, but the Good Shepherd knows them thoroughly and, wonderful to say, does not despise them.

Like a good shepherd, Christ cares tenderly for all his believing people. He provides for all their wants in the wilderness of this world and leads them by the right way to a city of habitation. He bears patiently with their many weaknesses and infirmities and does not cast them off because they are wayward, erring, sick, footsore or lame. He guards and protects them against all their enemies, as Jacob did the flock of Laban, and of those that the Father has given him he will be found at last to have lost none.

Like a good shepherd, Christ lays down his life for the sheep. He did it once for all, when he was crucified for them. When he saw that nothing but his blood could deliver them from hell and the devil he willingly made his soul an offering for their sins. The merit of that death he is now presenting before the Father's throne. The sheep are saved for evermore, because the Good Shepherd died for them. This is indeed a love that passeth knowledge! 'Greater love hath no man than this, that a man lay down his life for his friends' (John 15:13).

For meditation: *When a stranger enters a field of sheep they scatter in alarm. When their own shepherd comes they are confident. They know they can trust him.*

Suggested further reading: Isaiah 40:1-11

We should notice the name which Christ gives to true Christians. He uses a figurative expression which, like all his language, is full of deep meaning. He calls them 'my sheep'. The word 'sheep', no doubt, points to something in the character and ways of true Christians. It would be easy to show that weakness, helplessness, harmlessness, usefulness are all points of resemblance between the sheep and the believer. But the leading idea in our Lord's mind was the entire dependence of the sheep upon its shepherd. Just as sheep hear the voice of their own shepherd and follow him, so do believers follow Christ. By faith they listen to his call. By faith they submit themselves to his guidance. By faith they lean on him and commit their souls implicitly to his direction. The ways of a shepherd and his sheep are a most useful illustration of the relation between Christ and the true Christian.

The expression 'my sheep' points to the close connection that exists between Christ and believers. They are his by gift from the Father, his by purchase, his by calling and choice and his by their own consent and heart-submission. In the highest sense they are Christ's property and, just as a man feels a special interest in that which he has bought at a great price and made his own, so does the Lord Jesus feel a peculiar interest in his people.

Expressions like these should be carefully treasured up in the memories of true Christians. They will be found cheering and heart-strengthening in days of trial. The world may see no beauty in the ways of a godly man and may often pour contempt on him. But he who knows that he is one of Christ's sheep has no cause to be ashamed. He has within him a 'well of water springing up into everlasting life' (John 4:14).

For meditation: *The tender care of the Shepherd for the sheep should ever be their comfort in times of weakness and trial (Isa. 40:11).*

Suggested further reading: John 19:5-11

These verses show us that when Christ died, he died of his own voluntary free will. He uses a remarkable expression to teach this: 'I lay down my life that I might take it again. No man taketh it from me, but I lay it down of myself. I have power to lay it down and I have power to take it again.' The point before us is of no mean importance. We must never suppose for a moment that our Lord had no power to prevent his sufferings and that he was delivered up to his enemies and crucified because he could not help it. Nothing could be further from the truth than such an idea. The treachery of Judas, the armed band of priests' servants, the enmity of scribes and Pharisees, the injustice of Pontius Pilate, the rude hands of Roman soldiers, the scourge, the nails and the spear — all these could not have harmed a hair of our Lord's head, unless he had allowed them. Well might he say those remarkable words: 'Thinkest thou that I cannot now pray to my Father, and he shall presently give me more than twelve legions of angels? But how, then, shall the Scripture be fulfilled?' (Matt. 26:53.)

The plain truth is that our Lord submitted to death of his own free will, because he knew that his death was the only way of making atonement for man's sins. He poured out his soul unto death with all the desire of his heart, because he had determined to pay our debt to God and redeem us from hell. For the joy set before him he willingly endured the cross and laid down his life, in order that we, through his death, might have eternal life. His death was not the death of a martyr, who sinks at last overwhelmed by enemies, but the death of a triumphant conqueror, who knows that even in dying he wins for himself and his people a kingdom and a crown of glory.

Let us lean back our souls on these mighty truths and be thankful. If we hear his voice, repent and believe, he is our own.

For meditation: *On the day of Jesus' death Pilate thought he was in control (John 19:10) but our Lord knew otherwise (John 19:11).*

Suggested further reading: Acts 19:23-41

We should notice in this passage what strifes and controversies
our Lord occasioned when he was on earth. We read that
'There was a division among the Jews for his sayings,' and that
'Many of them said, He hath a devil, and is mad,' while others
took an opposite view. It may seem strange, at first sight, that
he who came to preach peace between God and man should be
the cause of contention. But herein were his own words literally
fulfilled: 'I came not to send peace, but a sword' (Matt. 10:34).
The fault was not in Christ or his doctrine, but in the carnal
mind of his Jewish hearers.

Let us never be surprised if we see the same thing in our own
day. Human nature never changes. So long as the heart of man
is without grace, so long we must expect to see it dislike the
gospel of Christ. Just as oil and water, acids and alkalies,
cannot combine, so in the same way unconverted people
cannot really like the people of God. 'The carnal mind is
enmity against God' (Rom. 8:7). 'The natural man receiveth
not the things of the Spirit of God' (1 Cor. 2:14).

The servant of Christ must think it no strange thing if he goes
through the same experience as his Master. He will often find
his ways and opinions in religion the cause of strife in his own
family. He will have to endure ridicule, hard words and petty
persecution from the children of this world. He may even discover that he is thought a fool or a madman on account of his
Christianity. Let none of these things move him. The thought
that he is a partaker of the afflictions of Christ ought to steel
him against every trial. 'If they have called the Master of the
house Beelzebub, how much more shall they call them of his
household' (Matt. 10:25).

One thing, at any rate, should never be forgotten. We must
not allow ourselves to think the worse of religion because of the
strifes and dissensions to which it gives rise. Whatever men
may please to say, it is human nature, and not religion, which is
to blame.

For meditation: *Our Lord divides humanity not just for time,
but for eternity. Are you with him or against him?*

Suggested further reading: *Isaiah 49:14-26*

Christ 'knows' his people with a special knowledge of appro-
bation, interest and affection. By the world around them they
are comparatively unknown, uncared for or despised. But they
are never forgotten or overlooked by Christ.

Christ 'gives' his people 'eternal life'. He bestows on them
freely a right and title to heaven, pardoning their many sins and
clothing them with a perfect righteousness. Money and health
and worldly prosperity he often wisely withholds from them.
But he never fails to give them grace, peace and glory.

Christ declares that his people 'shall never perish'. Weak as
they are, they shall all be saved. Not one of them shall be lost
and cast away; not one of them shall miss heaven. If they err,
they shall be brought back; if they fall, they shall be raised. The
enemies of their souls may be strong and mighty, but their
Saviour is mightier and none shall pluck them out of their
Saviour's hands.

A promise like this deserves the closest attention. If words
mean anything, it contains that great doctrine, the perseverance, or continuance in grace, of true believers. That doctrine is literally hated by worldly people. No doubt, like every
other truth of Scripture, it is liable to be abused. But the words
of Christ are too plain to be evaded. He has said it and he will
make it good: 'My sheep shall never perish.'

Whatever men may please to say against this doctrine, it is
one which God's children ought to hold fast and defend with
all their might. To all who feel within them the workings of the
Holy Spirit, it is a doctrine full of encouragement and consolation. Once inside the ark, they shall never be cast out. Once
converted and joined to Christ, they shall never be cut off from
his mystical body. Hypocrites and false professors shall doubtless make shipwreck for ever, unless they repent. But true
'sheep' shall never be confounded. Christ has said it, and Christ
cannot lie: 'They shall never perish.'

For meditation: *More happy, yet not more secure,*
                       The glorified spirits in heaven
                                              (A.M. Toplady).

Suggested further reading: 1 Kings 22:7-18

We should observe the extreme wickedness of human nature.
The unbelieving Jews at Jerusalem were neither moved by our
Lord's miracles, nor by his preaching. They were determined
not to receive him as their Messiah. Once more it is written that
'They took up stones to stone him.'

Our Lord had done the Jews no injury. He was no robber,
murderer or rebel against the law of the land. He was one
whose whole life was love and who 'went about doing good'
(Acts 10:38). There was no fault or inconsistency in his character. There was no crime that could be laid to his charge. So
perfect and spotless a man had never walked on the face of this
earth. But yet the Jews hated him and thirsted for his blood.
How true are the words of Scripture: 'They hated him without
a cause'! (John 15:25.) How just the remark of an old divine:
'Unconverted men would kill God himself if they could only
get at him'!

The true Christian has surely no right to wonder if he meets
with the same kind of treatment as our blessed Lord. In fact,
the more like he is to his Master and the more holy and spiritual
his life, the more probable is it that he will have to endure
hatred and persecution. Let him not suppose that any degree of
consistency will deliver him from this cross. It is not his faults,
but his graces, which call forth the enmity of men. The world
hates to see anything of God's image. The children of the world
are vexed and pricked in conscience when they see others better
than themselves. Why did Cain hate his brother Abel and slay
him? 'Because,' says St John, 'his own works were evil, and his
brother's righteous' (1 John 3:12). Why did the Jews hate
Christ? Because he exposed their sins and false doctrines and
they knew in their own hearts that he was right and they were
wrong.

For meditation: *Men will put up with anything except the truth
that exposes the evil of their hearts.*

Suggested further reading: Psalm 19:7-11

What high honour Jesus Christ puts on the Holy Scriptures! We find him using a text out of the Psalms as an argument against his enemies, in which the whole point lies in the single word 'gods'. And then, having quoted the text, he lays down the great principle: 'The Scripture cannot be broken.' It is as though he said , 'Wherever the Scripture speaks plainly on any subject, there can be no more question about it. The cause is settled and decided. Every jot and tittle of Scripture is true and must be received as conclusive.'

The principle here laid down by our Lord is one of vast importance. Let us grasp it firmly and never let it go. Let us maintain boldly the complete inspiration of every word of the original Hebrew and Greek Scriptures. Let us believe that not only every book of the Bible, but every chapter, and not only every chapter, but every verse, and not only every verse, but every word was originally given by inspiration of God. Inspiration, we must never shrink from asserting, extends not only to the thoughts and ideas of Scripture, but to the least words.

The principle before us, no doubt, is rudely assaulted in the present day. Let no Christian's heart fail because of these assaults. Let us stand our ground manfully and defend the principle of plenary inspiration as we would the apple of our eye. There are difficulties in Scripture, we need not shrink from conceding, things hard to explain, hard to reconcile and hard to understand. But in almost all these difficulties, the fault, we may justly suspect, is not so much in Scripture as in our own weak minds. In all cases we may well be content to wait for more light and believe that all shall be made clear at last.

The wisest course is to walk in the old path — the path of faith and humility — and say, 'I cannot give up a single word of my Bible.'

For meditation: *A small fault can render a whole machine unreliable in its work. If God's Word contains errors, how can we trust any of it?*

Suggested further reading: Exodus 4:1-9

What importance our Lord Jesus Christ attaches to his miracles! He appeals to them as the best evidence of his own divine mission. He bids the Jews look at them and deny them if they can. 'If I do not the works of my Father, believe me not. But if I do, though ye believe not me, believe the works.'

The mighty miracles which our Lord performed during the three years of his earthly ministry are probably not considered as much as they ought to be in the present day. These miracles were not few in number. Forty times and more we read in the Gospels of his doing things entirely out of the ordinary course of nature — healing sick people in a moment, raising the dead with a word, casting out devils, calming winds and waves in an instant, walking on the water as on solid ground. These miracles were not all done in private among friends. Many of them were wrought in the most public manner under the eyes of unfriendly witnesses. We are so familiar with these things that we are apt to forget the mighty lesson they teach. They teach that he who worked these miracles must be nothing less than very God. They stamp his doctrines and precepts with the mark of divine authority. He only who created all things at the beginning could suspend the laws of creation at his will. He who could suspend the laws of creation must be one who ought to be thoroughly believed and implicitly obeyed. To reject one who confirmed his mission by such mighty works is the height of madness and folly.

Hundreds of unbelieving men, no doubt, in every age, have tried to pour contempt on Christ's miracles and to deny that they were ever worked at all. But they labour in vain. Proofs upon proofs exist that our Lord's ministry was accompanied by miracles and that this was acknowledged by those who lived in our Lord's time.

For meditation: *Our Lord did not challenge his hearers with unverifiable miracles performed miles away, but with miracles before their very eyes.*

Suggested further reading: Romans 8:18-23

Nowhere shall we find such convincing proofs of our Lord's divine power. As God, he makes the grave itself yield up its tenants. Nowhere shall we find such striking illustrations of our Lord's ability to sympathize with his people. As man, he can be touched with the feelings of our infirmities. Such a miracle well became the end of such a ministry. It was meet and right that the victory of Bethany should closely precede the crucifixion at Calvary.

These verses teach us that true Christians may be sick and ill as well as others. We read that Lazarus of Bethany was one 'whom Jesus loved' and a brother of two well-known holy women. Yet Lazarus was sick, even unto death! The Lord Jesus, who had power over all diseases, could no doubt have prevented this illness, if he had thought fit. But he did not do so. He allowed Lazarus to be sick and in pain and weary and to languish and suffer like any other man.

The lesson is one which ought to be deeply graven in our memories. Living in a world full of disease and death, we are sure to need it some day. Sickness, in the very nature of things, can never be anything but trying to flesh and blood. Our bodies and souls are strangely linked together and that which vexes and weakens the body can hardly fail to vex the mind and soul. But sickness, we must always remember, is no sign that God is displeased with us; nay, more, it is generally sent for the good of our souls. It tends to draw our affections away from this world and to direct them to things above. It sends us to our Bibles and teaches us to pray better. It helps to prove our faith and patience and shows us the real value of our hope in Christ. It reminds us betimes that we are not to live always and tunes and trains our hearts for our great change. Let us believe that the Lord Jesus loves us when we are sick no less than when we are well.

For meditation: *By miraculous healing God grants us an insight into the disease-free age to come (Rom. 8:23). By leaving us ill he reminds us we are part of a fallen world (Rom. 8:18).*

Suggested further reading: 2 Chronicles 16:11-14

Jesus Christ is the Christian's best Friend in the time of need. We read that when Lazarus was sick, his sisters at once sent to Jesus and laid the matter before him. Beautiful, touching and simple was the message they sent. They did not ask him to come at once, or to work a miracle and command the disease to depart. They only said, 'Lord, he whom thou lovest is sick,' and left the matter there, in the full belief that he would do what was best. Here was the true faith and humility of saints! Here was gracious submission of will!

The servants of Christ, in every age and climate, will do well to follow this excellent example. No doubt when those whom we love are sick, we are to use diligently every reasonable means for their recovery. We must spare no pains to obtain the best medical advice. We must assist nature in every possible manner to fight a good fight against its enemy. But in all our doing, we must never forget that the best and ablest and wisest Helper is in heaven, at God's right hand. Like afflicted Job, our first action must be to fall on our knees and worship. Like Hezekiah, we must spread our matters before the Lord. Like the holy sisters at Bethany, we must send up a prayer to Christ.

Christ loves all who are true Christians. We read that 'Jesus loved Martha, and her sister, and Lazarus.' The characters of these three good people seem to have been somewhat different.

We must not undervalue others because they are not exactly like ourselves. The flowers in a garden may differ widely and yet the gardener feels interest in all. The children of a family may be curiously unlike one another and yet the parents care for all. It is just so with the church of Christ. There are degrees of grace and varieties of grace, but the least, the weakest, the feeblest disciples are all loved by the Lord Jesus.

For meditation: *Prayerlessness in times of need undoubtedly is an affront to God (2 Chron. 16:12).*

Suggested further reading: *2 Corinthians 12:7-10*

Christ knows best at what time to do anything for his people. We read that 'When he had heard that Lazarus was sick, he abode two days still in the same place where he was.' In fact, he purposely delayed his journey and did not come to Bethany till Lazarus had been four days in the grave. No doubt he knew well what was going on, but he never moved till the time came which he saw was best. For the sake of the church and the world, for the good of friends and enemies, he kept away.

The children of God must constantly school their minds to learn the great lesson now before us. Nothing so helps us to bear patiently the trials of life as an abiding conviction of the perfect wisdom by which everything around us is managed. Let us try to believe not only that all that happens to us is well done, but that it is done in the best manner, by the right instrument and at the right time. We are all naturally impatient in the day of trial. We are apt to say, like Moses, when beloved ones are sick, 'Heal her *now*, Lord, we beseech thee' (Num. 12:13). We forget that Christ is too wise a physician to make any mistakes. It is the duty of faith to say, 'My times are in thy hand. Do with me as thou wilt, how thou wilt and when thou wilt. Not my will, but thine be done.' The highest degree of faith is to be able to wait, sit still and not complain.

Let us turn from the passage with a settled determination to trust Christ entirely with all the concerns of this world, both public and private. Let us believe that he by whom all things were made at first is he who is managing all with perfect wisdom. The affairs of kingdoms, families and private individuals are all alike overruled by him. He chooses all the portions of his people. When we are sick, it is because he knows it to be for our good; when he delays coming to help us, it is for some wise reason. The hand that was nailed to the cross is too wise and loving to smite without a needs-be, or to keep us waiting for relief without a cause.

For meditation: *If God is all-wise, how can we ever think that he does not know best?*

Suggested further reading: Hebrews 11:8-16

How mysterious are the ways in which Christ sometimes leads his people! We are told that when he talked of going back to Judæa, his disciples were perplexed. It was the very place where the Jews had lately tried to stone their Master; to return thither was to plunge into the midst of danger. These timid Galileans could not see the necessity or prudence of such a step.

Things such as these are often going on around us. The servants of Christ are often placed in circumstances just as puzzling and perplexing as those of the disciples. They are led in ways of which they cannot see the purpose and object; they are called to fill positions from which they naturally shrink and which they would never have chosen for themselves. Thousands in every age are continually learning this by their own experience. The path they are obliged to walk in is not the path of their own choice. At present they cannot see its usefulness or wisdom.

At times like these a Christian must call into exercise his faith and patience. He must believe that his Master knows best by what road his servant ought to travel and that he is leading him by the right way to a city of habitation. He may rest assured that the circumstances in which he is placed are precisely those which are most likely to promote his graces and to check his besetting sins. He need not doubt that what he cannot see now he will understand hereafter. He will find one day that there was wisdom in every step of his journey, though flesh and blood could not see it at the time. If the twelve disciples had not been taken back into Judæa, they would not have seen the glorious miracle of Bethany. If Christians were allowed to choose their own course through life, they would never learn hundreds of lessons about Christ and his grace, which they are now taught in God's ways.

For meditation:
> *All the way my Saviour leads me.*
> *What have I to ask beside?*

Suggested further reading: 1 Corinthians 1:26-31

How much of natural temperament clings to a believer even after conversion! We read that when Thomas saw that Lazarus was dead and that Jesus was determined, in spite of all danger, to return into Judæa, he said, 'Let us also go, that we may die with him.' There can only be one meaning in that expression: it was the language of a despairing and desponding mind, which could see nothing but dark clouds in the picture. The very man who afterwards could not believe that his master had risen again and thought the news too good to be true is just the one of the twelve who thinks that if they go back to Judæa they must all die!

Things such as these are deeply instructive and are doubtless recorded for our learning. They show us that the grace of God in conversion does not so remould a man as to leave no trace of his natural bent of character. The sanguine do not altogether cease to be sanguine, nor the desponding to be desponding, when they pass from death to life and become true Christians. They show us that we must make large allowances for natural temperament in forming our estimate of individual Christians. We must not expect all God's children to be exactly one and the same. Each tree in a forest has its own peculiarities of shape and growth and yet all at a distance look one mass of leaf and verdure. Each member of Christ's body has his own distinctive bias and yet all in the main are led by one Spirit and love one Lord. The two sisters Martha and Mary, the apostles Peter and John and Thomas were certainly very unlike one another in many respects. But they had all one point in common: they loved Christ and were his friends.

Happy is the man of whom, with all his defects, Christ says to saints and angels, 'This is our friend.'

For meditation: *Christians are aptly described as God's 'peculiar' people in a number of senses. But the important thing is to be God's!*

Suggested further reading: *2 Corinthians 5:1-10*

How tenderly Christ speaks of the death of believers! He announces the fact of Lazarus being dead in language of singular beauty and gentleness: 'Our friend Lazarus sleepeth.'

Every true Christian has a Friend in heaven, of almighty power and boundless love. He is thought of, cared for, provided for, defended by God's eternal Son. He has an unfailing Protector, who never slumbers or sleeps and who watches continually over his interests. The world may despise him, but he has no cause to be ashamed. Father and mother even may cast him out, but Christ, having once taken him up, will never let him go. He is the 'friend of Christ' even after he is dead! The friendships of this world are often fair-weather friendships and fail us like summer-dried fountains, when our need is the sorest; but the friendship of the Son of God is stronger than death and goes beyond the grave. The Friend of sinners is a Friend that sticketh closer than a brother.

The death of true Christians is 'sleep' and not annihilation. It is a solemn and miraculous change, no doubt, but not a change to be regarded with alarm. They have nothing to fear for their souls in the change, for their sins are washed away in Christ's blood. The sharpest sting of death is the sense of unpardoned sin. Christians have nothing to fear for their bodies in the change; they will rise again by and by, refreshed and renewed, after the image of the Lord. The grave itself is a conquered enemy. It must render back its tenants safe and sound, the very moment that Christ calls for them at the last day.

To a mere worldly man death must needs be a terrible thing, but he that has Christian faith may boldly say, as he lays down life, 'I will lay me down in peace, and take my rest, for it is thou, Lord, that makest me dwell in safety.'

For meditation: *Do you know and believe that for you to die is gain? (Phil. 1:21.)*

Suggested further reading: Matthew 25:31-46

How great a blessing God sometimes bestows on actions of kindness and sympathy!
  It seems that the house of Martha and Mary at Bethany was filled with mourners when Jesus arrived. Many of these mourners, no doubt, knew nothing of the inner life of these holy women. Their faith, their hope, their love to Christ, their discipleship were things of which they were wholly ignorant. But they felt for them in their heavy bereavement and kindly came to offer what comfort they could. By so doing they reaped a rich and unexpected reward. They beheld the greatest miracle that Jesus ever wrought. They were eyewitnesses when Lazarus came forth from the tomb. To many of them, we may well believe, that day was a spiritual birth. The raising of Lazarus led to a resurrection in their souls. How small sometimes are the hinges on which eternal life appears to depend! If these people had not sympathized they might never have been saved.
  We need not doubt that these things were written for our learning. To show sympathy and kindness to the sorrowful is good for our own souls, whether we know it or not. To visit the fatherless and widows in their affliction, to weep with them that weep, to try to bear one another's burdens and lighten one another's cares — all this will make no atonement for sin and will not take us to heaven. Yet it is healthy employment for our hearts and employment which none ought to despise. Few perhaps are aware that one secret of being miserable is to live only for ourselves and one secret of being happy is to try to make others happy and to do a little good in the world.
  The saying of our Lord is too much overlooked: 'Whosoever shall give to drink unto one of these little ones a cup of cold water only in the name of a disciple, verily I say unto you, he shall in no wise lose his reward' (Matt. 10:42).

For meditation: *Sympathy is not merely to be a natural virtue. It is to be a Christian grace (1 Cor. 12:26).*

Suggested further reading: Galatians 2:11-14

What a strange mixture of grace and weakness is to be found even in the hearts of true believers! We see this strikingly illustrated in the language used by Martha and Mary. Both these holy women had faith enough to say, 'Lord, if thou hadst been here, my brother had not died.' Yet neither of them seems to have remembered that the death of Lazarus did not depend on Christ's absence and that our Lord, had he thought fit, could have prevented his death with a word, without coming to Bethany. Martha had knowledge enough to say, 'I know, that even now, whatsoever thou wilt ask of God, God will give it thee . . . I know that my brother shall rise again at the last day . . . I believe that thou art the Christ, the Son of God.' But even she could get no further. Her dim eyes and trembling hands could not grasp the grand truth that he who stood before her had the keys of life and death and that in her master dwelt 'all the fulness of the Godhead bodily' (Col. 2:9). She saw indeed, but through a glass darkly. She knew, but only in part. She believed, but her faith was mingled with much unbelief. Yet both Martha and Mary were genuine children of God and true Christians.

These things are graciously written for our learning. It is good to remember what true Christians really are. Many and great are the mistakes into which people fall by forming a false estimate of the Christian's character. Many are the bitter things which people write against themselves, by expecting to find in their hearts what cannot be found on this side of heaven. Let us settle it in our minds that saints on earth are not perfect angels, but only converted sinners. They are sinners renewed, changed, sanctified, no doubt, but they are yet sinners and will be till they die.

For meditation: *Where faults are seen attempts at loving restoration are to be made. Criticism is neither helpful nor meaningful if it does not aim at helping.*

Suggested further reading: *Colossians 1:9-14*

What need many believers have of clear views of Christ's person, office and power! This is a point which is forcibly brought out in the well-known sentence which our Lord addressed to Martha. In reply to her vague and faltering expression of belief in the resurrection at the last day, he proclaims the glorious truth: 'I am the resurrection and the life.' 'I, even I, thy Master, am he that has the keys of life and death in his hands.' And then he presses on her once more that old lesson, which she had doubtless often heard, but never fully realized: 'He that believeth in me, though he were dead, yet shall he live; and whosoever liveth and believeth in me shall never die.'

There is matter here which deserves the close consideration of all true Christians. Many of them complain of want of sensible comfort in their religion. They do not feel the inward peace which they desire. Let them know that vague and indefinite views of Christ are too often the cause of all their perplexities. They must try to see more clearly the great object on which their faith rests. They must grasp more firmly his love and power towards them that believe and the riches he has laid up for them even now in this world. We are many of us sadly like Martha. A little general knowledge of Christ as the only Saviour is often all that we possess. But of the fulness that dwells in him, of his resurrection, his priesthood, his intercession, his unfailing compassion, we have tasted little or nothing at all. They are things of which our Lord might well say to many, as he did to Martha, 'Believest thou this?'

Let us take shame to ourselves that we have named the name of Christ so long and yet know so little about him. What right have we to wonder that we feel so little comfort in our Christianity?

For meditation: *Is your great desire to know Christ above all else? (Phil. 3:10.)*

Suggested further reading: *Hebrews 4:14-5:10*

What a depth of tender sympathy there is in Christ's heart towards his people! We read that when our Lord saw Mary weeping and the Jews also weeping with her, 'He groaned in the spirit and was troubled.' We read even more than this. He gave outward expression to his feelings: he 'wept'. He knew perfectly well that the sorrow of the family of Bethany would soon be turned into joy and that Lazarus in a few minutes would be restored to his sisters. But though he knew all this, he 'wept'.

This weeping of Christ is deeply instructive. It shows us that it is not sinful to sorrow. Weeping and mourning are sadly trying to flesh and blood and make us feel the weakness of our mortal nature. But they are not in themselves wrong. Even the Son of God wept. It shows us that deep feeling is not a thing of which we need be ashamed. To be cold and stoical and unmoved in the sight of sorrow is no sign of grace. There is nothing unworthy of a child of God in tears. Even the Son of God could weep. It shows us, above all, that the Saviour in whom believers trust is a most tender and feeling Saviour. He is one who can be touched with sympathy for our infirmities. When we turn to him in the hour of trouble and pour out our hearts before him, he knows what we go through and can pity. And he is one who never changes. Though he now sits at God's right hand in heaven, his heart is still the same that it was upon earth. We have an Advocate with the Father who, when he was upon earth, could weep.

Let us strive to be men and women of a tender heart and a sympathizing spirit. If there were more Christians of this stamp and character, the church would be far more beautiful and the world would be far more happy.

For meditation: *The Christian is to become like Christ (Rom. 8:29). Christ has become like the Christian.*

Suggested further reading: *Romans 10:13-17*

These verses record one of the greatest miracles the Lord Jesus Christ ever worked and supply an unanswerable proof of his divinity. He whose voice could bring back from the grave one that had been four days dead must indeed have been very God! The miracle itself is described in such simple language that no human comment can throw light upon it. But the sayings of our Lord on this occasion are peculiarly interesting and demand special notice.

We should mark our Lord's words about the stone which lay upon the grave of Lazarus. We read that he said to those around him, when he came to the place of burial, 'Take ye away the stone.'

Now why did our Lord say this? It was doubtless as easy for him to command the stone to roll away untouched as to call a dead body from the tomb. But such was not his mode of proceeding. Here, as in other cases, he chose to give man something to do. Here, as elsewhere, he taught the great lesson that his almighty power was not meant to destroy man's responsibility. Even when he was ready and willing to raise the dead, he would not have man stand by altogether idle.

Let us treasure up this in our memories. It involves a point of great importance. In doing spiritual good to others, in training up our children for heaven, in following after holiness in our own daily walk — in all these things it is undoubtedly true that we are weak and helpless. 'Without Christ we can do nothing.' But still we must remember that Christ expects us to do what we can. 'Take ye away the stone' is the daily command which he gives us. Let us beware that we do not stand still in idleness, under the pretence of humility. Let us daily try to do what we can and in the trying Christ will meet us and grant his blessing.

For meditation: *Salvation is a work of God, but it must be preached by man and received by man. God does not leave us as passive spectators.*

Suggested further reading: *Matthew 9:27-31*

We should mark the words which our Lord addressed to Martha, when she objected to the stone being removed from the grave. The faith of this holy woman completely broke down, when the cave where her beloved brother lay was about to be thrown open. She could not believe that it was of any use. 'Lord,' she cries, 'by this time he stinketh.' And then comes in the solemn reproof of our Lord: 'Said I not unto thee that if thou wouldest believe thou shouldest see the glory of God?'

That sentence is rich in meaning. It is far from unlikely that it contains a reference to the message which had been sent to Martha and Mary, when their brother first fell sick. It may be meant to remind Martha that her Master had sent her word: 'This sickness is not unto death, but for the glory of God.' But it is perhaps more likely that our Lord desired to recall to Martha's mind the old lesson he had taught her all through his ministry, the duty of always believing. It is as though he said, 'Martha, Martha, thou art forgetting the great doctrine of faith, which I have ever taught thee. Believe, and all will be well. Fear not, only believe.'

The lesson is one which we can never know too well. How apt our faith is to break down in time of trial! How easy it is to talk of faith in the days of health and prosperity and how hard to practise it in the days of darkness, when neither sun, moon, nor stars appear! Let us lay to heart what our Lord says in this place. Let us pray for such stores of inward faith that, when our turn comes to suffer, we may suffer patiently and believe all is well. The Christian who has ceased to say, 'I must see, and then I will believe,' and has learned to say, 'I believe, and by and by I shall see,' has reached a high degree in the school of Christ.

For meditation: *Do your trials crush your faith or strengthen it?*

Suggested further reading: Hebrews 1:1-14

We should mark the words which our Lord addressed to God the Father when the stone was taken from the grave. We read that he said, 'Father, I thank thee that thou hast heard me. And I knew that thou hearest me always: but because of the people which stand by I said it, that they may believe that thou hast sent me.'

This wonderful language is totally unlike anything said by prophets or apostles when they worked miracles. In fact, it is not prayer, but praise. It evidently implies a constant mysterious communion going on between Jesus and his Father in heaven, which it is past the power of man either to explain or conceive. We need not doubt that here, as elsewhere in St John, our Lord meant to teach the Jews the entire and complete unity there was between him and his Father, in all that he did, as well as in all that he taught. Once more he would remind them that he did not come among them as a mere prophet, but as the Messiah who was sent by the Father and who was one with the Father. Once more he would have them know that as the words which he spake were the very words which the Father gave him to speak, so the works which he wrought were the very works which the Father gave him to do. In short, he was the promised Messiah, whom the Father always hears, because he and the Father are one.

Deep and high as this truth is, it is for the peace of our souls to believe it thoroughly and to grasp it tightly. Let it be a settled principle of our religion that the Saviour in whom we trust is nothing less than eternal God, one whom the Father hears always, one who in very deed is God's fellow. A clear view of the dignity of our Mediator's person is one secret of inward comfort. Happy is he who can say, 'I know whom I have believed, and that he is able to keep that which I have committed to him' (2 Tim. 1:12).

For meditation: *The Saviour who intercedes for us (Heb. 7:25) is always heard (John 11:42).*

Suggested further reading: 1 Corinthians 15:50-58

We should mark the words which our Lord addressed to Lazarus when he raised him from the grave. We read that 'He cried with a loud voice, Lazarus, come forth!' At the sound of that voice, the king of terrors at once yielded up his lawful captive and the insatiable grave gave up its prey. At once 'He that was dead came forth, bound hand and foot with grave-clothes.'

The greatness of this miracle cannot possibly be exaggerated. The mind of man can scarcely take in the vastness of the work that was done. Here, in open day and before many hostile witnesses, a man four days dead was restored to life in moment. Here was public proof that our Lord had absolute power over the material world! A corpse, already corrupt, was made alive! Here was public proof that our Lord had absolute power over the world of spirits! A soul that had left its earthly tenement was called back from Paradise and joined once more to its owner's body. Well may the church of Christ maintain that he who could work such works was 'God over all blessed for ever' (Rom. 9:5).

Let us turn from the whole passage with thoughts of comfort and consolation. Comfortable is the thought that the loving Saviour of sinners, on whose mercy our souls entirely depend, is one who has all power in heaven and earth and is mighty to save. Comfortable is the thought that there is no sinner too far gone in sin for Christ to raise and convert. He that stood by the grave of Lazarus can say to the vilest of men, 'Come forth: loose him, and let him go.' Comfortable, not least, is the thought that when we ourselves lie down in the grave, we may lie down in the full assurance that we shall rise again. The voice that called Lazarus forth will one day pierce our tombs and bid soul and body come together. 'The trumpet shall sound, and the dead shall be raised incorruptible, and we shall be changed' (1 Cor. 15:52).

For meditation: *The funerals of our loved ones only have the appearance of finality. There is a God who raises the dead.*

Suggested further reading: Luke 16:19-31

A man four days dead was raised to life in the sight of many witnesses. The fact was unmistakable and could not be denied and yet the chief priests and Pharisees would not believe that he who did this miracle ought to be received as the Messiah. In the face of overwhelming evidence, they shut their eyes and refused to be convinced. 'This man,' they admitted, 'does many miracles.' But so far from yielding to this testimony, they only plunged into further wickedness and 'took counsel to put him to death'. Great, indeed, is the power of unbelief!

Let us beware of supposing that miracles alone have any power to convert men's souls and to make them Christians. The idea is a complete delusion. To fancy, as some do, that if they saw something wonderful done before their eyes in confirmation of the gospel, they would at once cast off all indecision and serve Christ is a mere idle dream. It is the grace of the Spirit in our hearts, and not miracles, that our souls require. The Jews of our Lord's day are standing proof to mankind that men may see signs and wonders and yet remain hard as stone. It is a deep and true saying: 'If men believe not Moses and the prophets, neither would they be persuaded though one rose from the dead' (Luke 16:31).

We must never wonder if we see abounding unbelief in our own times and around our own homes. It may seem at first inexplicable to us how men cannot see the truth which seems so clear to ourselves and do not receive the gospel which appears so worthy of acceptation. But the plain truth is that man's unbelief is a far more deeply-seated disease than it is generally reckoned. It is proof against the logic of facts, against reasoning, against argument, against moral suasion. Nothing can melt it down but the grace of God. If we ourselves believe, we can never be too thankful.

For meditation: *Unbelief is not concerned with evidence. The only power to overcome it is the gift of a new heart.*

Suggested further reading: Psalm 2

These rulers of the Jews said to one another, 'If we let this Christ alone we shall be ruined. If we do not stop his course and make an end of his miracles, the Romans will interfere and make an end of our nation.' Never, the event afterwards proved, was there a more short-sighted and erring judgement than this. They rushed madly on the path they had chosen and the very thing they feared came to pass. They did not leave our Lord alone, but crucified and slew him. And what happened then? After a few years, the very calamity they had dreaded took place: the Roman armies did come, destroyed Jerusalem, burned the temple and carried away the whole nation into captivity.

The Roman emperors persecuted the Christians in the first three centuries and thought it a positive duty not to let them alone. But the more they persecuted them, the more they increased. The blood of the martyrs became the seed of the church. The English Papists, in the days of Queen Mary, persecuted the Protestants and thought that truth was in danger if they were let alone. But the more they burned our forefathers, the more they confirmed men's minds in steadfast attachment to the doctrines of the Reformation. In short, the words of the second Psalm are continually verified in this world: 'The kings of the earth set themselves, and the rulers take counsel together against the Lord.' But, 'He that sitteth in the heavens shall laugh; the Lord shall have them in derision.' God can make the designs of his enemies work together for the good of his people and cause the wrath of man to praise him. In days of trouble and rebuke and blasphemy, believers may rest patiently in the Lord. The very things that at one time seem likely to hurt them shall prove in the end to be for their gain.

For meditation: _The church is indestructible because it is built by Christ (Matt. 16:18)._

Suggested further reading: *Matthew 15:1-9*

What importance bad men sometimes attach to outward ceremonial, while their hearts are full of sin! We are told that many
Jews 'went up out of the country to Jerusalem, before the Passover, to purify themselves'. The most of them, it may be feared,
neither knew nor cared anything about inward purity of heart.
They made much ado about the washings and fastings and
ascetic observances which formed the essence of popular
Jewish religion in our Lord's time and yet they were willing in a
very few days to shed innocent blood. Strange as it may appear,
these very sticklers for outward sanctification were found
ready to do the will of the Pharisees and to put their own
Messiah to a violent death.
    Extremes like this meeting together in the same person are,
unhappily, far from uncommon. Experience shows that a bad
conscience will often try to satisfy itself by a show of zeal for the
cause of religion, while the 'weightier matters' of the faith are
entirely neglected. The very same man who is ready to compass
sea and land to attain ceremonial purity is often the very man
who, if he had fit opportunity, would not shrink from helping
to crucify Christ. Startling as these assertions may seem, they
are abundantly borne out by plain facts.
    Let us settle it firmly in our minds that a religion which
expends itself in zeal for outward formalities is utterly worthless in God's sight. The purity that God desires to see is not the
purity of bodily washing and fasting, of holy water and self-
imposed asceticism, but purity of heart. 'Blessed are the pure in
heart, for they shall see God' (Matt. 5:8).

For meditation: *Are you more concerned about what other
people **think** of you or what God **knows** about you?*

Suggested further reading: Luke 24:36-43

What abounding proofs exist of the truth of our Lord's greatest miracles! We read of a supper at Bethany, where Lazarus 'sat at the table' among the guests — Lazarus, who had been publicly raised from the dead after lying four days in the grave. No one could pretend to say that his resurrection was a mere optical delusion and that the eyes of the bystanders must have been deceived by a ghost or vision. Here was the very same Lazarus, after several weeks, sitting among his fellow men with a real material body and eating and drinking real material food. It is hard to understand what stronger evidence of a fact could be supplied. He that is not convinced by such evidence as this may as well say that he is determined to believe nothing at all.

It is a comfortable thought that the very same proofs which exist about the resurrection of Lazarus are the proofs which surround the still mightier fact, the resurrection of Christ from the dead. Was Lazarus seen for several weeks by the people of Bethany, going in and coming out among them? So was the Lord Jesus seen by his disciples. Did Lazarus take material food before the eyes of his friends? So did the Lord Jesus eat and drink before his ascension. No one, in his sober senses, who saw Jesus take 'broiled fish and a honeycomb' and eat it before several witnesses, would doubt that he had a real body (Luke 24:42).

We shall do well to remember this. In an age of abounding unbelief and scepticism, we shall find that the resurrection of Christ will bear any weight that we can lay upon it. Just as he placed beyond reasonable doubt the rising again of a beloved disciple within two miles of Jerusalem, so in a very few weeks he placed beyond doubt his own victory over the grave. If we believe that Lazarus rose again, we need not doubt that Jesus rose again also. If we believe that Jesus rose again, we need not doubt the truth of his Messiahship, the reality of his acceptance as our Mediator and the certainty of our own resurrection.

For meditation: *Surely only prejudice would reject over 500 eyewitnesses to an event? (1 Cor. 15:6.)*

Suggested further reading: *Jeremiah 38:1-6*

What unkindness and discouragement Christ's friends sometimes meet from man! We read that, at the supper in Bethany, Mary, the sister of Lazarus, anointed the feet of Jesus with precious ointment and wiped them with the hair of her head. Nor was this ointment poured on with a niggardly hand. She did it so liberally and profusely that 'The house was filled with the odour of the ointment.' She did it under the influence of a heart full of love and gratitude. She thought nothing too great and good to bestow on such a Saviour. Sitting at his feet in days gone by and hearing his words, she had found peace for her conscience and pardon for her sins. At this very moment she saw Lazarus, alive and well, sitting by her Master's side — her own brother Lazarus, whom he had brought back to her from the grave. Greatly loved, she thought she could not show too much love in return. Having freely received, she freely gave.

But there were some present who found fault with Mary's conduct and blamed her as guilty of wasteful extravagance. One especially, an apostle, a man of whom better things might have been expected, declared openly that the ointment would have been better employed if it had been sold and the price 'given to the poor'. The heart which could conceive such thoughts must have had low views of the dignity of Christ's person and still lower views of our obligations to him. A cold heart and a stingy hand will generally go together.

We must never allow ourselves to be moved from 'patient continuance in well-doing' by the unkind remarks of such persons. It is vain to expect a man to do much for Christ when he has no sense of debt to Christ. We must pity the blindness of our unkind critics and work on. He who pleaded the cause of loving Mary and said, 'Let her alone,' is sitting at the right hand of God and keeps a book of remembrance.

For meditation: *Christ's 'Well done' (Matt. 25:23) will more than compensate for every human rebuttal.*

Suggested further reading: 1 Timothy 6:3-10

What desperate hardness and unbelief there is in the heart of man! Unbelief appears in the chief priests, who 'consulted that they might put Lazarus to death'. They could not deny the fact of his having been raised again. Living and moving and eating and drinking within two miles of Jerusalem, after lying four days in the grave, Lazarus was a witness to the truth of Christ's Messiahship, whom they could not possibly answer or put to silence. Yet these proud men would not give way. They would rather commit a murder than throw down the arms of rebellion and confess themselves in the wrong. No wonder that the Lord Jesus in a certain place 'marvelled' at unbelief (Mark 6:6). Well might he say, in a well-known parable, 'If they believe not Moses and the prophets, neither will they be persuaded though one rose from the dead' (Luke 16:31).

Hardness appears in Judas Iscariot who, after being a chosen apostle and a preacher of the kingdom of heaven, turns out at last a thief and a traitor. So long as the world stands, this unhappy man will be a lasting proof of the depth of human corruption. That anyone could follow Christ as a disciple for three years, see all his miracles, hear all his teaching, receive at his hand repeated kindnesses, be counted an apostle and yet prove rotten at heart in the end — all this at first sight appears incredible and impossible! Yet the case of Judas shows plainly that the thing can be. Few things, perhaps, are so little realized as the extent of the fall of man.

Let us thank God if we know anything of faith and can say, with all our sense of weakness and infirmity, 'I believe.' Let us pray that our faith may be real, true, genuine and sincere and not a mere temporary impression, like the morning cloud and the early dew. Not least, let us watch and pray against the love of the world. It ruined one who basked in the full sunshine of privileges and heard Christ himself teaching every day.

For meditation: *How much is your heart welded to this world?*

Suggested further reading: *Zechariah 9:9-13*

The riding into Jerusalem on an ass, which is here recorded, might seem at first sight a simple action and in no way remarkable. But when we turn to the Old Testament, we find that this very thing had been predicted by the prophet Zechariah five hundred years before (Zech. 9:9). We find that the coming of a Redeemer some day was not the only thing which the Holy Ghost had revealed to the fathers, but that even the least particulars of his earthly career were predicted and written down with precise accuracy.

Such fulfilments of prophecy as this deserve the special attention of all who love the Bible and read it with reverence. They show us that every word of Holy Scripture was given by inspiration of God. They teach us to beware of the mischievous practice of spiritualizing and explaining away the language of Scripture. We must settle it in our minds that the plain, literal meaning of the Bible is generally the true and correct meaning. Here is a prediction of Zechariah literally and exactly fulfilled. Our Lord was not merely a very humble person, as some spiritualizing interpreters would have explained Zechariah's words to mean, but he literally rode into Jerusalem on an ass. Above all, such fulfilments teach us what we may expect in looking forward to the second advent of Jesus Christ. They show us that we must look for a literal accomplishment of the prophecies concerning that second coming and not for a figurative and a spiritual one. Forever let us hold fast this great principle. Happy is that Bible-reader who believes the words of the Bible to mean exactly what they seem to mean. Such a man has got the true key of knowledge in looking forward to things to come. To know that predictions about the second advent of Christ will be fulfilled literally, just as predictions about the first advent of Christ were fulfilled literally, is the first step towards a right understanding of unfulfilled prophecy.

For meditation: *The Scriptures stand detailed study because God is a God of detailed accuracy.*

Suggested further reading: John 18:1-8

How entirely voluntary the sufferings of Christ were! It is impossible not to see in the history before us that our Lord had a mysterious influence over the minds and wills of all around him, whenever he thought fit to use it. Nothing else can account for the effect which his approach to Jerusalem had on the multitudes which accompanied him. They seem to have been carried forward by a secret constraining power, which they were obliged to obey, in spite of the disapproval of the leaders of the nation. In short, just as our Lord was able to make winds and waves and diseases and devils obey him, so was he able, when it pleased him, to turn the minds of men according to his will.

For the case before us does not stand alone. The men of Nazareth could not hold him when he chose to 'pass through the midst of them and go his way' (Luke 4:30). The angry Jews of Jerusalem could not detain him when they would have laid violent hands on him in the temple, but 'going through the midst of them, he passed by' (John 8:59). Above all, the very soldiers who apprehended him in the garden at first 'went backward and fell to the ground' (John 18:6). In each of these instances there is but one explanation. A divine influence was put forth. There was about our Lord during his whole earthly ministry a mysterious 'hiding of his power' (Hab. 3:4). But he had almighty power when he was pleased to use it.

Why then, did he not resist his enemies at last? Why did he not scatter the band of soldiers who came to seize him like chaff before the wind? There is but one answer. He was a willing sufferer. He did not bleed and suffer and die because he was vanquished by superior force and could not help himself, but because he loved us and rejoiced to give himself for us as our Substitute.

For meditation: *'How willing was Jesus to die that we poor sinners might live!'*

Suggested further reading: Acts 26:19-29

A careful reader of the Gospels can hardly fail to observe that our Lord Jesus Christ's conduct at this stage of his earthly ministry is very peculiar. It is unlike anything else recorded of him in the New Testament. Hitherto we have seen him withdrawing as much as possible from public notice, retiring into the wilderness and checking those who would have brought him forward and made him a king. As a rule he did not court popular attention. He did not 'cry or strive, or cause his voice to be heard in the streets' (Matt. 12:19). Here, on the contrary, we see him making a public entry into Jerusalem, attended by an immense crowd of people and causing even the Pharisees to say, 'Behold, the world has gone after him.'

The explanation of this apparent inconsistency is not hard to find out. The time had come at last when Christ was to die for the sins of the world. The time had come when the true Passover Lamb was to be slain, when the true blood of atonement was to be shed, when Messiah was to be 'cut off' according to prophecy (Dan. 9:26), when the way into the holiest was to be opened by the true High Priest to all mankind. Knowing all this, our Lord purposely drew attention to himself. Knowing this, he placed himself prominently under the notice of the whole Jewish nation. It was only meet and right that this thing should not be 'done in a corner' (Acts 26:26). If ever there was a transaction in our Lord's earthly ministry which was public, it was the sacrifice which he offered up on the cross of Calvary. He died at the time of year when all the tribes were assembled at Jerusalem for the Passover feast. Nor was this all. He died in a week when, by his remarkable public entry into Jerusalem, he had caused the eyes of all Israel to be specially fixed upon himself.

For meditation: *Our Lord was not interested in gaining publicity for himself, but in focusing attention on his saving death.*

Suggested further reading: Hebrews 2:14-18

Who would have thought when Christ was on earth that
foreigners from a distant land would have come forward in
Jerusalem and said, 'Sir, we would see Jesus'? Who these
Greeks were, what they meant, why they desired to see Jesus,
what their inward motives were — all these are questions we
cannot answer. Enough for us to know that they showed more
interest in Christ than Caiaphas and all his companions. Death
is the way to spiritual life and glory. 'Except a corn of wheat fall
into the ground, it abideth alone; but if it die, it bringeth forth
much fruit.' This sentence was primarily meant to teach the
wondering Greeks the true nature of Messiah's kingdom. If
they thought to see a king like the kings of this world, they were
greatly mistaken. Our Lord would have them know that he
came to carry a cross and not to wear a crown. He came not to
live a life of honour, ease and magnificence, but to die a shame-
ful and dishonoured death. The kingdom he came to set up was
to begin with a crucifixion and not with a coronation. Its glory
was to take its rise not from victories won by the sword and
from accumulated treasures of gold and silver, but from the
death of its King.

But this sentence was also meant to teach a wider and
broader lesson still. It revealed, under a striking figure, the
mighty foundation truth that Christ's death was to be the
source of spiritual life to the world. From his cross and
passions was to spring up a mighty harvest of benefit to all
mankind. His death, like a grain of seed corn, was to be the root
of blessings and mercies to countless millions of immortal
souls. In short, the great principle of the gospel was once more
exhibited — that Christ's vicarious death (not his life, or
miracles, or teaching, but his *death*) was to bring forth fruit to
the praise of God and to provide redemption for a lost world.

For meditation: *Paul did not simply preach Christ, but Christ
and him crucified (1 Cor. 2:2).*

Suggested further reading: Galatians 6:12-18

'He that hateth his life shall keep it.' He that would be saved must be ready to give up life itself, if necessary, in order to obtain salvation. He must bury his love of the world, with its riches, honours, pleasures and rewards, with a full belief that in so doing he will reap a better harvest, both here and hereafter. He who loves the life that now is so much that he cannot deny himself anything for the sake of his soul will find at length that he has lost everything. He, on the contrary, who is ready to cast away everything most dear to him in this life, if it stands in the way of his soul, and to crucify the flesh with its affections and lusts will find at length that he is no loser. In a word, his losses will prove nothing in comparison to his gains.

Truths such as these should sink deeply into our hearts and stir up self-inquiry. It is as true of Christians as it is of Christ — there can be no life without death, there can be no sweet without bitter, there can be no crown without a cross. Without Christ's death there would have been no life for the world. Unless we are willing to die to sin and crucify all that is most dear to flesh and blood, we cannot expect any benefit from Christ's death. Let us remember these things and take up our cross daily like men. Let us for the joy set before us endure the cross and despise the shame and in the end we shall sit down with our Master at God's right hand. The way of self-crucifixion and sanctification may seem foolishness and waste to the world, just as burying good seed corn seems waste to the child and the fool. But there never lived the man who did not find that by sowing to the Spirit he reaped life everlasting.

For meditation: *We must beware of that mentality which always talks of the sacrifices it has made for Christ. They always pale into insignificance in the light of his sacrifice.*

Suggested further reading: Matthew 5:10-12

If we profess to serve Christ, we must follow him. That expression, 'following', is one of wide signification and brings before our minds many familiar ideas. As the soldier follows his general, as the servant follows his master, as the scholar follows his teacher, as the sheep follows its shepherd, just so ought the professing Christian to follow Christ. Faith and obedience are the leading marks of real followers and will always be seen in true believing Christians. Their knowledge may be very small and their infirmities very great, their grace very weak and their hope very dim. But they believe what Christ says and strive to do what Christ commands. And of such Christ declares, 'They serve me; they are mine.'

Christianity like this receives little from man. It is too thorough, too decided, too strong, too real. To serve Christ in name and form is easy work and satisfies most people, but to follow him in faith and life demands more trouble than the generality of men will take about their souls. Laughter, ridicule, opposition, persecution are often the only reward which Christ's followers get from the world. Their religion is one 'whose praise is not of men, but of God' (Rom. 2:29).

Yet to him that followeth, let us never forget, the Lord Jesus holds out abundant encouragement: 'Where I am,' he declares, 'there also shall my servant be; if any man serve me, him will my Father honour.' Let us lay to heart these comfortable promises and go forward in the narrow way without fear. The world may cast out our name as evil and turn us out of its society, but when we dwell with Christ in glory, we shall have a home from which we can never be ejected. The world may pour contempt on our religion and laugh us and our Christianity to scorn, but when the Father honours us at the last day, before the assembly of angels and men, we shall find that his praise makes amends for all.

For meditation: *To suffer is difficult enough, but to rejoice in suffering is a Christian virtue (Acts 5:41).*

Suggested further reading: Romans 5:12-21

We have in these verses a great doctrine indirectly proved. That doctrine is the imputation of man's sin to Christ. We see the Saviour of the world, the eternal Son of God, troubled and disturbed in mind: 'Now is my soul troubled.' We see him who could heal diseases with a touch, cast out devils with a word and command the waves and winds to obey him in great agony and conflict of spirit. Now how can this be explained?

To say, as some do, that the only cause of our Lord's trouble was the prospect of his own painful death on the cross is a very unsatisfactory explanation. At this rate it might justly be said that many a martyr has shown more calmness and courage than the Son of God. Such a conclusion is, to say the least, most revolting. Yet this is the conclusion to which men are driven if they adopt the modern notion that Christ's death was only a great example of self-sacrifice.

Nothing can ever explain our Lord's trouble of soul, both here and in Gethsemane, except the old doctrine that he felt the burden of man's sin pressing him down. It was the mighty weight of a world's guilt imputed to him and meeting on his head which made him groan and agonize and cry, 'Now is my soul troubled.' Forever let us cling to that doctrine, not only as untying the knot of the passage before us, but as the only ground of solid comfort for the heart of a Christian. That our sins have been really laid on our divine Substitute and borne by him and that his righteousness is really imputed to us and accounted ours — this is the real warrant for Christian peace. And if any man asks how we know that our sins were laid on Christ, we bid him read such passages as that which is before us and explain them on any other principle if he can. Christ has borne our sins, carried our sins, groaned under the burden of our sins, been 'troubled' in soul by the weight of our sins and really taken away our sins. This, we may rest assured, is sound doctrine; this is scriptural theology.

For meditation: *Christ had no sin but our sin for which to die (2 Cor. 5:21).*

Suggested further reading: Galatians 5:13-25

We cannot fail to see in the passage before us a mighty mental struggle in our blessed Saviour. Of its depth and intensity we can probably form very little conception. But the agonizing cry, 'My soul is troubled,' the solemn question, 'What shall I say?' the prayer of suffering flesh and blood, 'Father, save me from this hour,' the meek confession, 'For this cause came I unto this hour,' the petition of a perfectly submissive will, 'Father, glorify thy name' — what does all this mean? Surely there can be only one answer. These sentences tell of a struggle within our Saviour's breast, a struggle arising from the natural feelings of one who was perfect man and as man could suffer all that man is capable of suffering. Yet he in whom this struggle took place was the holy Son of God. 'In him is no sin' (1 John 3:5). There is a fountain of comfort here for all true servants of Christ which ought never to be overlooked. Let them learn from their Lord's example that inward conflict of soul is not necessarily in itself a sinful thing. Too many, we believe, from not understanding this point, go heavily all their days on their way to heaven. They fancy they have no grace because they find a fight in their own hearts. They refuse to take comfort in the gospel because they feel a battle between the flesh and the Spirit. Let them mark the experience of their Lord and Master and lay aside their desponding fears. Let them study the experience of his saints in every age, from St Paul downwards, and understand that, as Christ had inward conflicts, so must Christians expect to have them also. To give way to doubts and unbelief, no doubt, is wrong and robs us of our peace. There is a faithless despondency, unquestionably, which is blame-worthy and must be resisted, repented of and brought to the fountain for all sin that it may be pardoned. But the mere presence of fight and strife and conflict in our hearts is in itself no sin. The believer may be known by his inward warfare as well as by his inward peace.

For meditation: *Our Lord's identification with us in our humanity means that he knew inner struggles too.*

Suggested further reading: 2 Peter 1:16-18

We have in these verses a great miracle exhibited. That miracle is the heavenly voice described in this passage — a voice which was heard so plainly that people said it thundered — proclaiming, 'I have glorified my name, and will glorify it again.' This wondrous voice was heard three times during our Lord's earthly ministry. Once it was heard at his baptism, when the heavens were opened and the Holy Ghost descended on him. Once it was heard at his transfiguration, when Moses and Elias appeared for a season with him before Peter, James and John. Once it was heard here at Jerusalem in the midst of a mixed crowd of disciples and unbelieving Jews. On each occasion we know that it was the voice of God the Father. But why and wherefore this voice was only heard on these occasions we are left to conjecture. The thing was a deep mystery and we cannot now speak particularly of it.

Let it suffice us to believe that this miracle was meant to show the intimate relations and unbroken union of God the Father and God the Son throughout the period of the Son's earthly ministry. At no period during his incarnation was there a time when the eternal Father was not close to him, though unseen by man. Let us also believe that this miracle was meant to signify to bystanders the entire approval of the Son by the Father, as the Messiah, the Redeemer and the Saviour of man. That approval the Father was pleased to signify by voice three times, as well as to declare by signs and mighty deeds, performed by the Son in his name. These things we may well believe. But when we have said all, we must confess that the voice was a mystery. We may read of it with wonder and awe, but we cannot explain it.

For meditation: *God has usually revealed himself through men, but has added to this the witness of his own voice.*

Suggested further reading:　Revelation 7:9-12

We have in these verses a great prophecy delivered. The Lord Jesus declared, 'I, if I be lifted up from the earth, will draw all men unto me.'

Concerning the true meaning of these words there can be but one opinion in any candid mind. They do not mean, as is often supposed, that if the doctrine of Christ crucified is lifted up and exalted by ministers and teachers, it will have a drawing effect on hearers. This is undeniably a truth, but it is not the truth of the text. They simply mean that the death of Christ on the cross would have a drawing effect on all mankind. His death as our Substitute and the sacrifice for our sins would draw multitudes out of every nation to believe on him and receive him as their Saviour. By being crucified for us, and not by ascending a temporal throne, he would set up a kingdom in the world and gather subjects to himself.

How thoroughly this prophecy has been fulfilled for nineteen centuries, the history of the church is an abundant proof. Whenever Christ crucified has been preached and the story of the cross fully told, souls have been converted and drawn to Christ, just as iron filings are drawn to a magnet, in every part of the world. No truth so exactly suits the wants of all children of Adam, of every colour, climate and language, as the truth about Christ crucified.

And the prophecy is not yet exhausted. It shall yet receive a more complete accomplishment. A day shall come when every knee shall bow before the Lamb that was slain and every tongue confess that he is Lord to the glory of God the Father. He that was 'lifted up' on the cross shall yet sit on the throne of glory and before him shall be gathered all nations. Friends and foes, each in their own order, shall be 'drawn' from their graves and appear before the judgement-seat of Christ. Let us take heed in that day that we are found on his right hand!

For meditation:　*All the ransomed church of God shall be saved to sin no more.*

Suggested further reading: 2 Corinthians 5:16-6:2

We may learn from these verses the duty of using present opportunities. The Lord Jesus says to us all, 'Yet a little while is the light with you. Walk while ye have the light, lest darkness come upon you . . . While ye have light believe in the light.' Let us not think that these things were only spoken for the sake of the Jews. They were written for us also, upon whom the ends of the world are come.

The lesson of the words is generally applicable to the whole professing church of Christ. Its time for doing good in the world is short and limited. The throne of grace will not always be standing; it will be removed one day and the throne of judgement will be set up in its place. The door of salvation by faith in Christ will not always be open; it will be shut one day for ever and the number of God's elect will be completed. The fountain for all sin and uncleanness will not always be accessible; the way to it will one day be barred and there will remain nothing but the lake that burns with fire and brimstone.

These are solemn thoughts, but they are true. They cry aloud to sleeping churchmen and drowsy congregations and ought to arouse great searchings of heart. 'Can nothing more be done to spread the gospel at home and abroad? Has every means been tried for extending the knowledge of Christ crucified? Can we lay our hands on our hearts and say that the churches have left nothing undone in the matter of missions? Can we look forward to the second advent with no feelings of humiliation and say that the talents of wealth and influence and opportunities have not been buried in the ground?' Such questions may well humble us when we look, on one side, at the state of professing Christendom and, on the other, at the state of the heathen world. We must confess with shame that the church is not walking worthy of its light.

For meditation: *Salvation is not something to put off to tomorrow. There is an urgency about its reception.*

Suggested further reading: *Exodus 7:1-5*

We may learn from these verses the desperate hardness of the human heart. It is written of our Lord's hearers at Jerusalem that, 'Though he had done so many miracles before them, yet they believed not on him.'

We err greatly if we suppose that seeing wonderful things will ever convert souls. Thousands live and die in this delusion. They fancy if they saw some miraculous sight, or witnessed some supernatural exercise of divine grace, they would lay aside their doubts and at once become decided Christians. It is a total mistake. Nothing short of a new heart and a new nature implanted in us by the Holy Ghost will ever make us real disciples of Christ. Without this, a miracle might raise within us a little temporary excitement, but, the novelty once gone, we should find ourselves just as cold and unbelieving as the Jews.

The prevalence of unbelief and indifference in the present day ought not to surprise us. It is just one of the evidences of that mighty foundation doctrine, the total corruption and fall of man. How feebly we grasp and realize that doctrine is proved by our surprise at human incredulity. We only half believe the heart's deceitfulness. Let us read our Bibles more attentively and search their contents more carefully. Even when Christ wrought miracles and preached sermons, there were numbers of his hearers who remained utterly unmoved. What right have we to wonder if the hearers of modern sermons in countless instances remain unbelieving? 'The disciple is not greater than his Master.' If even the hearers of Christ did not believe, how much more should we expect to find unbelief among the hearers of his ministers! Let the truth be spoken and confessed. Man's obstinate unbelief is one among many indirect proofs that the Bible is true. The clearest prophecy in Isaiah begins with the solemn question: 'Who hath believed?' (Isa. 53:1.)

For meditation: *Pharaoh saw mighty miracles but repeatedly hardened his heart. 'Mere' miracles do not change hearts.*

Suggested further reading: Genesis 13:5-18

We may learn from these verses the amazing power which the love of the world has over men. We read that 'Among the chief rulers many believed on Christ; but because of the Pharisees they did not confess him, lest they should be put out of the synagogue. For they loved the praise of men more than the praise of God.'

These unhappy men were evidently convinced that Jesus was the true Messiah. Reason and intellect and mind and conscience obliged them secretly to admit that no one could do the miracles which he did unless God was with him and that the preacher of Nazareth really was the Christ of God. But they had not courage to confess it. They dared not face the storm of ridicule, if not of persecution, which confession would have entailed. And so, like cowards, they held their peace and kept their convictions to themselves.

Their case, it may be feared, is a sadly common one. There are thousands of people who know far more in religion then they act up to. They know they ought to come forward as decided Christians. They know that they are not living up to their light. But the fear of man keeps them back. They are afraid of being laughed at, jeered at and despised by the world. They dread losing the good opinion of society and the favourable judgement of men and women like themselves. And so they go on from year to year, secretly ill at ease and dissatisfied with themselves, knowing too much of religion to be happy in the world and clinging too much to the world to enjoy any religion.

Faith is the only cure for soul ailments like this. A believing view of an unseen God, an unseen Christ, an unseen heaven and an unseen judgement day — this is the grand secret of overcoming the fear of man. The expulsive power of a new principle is required to heal the disease. 'This is the victory that overcometh the world, even our faith' (1 John 5:4).

For meditation: *Lot wanted the best land for himself and got Sodom. Abram gave up his rights and received the land from God.*

Suggested further reading: John 14:8-11

One thing shown in these verses is the dignity of our Lord Jesus Christ. We find him saying, 'He that seeth me, seeth him that sent me. I am come a light into the world, that whosoever believeth on me should not abide in darkness.' Christ's oneness with the Father and Christ's office are clearly exhibited in these words.

Concerning the unity of the Father and the Son, we must be content to believe reverently what we cannot grasp mentally or explain distinctly. Let it suffice us to know that our Saviour was not like the prophets and patriarchs, a man sent by God the Father, a friend of God and a witness for God. He was something far higher and greater than this. He was in his divine nature essentially one with the Father and, in seeing him, men saw the Father that sent him. This is a great mystery, but a truth of vast importance to our souls. He that casts his sins on Jesus Christ by faith is building on a rock. Believing on Christ, he believes not merely on him, but on him that sent him.

Concerning the office of Christ, there can be little doubt that in this place he compares himself to the sun. Like the sun, he has risen on this sin-darkened world with healing in his wings and shines for the common benefit of all mankind. Like the sun, he is the great source and centre of all spiritual life, comfort and fertility. Like the sun, he illuminates the whole earth, and no one need miss the way to heaven, if he will only use the light offered for his acceptance.

Forever let us make much of Christ in all our religion. We can never trust him too much, follow him too closely or commune with him too unreservedly. He has all power in heaven and earth. He is able to save to the uttermost all who come to God by him. None can pluck us out of the hand of him who is one with the Father. He can make all our way to heaven bright and plain and cheerful like the morning sun cheering the traveller.

For meditation: *The Father and the Son are one (John 10:30). To have one is to have both (2 John 9).*

Suggested further reading: _Revelation 20:11-15_

In these verses there is the certainty of a judgement to come. We find our Lord saying, 'He that rejecteth me, and receiveth not my words, hath one that judgeth him: the word that I have spoken, the same shall judge him in the last day.'

There is a last day! The world shall not always go on as it does now. Buying and selling, sowing and reaping, planting and building, marrying and giving in marriage — all this shall come to an end at last. There is a time appointed by the Father when the whole machinery of creation shall stop and the present dispensation shall be changed for another. It had a beginning and it shall also have an end. Banks shall at length close their doors for ever. Stock exchanges shall be shut. Parliaments shall be dissolved. The very sun, which since Noah's flood has done his daily work so faithfully, shall rise and set no more. Well would it be if we thought more of this day! Rent days, birthdays, wedding days are often regarded as days of absorbing interest, but they are nothing compared to the last day.

There is a judgement coming! Men have their reckoning days and God will at last have his. The trumpet shall sound. The dead shall be raised incorruptible. The living shall be changed. All, of every name and nation and people and tongue, shall stand before the judgement-seat of Christ. The books shall be opened and the evidence brought forth. Our true character will come out before the world. There will be no concealment, no evasion, no false colouring. Everyone shall give account of himself to God and all shall be judged according to their works. The wicked shall go away into everlasting fire and the righteous into life eternal.

These are awful truths! But they are truths and ought to be told. No wonder that the Roman governor Felix trembled when Paul the prisoner discoursed about 'righteousness, temperance and judgement to come' (Acts 24:25).

For meditation: _How much does the reality of judgement affect the way you live?_

Suggested further reading: _Exodus 12:1-13_

The passage we have now read begins one of the most interesting portions of St John's Gospel. For five consecutive chapters we find the evangelist recording matters which are not mentioned by Matthew, Mark and Luke. We can never be thankful enough that the Holy Ghost has caused them to be written for our learning! In every age the contents of these chapters have been justly regarded as one of the most precious parts of the Bible. They have been the meat and drink, the strength and comfort of all true-hearted Christians. Let us ever approach them with peculiar reverence. The place whereon we stand is holy ground.

We should observe that the Feast of the Passover is always carefully mentioned by each Gospel writer as the precise time of the year when Jesus was crucified. It was ordered of God that it should be at this particular time for two good reasons. For one thing, the Passover lamb was the most striking and remarkable type in the whole Jewish ceremonial of Christ himself, and the history of the Passover of Christ's work of redemption. For another thing, it secured the greatest assembly of Israelites to be eyewitnesses of our Lord's crucifixion. At no time of the Jewish year were so many Jews gathered at Jerusalem. Anything that happened at the Passover would be reported by Jewish worshippers, on returning home, all over the civilized world. For these two reasons 'the Lamb of God' was slain at this feast, in spite of the priests, who said, 'Not on the feast day.'

Let us note that our Lord knew perfectly beforehand when and how he should suffer. This, whatever we may think, is a great addition to suffering. Our ignorance of things before us is a great blessing. Our Lord saw the cross clearly before him and walked straight up to it. His death was not a surprise to him, but a voluntary, foreknown thing.

For meditation: _Christ is our Passover Lamb (1 Cor.5:7)._

Suggested further reading: John 10:25-30

Let us observe how death is spoken of here. It is taking a journey — a going from one place to another. In the case of our Lord, it was a return to his Father's house and a going home after finishing the work he came to do. So a believer's death, in a lower sense, is going home. Calvin observes, 'This definition of death belongs to the whole body of the church. It is to the saints a passage to the Father, an inlet to eternal life.'

It is written that 'Having loved his own which were in the world, he loved them unto the end.' The meaning of this seems to be 'Having always loved his own disciples and having given many proofs of his singular affection, he now, before leaving them alone like orphans in the world, gave one more striking proof of his love by washing their feet and thus on the last evening before his death showed that he loved them to the very end of his ministry and was not weary of them.'

He knew perfectly that they were going to forsake him and act like cowards, but that did not prevent him loving them, with all their weakness, to the very end. He knew perfectly that he was about to suffer within twenty-four hours, but the knowledge and foresight of it did not absorb his thoughts so as to make him forget his little flock of followers.

The expression 'his own', applied to believers, is very noteworthy. They are Christ's peculiar property, given to him by the Father and his own special care as members of his body.

The expression 'which were in the world' is another great depth. Believers are not in heaven yet and find it out to their cost. They are in a cold, unkind, persecuting world. Let them take comfort in the thought that Jesus knows and remembers it. 'I know thy works and where thou dwellest' (Rev.2:13).

For meditation: *Christ remains faithful even when we are faltering and failing.*

Suggested further reading: *1 John 4:7-16*

The love of Christ to sinners is the very essence and marrow of the gospel. That he should love us at all and care for our souls, that he should love us before we love him, or even know anything about him, that he should love us so much as to come into the world to save us, take our nature on him, bear our sins and die for us on the cross — all this is wonderful indeed! It is a kind of love to which there is nothing like among men. The narrow selfishness of human nature cannot fully comprehend it. It is one of those things which even the angels of God 'desire to look into'. It is a truth which Christian preachers and teachers should proclaim incessantly and never be weary of proclaiming.

The love of Christ to saints is no less wonderful, in its way, than his love to sinners, though far less considered. That he should bear with all their countless infirmities from grace to glory, that he should never be tired of their endless inconsistencies and petty provocations, that he should go on forgiving and forgetting incessantly and never be provoked to cast them off and give them up — all this is marvellous indeed! No mother watching over the waywardness of her feeble babe, in the days of its infancy, has her patience so thoroughly tried as the patience of Christ is tried by Christians. Yet his longsuffering is infinite. His compassions are a well that is never exhausted. His love is 'a love that passeth knowledge'.

Let no man be afraid of beginning with Christ, if he desires to be saved. The chief of sinners may come to him with boldness and trust him for pardon with confidence. This loving Saviour is one who delights to 'receive sinners' (Luke 15:2). Let no man be afraid of going on with Christ after he has once come to him and believed.

For meditation: *'There is no love like the love of Jesus.'*

Suggested further reading: Jude 5-16

What deep corruption may sometimes be found in the heart of a great professor of religion! It is written that 'the devil put into the heart of Judas Iscariot, Simon's son, to betray Christ.'

This Judas, we must always remember, was one of the twelve apostles. He had been chosen by Christ himself, at the same time with Peter, James, John and their companions. For three years he had walked in Christ's society, had seen his miracles, had heard his preaching, had experienced many proofs of his lovingkindness. He had even preached himself and wrought miracles in Christ's name and when our Lord sent out his disciples two and two, Judas Iscariot no doubt must have been one of some couple that was sent. Yet here we see this very man possessed by the devil and rushing headlong to destruction.

He shows us what length a man may go in religious profession and yet turn out a rotten hypocrite at last and prove never to have been converted. He shows us the uselessness of the highest privileges unless we have a heart to value them and turn them to good account. Privileges alone without grace save nobody and will only make hell deeper. He shows us the uselessness of mere head-knowledge. To know things with our brains and be able to talk and preach and speak to others is no proof that our own feet are in the way of peace. These are terrible lessons, but they are true.

Let us never be surprised if we see hypocrisy and false profession among Christians in modern days. There is nothing new in it, nothing peculiar, nothing that did not happen even among Christ's own immediate followers and under Christ's own eyes.

For meditation: *Boastful claims do not make up for inner unreality.*

Suggested further reading: Genesis 3:1-7

Verse 2 does not mean that Judas now for the first time left the faith and became an apostate. Our Lord long before had spoken of him as one that was 'a devil' (John 6:70). But it means that now at length the devil suggested into the heart of this unhappy man the atrocious idea of betraying his Master. It was the last and final heading up of his apostasy.

The word rendered 'put' is literally 'cast'. This graphically describes the way in which Satan works. He casts into the heart of those he tempts the seeds of evil. The heart is the seed plot which he sows. Suggestion is one of his chief weapons. The sin of man consists in opening his heart to the suggestion, giving it a place and letting it sink down. This is obvious in the first temptation of Eve in the garden of Eden.

There seems no need for regarding Judas' betrayal of his Master as anything but the wicked act of a wicked man who loved money more than his soul. The theory that he was a high-minded, impatient disciple, who wished his Master no harm, but desired to hasten his kingdom and expected him to work a miracle and save himself at the last, is ingenious, but lacks foundation. Our Lord's word applied to him, 'a devil', and the word of St John, 'a thief', appear to me to overturn the theory altogether. Judas betrayed Jesus because he loved money better than his Master. He probably did not realize the full consequence of his act. But this is often the case with wicked men.

Melancthon shows that the three greatest marks of pity and compassion are (1) to tolerate the wicked for a season; (2) to abstain from exposing their sins as long as possible; (3) to warn them plainly and gently before leaving them for ever. All this appears in our Lord's dealings with Judas in this chapter.

For meditation: *We must never undermine the truth that Satan exists, nor underestimate his power.*

Suggested further reading: Genesis 18:1-5

The object of verse 3 is to show the extent and depth of our Lord's infinite condescension and love to his disciples. With a full knowledge that the Father had committed all power into his hands, that he had been from eternity with God and was going back to God, knowing all the dignity and majesty of his person and office, he yet condescended to perform the most menial office and to minister like a servant to his disciples.

Wonderful as all this transaction seems and no doubt is, when we remember who our Lord was, one thing must never be forgotten. The actions here described would not seem nearly so strange to the disciples as they do to us. They were simply the courteous actions of a host who desired to show the utmost degree of hospitable attention to the guests. Thus Abraham washed the feet of the three angelic messengers (Gen. 18:4; so also 1 Sam. 25:41). In a hot country like Palestine, where people wore no stockings and the heat was very scorching to the skin, frequent washing of the feet was an absolute necessity and to wash the feet of guests was a common piece of hospitality. It is one mark of a deserving widow that she has 'washed the saints' feet' (1 Tim. 5:10). The real wonder was that such a Master, on such a solemn occasion, should do such a condescending act to such weak disciples. It was not so much the action as the doer of it that was remarkable.

After all, there was a touching fitness in our Lord's choice of an instructive action on this solemn occasion. He knew that he was leaving his disciples, like poor feeble travellers, in a weary, wicked world. He would therefore wash their feet before parting and strengthen and refresh them for their journey.

It will be observed that the work was not left unfinished and half done. Like a perfect servant, our Lord 'wiped' the feet as well as 'washed' them.

For meditation: *The Son of man did not come to be served, but to serve (Mark 10:45).*

Suggested further reading: Luke 24:25-35

The English language here fails to give the full emphasis of the Greek. Verse 6 should be rendered: 'Dost thou, of me, wash the feet?' 'Such a one as thou art wash the feet of such a one as I am!' It is like John the Baptist's exclamation when our Lord came to his baptism: 'Comest thou to me?' (Matt. 3:14.) In verse 8 one sentence would be rendered literally: 'Thou shalt never wash my feet for ever,' or 'unto eternity'.

We should notice the hasty ignorance of the apostle Peter. One moment we find him refusing to allow his Master to do such a servile work as he is about to do: 'Dost thou wash my feet? . . . Thou shalt never wash my feet.' Another moment we find him rushing with characteristic impetuosity into the other extreme: 'Lord, wash not my feet only, but my hands and my head.' But throughout the transaction we find him unable to take in the real meaning of what his eyes behold. He sees, but he does not understand.

Let us gather from Peter's conduct that a man may have plenty of faith and love and yet be sadly destitute of clear knowledge. We must not set down men as graceless and godless because they are dull and stupid and blundering in their religion. The heart may often be quite right when the head is quite wrong. We must make allowances for the corruption of the understanding as well as of the will. We must not be surprised to find that the brains as well as the affections of Adam's children have been hurt by the Fall. It is a humbling lesson and one seldom fully learned except by long experience. But the longer we live, the more true shall we find it that a believer, like Peter, may make many mistakes and lack understanding and yet, like Peter, have a heart right before God and get to heaven at last.

For meditation: *Ignorance and slowness to learn are not to be confused with the absence of grace.*

Suggested further reading: 2 Timothy 3:10-17

The famous saying of verse 7 stretches far beyond the literal application of the words. Primarily, of course, it means, 'This action of mine has a meaning which in a few minutes I will explain and you will understand, though at present it may seem to you strange and unsuitable.' But in every age true Christians have seen a higher, deeper, broader meaning in the words and a pious mind cannot doubt that they were intended to bear that meaning. It supplies the key to many things which we cannot understand in the providential government of the world, in the history of the church, in the events of our own lives. We must make up our minds to see many things happening which we do not know and understand now and of which we cannot at present see the wisdom. But we must believe that 'we shall know hereafter' the full purposes, the why and wherefore and needs-be, of each and all. It is a golden sentence to store up in our memories. God's eternal counsels, the wisdom of the great Head of the church, must never be forgotten. All is going on well, even when we think all is going on ill. When we cannot see it, we must believe. In sickness, sorrow, bereavement, disappointment, we must summon up faith and patience and hear Christ saying to us, 'What I do thou knowest not now, but thou shalt know hereafter.'

The 'why' and 'wherefore' of many a providence will often puzzle and perplex us quite as much as the washing puzzled Peter. The wisdom and fitness and necessity of many a thing will often be hidden from our eyes. There came days, long after Christ had left the world, when Peter saw the full meaning of all that happened on the memorable night before the crucifixion. Even so, there will be a day when every dark page in our life's history will be explained and when, as we stand with Christ in glory, we shall know all.

For meditation: *We have often to wait for our questions to be answered. All we **need** to know we have revealed (2 Tim. 3:15-17).*

Suggested further reading: *Hebrews 9:11-14*

We need not doubt that verse 8 was meant to bear a deep and full meaning and to reach far beyond the primary application. It would be a very cold and tame exposition to say that our Lord only meant, 'Unless thy feet are washed by me tonight, thou art not one of my disciples.' It means a great deal more. Our Lord seems in effect to say, 'Thou wilt not be wise to object to the symbolical action which I am performing. Remember no one can be saved, or have any part in me and my work of redemption, unless I wash away his sins. Except I wash away thy many sins, even thou, Simon Peter, hast no part in me. I must wash every saved soul and every saved soul must be washed. Surely, therefore, it does not become thee to object to my doing an instructive and figurative act to thy feet, when I must needs do a far greater work to thy soul.'

The sentence is one of wide, deep and sweeping application. It is true of every Christian of every rank and position. To each one Christ says, 'If I wash thee not, thou hast no part in me.' It is not enough that we are churchmen, professed communicants and the like. The great question for everyone is this: 'Am I washed and justified?'

The common assertion that this 'washing' here spoken of is baptism seems to me unwarrantable. Our Lord never baptized anyone, so far as we can learn from Scripture. Where is it said that he baptized Peter? Moreover, if baptism were meant, the past tense would have been used: 'If I had not washed thee, thou wouldst have no part in me.' The washing here spoken of is something far above baptism.

No man or woman can be saved unless his sins are washed away in Christ's precious blood. Nothing else can make us clean or acceptable before God.

For meditation:
> *What can wash away my sin?*
> *Nothing but the blood of Jesus.*

Suggested further reading: 1 John 1:5-10

The exclamation of Peter in verse 9 is highly characteristic of the man. Impulsive, excitable, zealous, ardent, with more love than knowledge and more feeling than spiritual discernment, he is horrified at the very idea of 'having no part in Christ'. Anything rather than that! Not seeing clearly the deep meaning of his Master's words and still sticking to a carnal, literal interpretation of the word 'washing', he cries out that his Master may wash him all over, hands and head as well as feet, if an interest in Christ depends on that.

Verse 10 conveys a latent rebuke of Peter's spiritual dullness. It is as though Jesus said, 'The washing of head and hands whereof thou speakest is not needed. Even assuming that a literal washing is all I meant in saying, "If I wash thee not", it is well known that he who is washed needs only to wash his feet after a journey and is accounted clean entirely after such a partial washing. But this is far more true of the washing of pardon and justification. He that is pardoned and justified by me is entirely washed from all his sins and only needs the daily forgiveness of the daily defilement he contracts in travelling through a sinful world. Once washed, justified and accepted by me, ye are clean before God, although not all of you. There is one painful exception.'

The great practical truth contained in this sentence ought to be carefully noted and treasured up by all believers. Once joined to Christ and cleansed in his blood, they are completely absolved and free from all spot of guilt and are counted without blame before God. But, for all this, they need every day, as they walk through this world, to confess their daily failures and to sue for daily pardon. They require, in short, a daily washing of their feet, over and above the great washing of justification, which is theirs the moment they first believe.

For meditation: _Our sin needs to be confessed (1 John 1:9)._

Suggested further reading: Matthew 20:20-28

What did our Lord really mean? Did he mean that we all ought literally to do the very same thing that he did? Or did he only mean that we are to imitate the spirit of his action?
   The church of Rome, it is well known, puts a literal sense on our Lord's language. Once every year, about Easter, the head of the Romish church publicly washes the feet of certain poor persons got ready for the occasion. The absurdity, to say the least, of this view is evident on a moment's reflection.
   It seems absurd to take our Lord's words literally and to suppose that the pope's literal washing of a few feet at Easter can supersede the duty of all Christians to do the same. It is in any case absurd to suppose that our Lord would require his disciples to perform a duty which the young and the feeble would be physically unable to do.
   It is inconsistent with the general tenor of our Lord's teaching to suppose that he would ever attach so much importance to a mere bodily action. 'Bodily exercise profiteth little' (1 Tim. 4:8). A formal performance of bodily acts of religion is just the easiest thing that can be imposed on people. The thing that is really hard, and yet always required, is the service of the heart.
   The true interpretation of the two verses is that which places a spiritual sense on our Lord's words. It is a practical illustration of Matthew 20:26-28. He wished to teach his disciples that they ought to be willing to wait on one another, serve one another, minister to one another, even in the least and lowest things. They should think nothing too low, or humble, or menial to undertake, if they can show love, kindness and condescension to another. Doctrinal orthodoxy without practical love and humility is utterly worthless before God.

For meditation: *Copying actions to the letter in a mimicking way is not as helpful as applying the principle of the action to each situation.*

Suggested further reading: Philippians 2:1-8

If the only-begotten Son of God, the King of kings, did not think it beneath him to do the humblest work of a servant, there is nothing which his disciples should think themselves too great or too good to do. No sin is so offensive to God and so injurious to the soul as pride. No grace is so commended, both by precept and example, as humility. 'Be clothed with humility' (1 Peter 5:5). 'He that humbleth himself shall be exalted' (Luke 18:14). 'Let this mind be in you, which was also in Christ Jesus: who, being in the form of God, thought it not robbery to be equal with God: but made himself of no reputation, and took upon him the form of a servant, and was made in the likeness of men: and being found in fashion as a man, he humbled himself' (Phil. 2:5-8). Well would it be for the church if this very simple truth was more remembered and real humility was not so sadly rare. Perhaps there is no sight so displeasing in God's eyes as a self-conceited, self-satisfied, self-contented, stuck-up professor of religion.

Love is manifestly the other part of the great practical lesson. Our Lord would have us love others so much that we should delight to do anything which can promote their happiness. We ought to rejoice in doing kindnesses, even in little things. We ought to count it a pleasure to lessen sorrow and multiply joy, even when it costs us some self-sacrifice and self-denial. We ought to love every child of Adam so well, that if in the least trifle we can do anything to make him more happy and comfortable, we should be glad to do it. This was the mind of the Master and this the ruling principle of his conduct upon earth. There are but few who walk in his steps, it may be feared, but these few are men and women after his own heart.

For meditation: *Do other people think of you as selfish of selfless?*

Suggested further reading: Matthew 18:1-5

Christians must never be ashamed of doing anything that Christ has done. We read, 'Verily, I say unto you, The servant is not greater than his Lord; neither he that is sent greater than he that sent him.'

There seems little doubt that our Lord's all-seeing eye saw a rising unwillingness in the minds of the apostles to do such menial things as they had just seen him do. Puffed up with their old Jewish expectation of thrones and kingdoms in this world, secretly self-satisfied with their own position as our Lord's friends, these poor Galileans were startled at the idea of washing people's feet! They could not bring themselves to believe that Messiah's service entailed work like this. They could not yet take in the grand truth that true Christian greatness consisted in doing good to others. And hence they needed our Lord's word of warning. If he had humbled himself to do humbling work, his disciples must not hesitate to do the same.

The lesson is one of which we all need to be reminded. We are all too apt to dislike any work which seems to entail trouble, self-denial and going down to our inferiors. We are only too ready to depute such work to others and to excuse ourselves by saying, 'It is not in our way.' When feelings of this kind arise within us we shall find it good to remember our Lord's words in this passage, no less than our Lord's example. We ought never to think it beneath us to show kindness to the lowest of men. We ought never to hold our hand because the objects of our kindness are ungrateful or unworthy. Such was not the mind of him who washed the feet of Judas Iscariot as well as Peter. He who in these matters cannot stoop to follow Christ's example gives little evidence of possessing true love or true humility.

For meditation: *'I don't mind helping out but . . .'*   *But what? And why?*

Suggested further reading: Romans 2:17-24

We read, 'If ye know these things, happy are ye if ye do them.' It sounds as if our Lord would warn his disciples that they would never be really happy in his service if they were content with a barren head-knowledge of duty and did not live according to their knowledge.

Nothing is more common than to hear people saying of doctrine or duty, 'We know it, we know it,' while they sit still in unbelief or disobedience. They actually seem to flatter themselves that there is something creditable and redeeming in knowledge, even when it bears no fruit in heart, character, or life. Yet the truth is precisely the other way. To know what we ought to be, believe and do, and yet to be unaffected by our knowledge, only adds to our guilt in the sight of God. To know that Christians should be humble and loving, while we continue proud and selfish, will only sink us deeper in the pit unless we awake and repent. Practice, in short, is the very life of religion. 'To him that knoweth to do good, and doeth it not, to him it is sin' (James 4:17).

Of course, we must never despise knowledge. It is in one sense the beginning of Christianity in the soul. So long as we know nothing of sin, or God, or Christ, or grace, or repentance, or faith, or conscience, we are, of course, nothing better than heathens. But we must not overrate knowledge. It is perfectly valueless unless it produces results in our conduct and influences our lives and moves our wills. In fact knowledge without practice does not raise us above the level of the devil.

Satan knows truth, but has no will to obey it and is miserable. He that would be happy in Christ's service must not only know, but do.

For meditation: *'Knowledge puffs up but love edifies' (1 Cor. 8:1).*

Suggested further reading: *Matthew 22:1-14*

We are taught in these verses the perfect knowledge which Christ has of all his people. He can distinguish between false profession and true grace. The church may be deceived and rank men as apostles who are nothing better than brethren of Judas Iscariot. But Jesus is never deceived, for he can read hearts. And here he declares with peculiar emphasis, 'I know whom I have chosen.'

This perfect knowledge of our Lord Jesus Christ is a very solemn thought and one which cuts two ways. It ought to fill the hypocrite with alarm and drive him to repentance. Let him remember that the eyes of the all-seeing Judge already see him through and through and detect the lack of a wedding garment. If he would not be put to shame before assembled worlds, let him cast aside his false profession and confess his sin before it is too late. Believers, on the other hand, may think of an all-knowing Saviour with comfort. They may remember, when misunderstood and slandered by an evil world, that their Master knows all. He knows that they are true and sincere, however weak and failing. A time is coming when he will confess them before his Father and bring forth their characters clear and bright as the summer sun at noonday.

The forty-first Psalm is here shown to apply to one greater than David and one worse than Ahithophel. The ninth verse here quoted says, 'Mine own familiar friend, which did eat of my bread, hath lifted up his heel against me.' The expression implies the act of one who, like a stubborn and vicious horse, suddenly turns round against his master and kicks at him. 'This,' our Lord says, 'is about to be fulfilled in the conduct of Judas Iscariot to me.'

The grand lesson that we must be prepared for much disappointment in friends and companions in this life is very plain in this passage. The less we expect from man, the better.

For meditation: *Hebrews 4:13.*

Suggested further reading: *Matthew 10:5-15*

We are taught in these verses the true dignity of Christ's disciples. The world may despise and ridicule the apostles because they care more for works of love and humility than the pursuits of the world. But the Master bids them remember their commission and not be ashamed. They are God's ambassadors and have no cause to be cast down. 'Verily, verily,' he declares, 'He that receiveth whomsoever I send receiveth me, and he that receiveth me receiveth him that sent me.'

The doctrine here laid down is full of encouragement. It ought to cheer and hearten all who lay themselves out to do good and specially to do good to the fallen and the poor. Work of this kind gets little praise from men and they who give themselves up to it are often regarded as miserable enthusiasts and meet with much opposition. Let them, however, work on and take comfort in the words of Christ which we are now considering. To spend and be spent in trying to do good makes a man far more honourable in the eyes of Jesus than to command armies or amass a fortune. The few who work for God in Christ's way have no cause to be ashamed. Let them not be cast down if the children of the world laugh and sneer and despise them. A day comes when they will hear the words: 'Come ye blessed children of my Father, inherit the kingdom prepared for you' (Matt. 25:34).

Let us note that it is no light matter to reject and despise a faithful minister of Christ. A weak and ignorant servant may carry a message for a royal master and, for his master's sake, ought not to be lightly esteemed. Contempt for Christ's ministers, when they are really faithful, is a bad symptom in a church or nation.

For meditation: *Do you give your minister joy before God?*
(Heb. 13:17.)

Suggested further reading: Job 6:1-13

The subject of the verses before us is a very painful one. They describe the last scene between our Lord Jesus Christ and the false apostle Judas Iscariot. They contain the last words which passed between them before they parted for ever in this world. They never seem to have met again on earth, excepting in the garden when our Lord was taken prisoner. Within a short time both the holy Master and the treacherous servant were dead. They will never meet again in the body till the trumpet sounds and the dead are raised and the judgement is set and the books are opened. What an awful meeting will that be!

What trouble our Lord Jesus went through for the sake of our souls! We are told that, shortly after washing the disciples' feet, he 'was troubled in spirit, and said, One of you shall betray me'.

This expression applied to our Lord is peculiar to St John. We find it only in his Gospel, here and at 11:33 and 12:27. Here it seems to mean principally the pain and sorrow which our Lord experienced on seeing one of his own chosen apostles about to betray him. In addition to this, it probably includes that peculiar agony and distress of soul which our Lord was subject to under the presence of a world's sin laid upon him and which we see intensified in the garden of Gethsemane.

Let it be noted, that, of all the Gospel writers, John is the one who dwells most fully on the divine nature of our Lord and also is the one who describes most fully the reality of his human affections.

Observe that to be troubled and disturbed in mind is not in itself sinful. How foolish were the Stoic philosophers, who taught that a wise man is never disturbed in mind!

For meditation: _Neither physical sickness nor mental distress are necessarily sinful. We must not condemn the innocent._

Suggested further reading: Psalm 22:1-11

The whole length and breadth and depth of our Master's troubles during his earthly ministry are far beyond the conception of most people. His death and suffering on the cross were only the heading up and completion of his sorrows. But all throughout his life, partly from the general unbelief of the Jews, partly from the special hatred of the Pharisees and Sadducees, partly from the weakness and infirmity of his few followers, he must have been in a peculiar degree 'a man of sorrows and acquainted with grief' (Isa. 53:3).

But the trouble before us was a singular and exceptional one. It was the bitter sorrow of seeing a chosen apostle deliberately becoming an apostate, a backslider and an ungrateful traitor. That it was foreseen sorrow from the beginning we need not doubt, but sorrow is not less acute because long foreseen. That it was a peculiarly cutting sorrow is very evident. Nothing is found so hard for flesh and blood to bear as ingratitude. Even a poet of our own has said that it is 'sharper than a serpent's tooth to have a thankless child'. Absalom's rebellion seems to have been David's heaviest trouble and Judas Iscariot's treachery seems to have been one of the heaviest trials of the Son of David. When he saw it drawing near, he was 'troubled in spirit'.

Passages like these should make us see the amazing love of Christ to sinners. How many cups of sorrow he drained to the dregs in working out our salvation, beside the mighty cup of bearing our sins! They show us how little reason we have for complaining when friends fail us and men disappoint us. If we share our Master's lot, we have no cause to be surprised. Above all, they show us the perfect suitableness of Christ to be our Saviour. He can sympathize with us. He has suffered himself and can feel for those who are ill-used and forsaken.

For meditation: _'Judas' is a synonym for treachery, a term of utter contempt._

Suggested further reading: James 2:21-23

We notice from verse 22 that the first effect of our Lord's declaration seems to have been silence. Like men stunned and amazed, the disciples looked at one another in astonishment. The thing announced was the last thing they expected to hear.

Let us note that neither here nor afterwards does any suspicion appear to have fallen on Judas. For anything we can see, he looked as good as Peter, James and John, and as unlikely to betray his Master. The length to which hypocrisy can go is very awful.

To understand verse 23 we must remember the customs of the East in the time of our Lord about the position and attitude of the guests at a meal. They did not sit, but reclined.

The disciple that Jesus loved was John, the writer of this Gospel. It is the first time he speaks of himself in this way and the expression occurs afterwards four times (John 19:26; 20:2; 21:7,20).

The Greek word rendered 'loved' deserves notice. It signifies the higher, nobler and more refined kind of love. There are two words in the Greek language translated 'love' in the New Testament.

Let it be noted that the general special love with which our Lord loves all his disciples did not prevent his having a particular love for one individual. Why he specially loved John we are not told. Gifts certainly do not appear so much in John as grace. But it is worth noticing that love seems more the characteristic of John than of any disciple and that in this he showed more of the mind of Christ. It is quite clear that special friendship for one individual is quite consistent with love for all.

It is noteworthy that, of all the writers of the New Testament, none goes so deep and reveals so much of the hidden things of God as he who lay in the bosom of Christ.

For meditation: *What greater title could be given than 'the disciple that Jesus loved'?*

Suggested further reading: Romans 2:1-10

The characteristic forwardness and zeal of Peter come out strikingly (v.24). None seem so excited by our Lord's announcement as he is. None is so anxious to know of whom our Lord can be speaking. He cannot wait silently like the others. He makes a sign to John to ask privately who it can be. A fisherman by early training, like John, he was probably intimate with him and could make himself understood by signs.

In verse 25 the idea is evidently of one moving and leaning towards another, so as to get closer to him and whisper a question, so as not to be heard or observed. That this is what John did is evident. It is plain that he did not say out aloud, 'Lord, who is it?'

The action by which our Lord told John he would indicate the traitor to him was probably so common at an Eastern banquet that no one at the table would remark anything about it. That it was a common way of eating is shown by Ruth 2:14. Hengstenberg observes that by this act of kindness and attention Jesus 'would touch the heart of Judas once more, if haply he might be susceptible of better emotions'. That our Lord's answer was whispered is evident. No one seems to have noticed it, except John.

The word 'gave' is literally 'gives' in the present tense, showing the immediate action which followed our Lord's reply to John's question.

Here, as elsewhere, it is noteworthy that John specially calls Judas 'the son of Simon', in order to make it quite clear what Judas it was who did this foul deed.

Bengel remarks, 'How very near to Jesus was Judas on this occasion! But in a short time after, by what a wide gulf did glory separate Jesus from Judas, and destruction separate Judas from Jesus!'

For meditation: *Even God is finally impatient with the stubbornly impenitent.*

Suggested further reading: *Genesis 3:1-6*

Let us mark in these verses the power and malignity of our great enemy the devil. We re told in the beginning of the chapter that he 'put it into the heart' of Judas to betray our Lord. We are told here that he 'entered into' him. First he suggests; then he commands. First he knocks at the door and asks permission to come in; then, once admitted, he takes complete possession and rules the whole inward man like a tyrant.

Let us take heed that we are not 'ignorant of Satan's devices'. He is still going to and fro in the earth, seeking whom he may devour. He is about our path and about our bed and spies out all our ways. Our only safety lies in resisting him at the first and not listening to his first advances. For this we are all responsible. Strong as he is, he has no power to do us harm, if we cry to the stronger one in heaven and use the means which he has appointed. It is a standing principle of Christianity and will ever be found true: 'Resist the devil, and he will flee from you' (James 4:7).

Once let a man begin tampering with the devil and he never knows how far he may fall. Trifling with the first thoughts of sin, making light of evil ideas when first offered to our hearts, allowing Satan to talk to us and flatter us and put bad notions into out hearts — all this may seem a small matter to many. It is precisely at this point that the road to ruin often begins. He that allows Satan to sow wicked thoughts will soon find within his heart a crop of wicked habits. Happy is he who really believes that there is a devil and, believing, watches and prays daily that he may be kept from his temptations.

For meditation: *We can believe Satan has too much power and dishonour God, or believe he has too little and be defeated by him.*

Suggested further reading: *Hebrews 10:26-39*

Let us mark in these verses the extreme hardness which comes over the heart of a backsliding professor of religion. This is a thing which is most painfully brought out in the case of Judas Iscariot. One might have thought that the sight of our Lord's trouble and the solemn warning, 'One of you shall betray me,' would have stirred the conscience of this unhappy man. But it did not do so. One might have thought that the solemn words, 'That thou doest, do quickly,' would have arrested him and made him ashamed of his intended sin. But nothing seems to have moved him. Like one whose conscience was dead, buried and gone, he rises and goes out to do his wicked work and parts with his Lord for ever.

The extent to which we may harden ourselves by resisting light and knowledge is one of the most fearful facts in our nature. We may become past feeling, like those whose limbs are mortified before they die. We may lose entirely all sense of fear, or shame, or remorse and have a heart as hard as the nether millstone, blind to every warning and deaf to every appeal. It is a sore disease, but one which unhappily is not uncommon among professing Christians. None seem so liable to it as those who, having great light and privilege, deliberately turn their backs on Christ and return to the world. Nothing seems likely to touch such people, but the voice of the archangel and the trump of God.

Let us watch jealously over our hearts and beware of giving way to the beginnings of sin. Happy is he who feareth always and walks humbly with his God. The strongest Christian is the one who feels his weakness most and cries most frequently, 'Hold thou me up, and I shall be safe' (Ps. 119:117; Prov. 28:14).

For meditation: *Persistence in sin is a guaranteed road to disaster.*

Suggested further reading: Matthew 19:23-30

The statement that 'Judas had the bag' shows the position he occupied among the apostles. He was so far from being suspected that he had the charge of the common store of money.

The supposition of some that Jesus told Judas to 'buy the things needed against the feast' shows clearly that our Lord did not work miracles in order to procure the necessaries required by himself and his disciples. Christians must buy and sell like other people and must manage their money affairs with prudence and economy. It shows how little the disciples realized that their Master's death was close at hand.

The supposition of others that Jesus told Judas to 'give something to the poor' shows plainly what was our Lord's custom in the matter of almsgiving. He sanctified and adorned the practice of caring for the poor by his own example. This passage and Galatians 2:10 deserve careful consideration.

Let us mark the snares which attend the possession, fingering and handling of money. The man who has care of the money in our Lord's little company of followers is the very man who makes shipwreck of his soul for ever through the love of money. 'Give me neither poverty nor riches,' should be a Christian's frequent prayer (Prov. 30:8).

The hasty departure of Judas as soon as our Lord had given him the morsel and spoken the remarkable words already commented on may easily be explained. He saw at once that our Lord knew all his plot and dreaded exposure. His conscience condemned him and he dared no longer sit in our Lord's company. He, at any rate, understood what our Lord meant, if nobody else did. He felt himself detected and discovered and for very shame got up and went away.

It is curious and noteworthy that John, at all events, must have known Judas to be the traitor and yet he seems to have said nothing.

For meditation: *No one has ever successfully served God and money (Matt. 6:24).*

Suggested further reading: Isaiah 53

The crucifixion brought glory to the Father. It glorified his wisdom, faithfulness, holiness and love. It showed him wise in providing a plan whereby he could be just and yet the justifier of the ungodly. It showed him faithful in keeping his promise that the seed of the woman should bruise the serpent's head. It showed him holy in requiring his law's demands to be satisfied by our great Substitute. It showed him loving, in providing such a Mediator, such a Redeemer and such a Friend for sinful man as his co-eternal Son.

The crucifixion brought glory to the Son. It glorified his compassion, his patience and his power. It showed him most compassionate, in dying for us, suffering in our stead, allowing himself to be counted sin and a curse for us and buying our redemption with the price of his own blood. It showed him most patient, in not dying the common death of most men, but in willingly submitting to such horrors and unknown agonies as no mind can conceive, when with a word he could have summoned his Father's angels and been set free. It showed him most powerful in bearing the weight of all a world's transgressions and vanquishing Satan and despoiling him of his prey.

Forever let us cling to these thoughts about the crucifixion. Let us remember that painting and sculpture can never tell a tenth part of what took place on the cross. Crucifixes and pictures at best can only show us a human being agonizing in a painful death. But of the length and breadth and depth and height of the work transacted on the cross, of God's law honoured, man's sins borne, sin punished in a substitute, free salvation bought for man — of all this they can tell nothing. Yet all this lies hid under the crucifixion. No wonder St Paul cries, 'God forbid that I should glory, save in the cross of our Lord Jesus Christ' (Gal. 6:14).

For meditation: *Humans delight in strength. God saved us through weakness (2 Cor. 13:4).*

Suggested further reading: John 17:20-26

This is the only time our Lord ever calls his disciples his children. It was evidently a term of affection and compassion, like the language of a father speaking to children whom he is about to leave alone as orphans in the world: 'My believing followers, whom I love and regard as my children.' Observe that the expression is not used till Judas has gone away. Unbelievers are not to be addressed as Christ's children.

'Yet a little while and I am with you' seems to mean, 'I am only staying a very little longer with you. The time is short. The hour approaches when we must part. Give me your best attention while I talk to you for the last time before I go.'

It is not clear what 'You will seek me' means. Of course, it cannot refer to the time after the resurrection when the disciples were fully convinced that the Lord had risen. Much less can it refer to the time after the ascension. I can only suppose it means, 'After my death ye shall be perplexed, amazed and confounded for a little season, wanting me, seeking me, wishing for me and wondering where I am gone. The very moment the little child is left alone by mother or nurse, it begins to cry after her and want her. So will it be with you.'

The closing words of verse 33 applied to the Jews meant that Jesus was going to a place where spiritually and morally the Jews were unfit to go and in their impenitent state could not go. The words applied to the disciples only meant that Jesus was going into a world where they could not follow him till they died. They were remaining on earth and he was going to heaven.

Hengstenberg observes that this is the only place in which Jesus ever spoke to his disciples concerning 'the Jews'. Elsewhere he uses the expression in speaking to the Samaritan woman (John 4:22) and before Caiaphas and Pilate.

For meditation: *Where unbelievers cannot go, believers surely shall (John 17:24).*

Suggested further reading: *1 John 3:10-15*

What great importance our Lord Jesus attaches to the grace of brotherly love! Almost as soon as the false apostle had left the faithful eleven, comes the injunction, 'Love one another.' Immediately after the sad announcement that he would leave them soon, the commandment is given, 'Love one another.' It is called a 'new' commandment, not because it had never been given before, but because it was to be more honoured, to occupy a higher position, to be backed be a higher example than it ever had been before. Above all, it was to be the test of Christianity before the world. 'By this shall all men know that ye are my disciples, if ye have love one to another.'

Let us take heed that this well-known Christian grace is not merely a notion in our heads, but a practice in our lives. Of all the commands of our Master, there is none which is so much talked about and so little obeyed as this. Yet, if we mean anything when we profess to have charity and love towards all men, it ought to be seen in our tempers and our words, our bearing and our doing, our behaviour at home and abroad, our conduct in every relation of life. Specially it ought to show itself forth in all our dealings with other Christians. We should regard them as brethren and sisters and delight to do anything to promote their happiness. We should abhor the idea of envy, malice and jealousy towards a member of Christ and regard it as a downright sin. This is what our Lord meant when he told us to love one another.

Christ's cause in the earth would prosper far more than it does if this simple law was more honoured. There is nothing that the world understands and values more than true love.

For meditation: *Do your neighbours see that you love your fellow Christians?*

Suggested further reading: *1 John 4:7-11*

There can be no mistake about these words. Love was to be the grand characteristic, the distinguishing mark of Christ's disciples.

Let us note that our Lord does not name gifts, or miracles, or intellectual attainments, but love, the simple grace of love, a grace within reach of the poorest, lowliest believer, as the evidence of discipleship. No love, no grace, no regeneration, no true Christianity!

Let us note what a heavy condemnation this verse pronounces on sectarianism, bigotry, narrow-mindedness, party-spirit, strife, bitterness, needless controversy between Christian and Christian.

Let us note how far from satisfactory is the state of those who are content with sound doctrinal opinions and orthodox correct views of the gospel, while in their daily life they give way to ill-temper, ill-nature, malice, envy, quarrelling, squabbling, bickering, surliness, passion, snappish language and crossness of word and manner. Such persons, whether they know it or not, are daily proclaiming that they are not Christ's disciples. It is nonsense to talk about justification and regeneration and election and conversion and the uselessness of works, unless people can see in us practical Christian love.

In verse 36, as elsewhere, the forward, impulsive spirit of Peter prompts him to ask anxiously what our Lord meant by talking of going: 'Whither goest thou?' Can we doubt, however, that in this question he was the spokesman of all?

How very little the disciples had ever comprehended our Lord's repeated saying that he must be taken prisoner, crucified and die, we see in this place. Often as he had told them he must die, they had never realized it and are startled when he talks of going away. It is marvellous how much religious teaching men may have and yet not take it in, receive or believe it, especially when it contradicts preconceived notions.

For meditation: *Do your fellow Christians know that you love them?*

Suggested further reading:　1 Corinthians 10:1-13

It is not unlikely, as Cyril observes, that these words, 'Thou shalt follow me,' pointed to the manner of Peter's death by crucifixion. He was to walk in his Master's steps and enter heaven by the same road.

Verse 37 shows how little Peter realized what our Lord fully meant and the nearness of his death on the cross. 'Why cannot I follow thee now? Where is the place thou art going to on earth, where I am not willing and ready to follow thee? I love thee so much and am so determined to cling to thee, that I am ready to lay down my life rather than be separate from thee.'

These words were well meant and Peter never doubted, perhaps, that he could stand to them. But he did not know his own heart. There was more feeling than principle in his declaration. He did not see all that was in himself. Let us note the mischief of self-ignorance. Let us pray for humility. Let us beware of over-confidence in our own courage and steadfastness. Pride goeth before a fall.

The meaning of our Lord's answer to Peter appears to be 'Wilt thou really and truly lay down thy life for me? Thou little knowest thy own weakness and feebleness. I tell thee in the most solemn answer that this very night, before the cock crow, before sunrise, thou, even thou, wilt deny three times that thou knowest me. So far from laying down thy life, thou wilt try to save thy life by cowardly denying that thou hast anything to do with me.'

Let us note the wonderful foreknowledge of our Lord. What an unlikely thing it seemed that such a professor should fall so far and so soon. Yet our Lord foresaw it all!

Let us note the wonderful kindness and condescension of Jesus. He knew perfectly well the weakness and feebleness of his chief disciple and yet never rejected him and even raised him again after his fall. Christians should be men of very pitiful and tender feelings towards weak brethren.

For meditation:　*Self-confidence is a cliff from which many fall very far.*

Suggested further reading: John 14:7-27

Our Lord's great object throughout this and the two following chapters seems clear and plain. He desired to comfort, stablish and build up his downcast disciples. He saw their 'hearts were troubled' from a variety of causes — partly by seeing their Master 'troubled in spirit' (13:21), partly by hearing that one of them should betray him, partly by the mysterious departure of Judas, partly by their Master's announcement that he should only be a little time longer with them and that at last they could not come with him and partly by the warning addressed to Peter that he would deny his Master thrice. For all these reasons this little company of weak believers was disquieted and cast down and anxious. Their gracious Master saw it and proceeded to give them encouragement: 'Let not your heart be troubled.'

Hengstenberg gives the following list of the grounds of comfort which the chapter contains, in systematic order, which well deserve attention.

a. The first encouragement is that to the disciples of Christ heaven is sure (vv.2,3).

b. The second encouragement is that disciples have in Christ a certain way to heaven (vv.4-11).

c. The third encouragement is that disciples need not fear that with the departure of Christ his work will cease (vv.12-14).

d. The fourth encouragement is that in the absence of Christ disciples will have the help of the Spirit (vv.15-17).

e. The fifth encouragement is that Christ will not leave his people for ever, but will come back again (vv.18-24).

f. The sixth encouragement is that the Spirit will teach the disciples and supply their want of understanding when left alone (vv.25,26).

g. Finally, the seventh encouragement is that the legacy of peace will be left to cheer them in their Master's absence (v.27).

For meditation: *God never forgets to comfort his people and care for them (Ps. 121:4).*

Suggested further reading: Philippians 4:1-7

Heart trouble is the commonest thing in the world. No rank or class or condition is exempt from it. No bars or bolts or locks can keep it out. Partly from inward causes and partly from the mind, partly from what we love and partly from what we fear, the journey of life is full of trouble. Even the best of Christians have many bitter cups to drink between grace and glory. Even the holiest saints find the world a vale of tears.

Faith in the Lord Jesus is the only sure medicine for troubled hearts. To believe more thoroughly, trust more entirely, rest more unreservedly, lay hold more firmly, lean back more completely — this is the prescription which our Master urges on the attention of all his disciples. No doubt the members of that little band which sat round the table at the Last Supper had believed already. They had proved the reality of their faith by giving up everything for Christ's sake. Yet what does their Lord say to them here? Once more he presses on them the old lesson, the lesson with which they first began: 'Believe! Believe more! Believe on me!' (Isa. 26:3.)

Never let us forget that there are degrees in faith and that there is a wide difference between weak and strong believers. The weakest faith is enough to give a man a saving interest in Christ and ought not to be despised, but it will not give a man such inward comfort as a strong faith. Vagueness and dimness of perception are the defect of weak believers. They do not see clearly what they believe and why they believe. In such cases more faith is the one thing needed. Like Peter on the water, they need to look more steadily at Jesus and less at the waves and wind.

For meditation: *When our mind is fixed on God our heart can be at peace (Isa. 26:3).*

Suggested further reading: *2 Corinthians 5:1-11*

Heaven is 'a Father's house', the house of that God of whom
Jesus says, 'I go to my Father, and your Father.' It is, in a word,
home, the home of Christ and Christians. This is a sweet and
touching expression. Home, as we all know, is the place where
we are generally loved for our own sakes, and not for our gifts
or possessions, the place where we are loved to the end, never
forgotten and always welcome. This is one idea of heaven.
Believers are in a strange land and at school in this life. In the
life to come they will be at home.

Heaven is a place of 'mansions', of lasting, permanent and
eternal dwellings. Here in the body we are in lodgings, tents
and tabernacles and must submit to many changes. In heaven
we shall be settled at last and go out no more. 'Here we have no
continuing city' (Heb. 13:14). Our house not made with hands
shall never be taken down.

Heaven is a place of 'many mansions'. There will be room for
all believers and room for all sorts, for little saints as well as
great ones, for the weakest believer as well as for the strongest.
The feeblest child of God need not fear there will be no place
for him. None will be shut out but impenitent sinners and
obstinate unbelievers.

Heaven is a place where Christ himself shall be present. He
will not be content to dwell without his people: 'Where I am,
there ye shall be also.' We need not think that we shall be alone
and neglected. Our Saviour, our elder Brother, our Redeemer,
who loved us and gave himself for us, shall be in the midst of us
for ever. What we shall see and whom we shall see in heaven, we
cannot fully conceive yet, while we are in the body. But one
thing is certain: we shall see Christ.

For meditation: *When the Christian leaves his body in the grave
he is at home with the Lord (2 Cor. 5:8).*

Suggested further reading: *Titus 2:11-14*

We have in this passage a solid ground for expecting good things to come. The evil heart of unbelief within us is apt to rob us of our comfort about heaven. 'We wish we could think it was all true.' 'We fear we shall never be admitted into heaven.' Let us hear what Jesus says to encourage us.

One cheering word is this: 'I go to prepare a place for you.' Heaven is a prepared place for a prepared people: a place which we shall find Christ himself has made ready for true Christians. He has prepared it by procuring a right for every sinner who believes to enter in. None can stop us and say we have no business there. He has prepared it by going before us as our Head and Representative and taking possession of it for all the members of his mystical body. As our Forerunner he has marched in, leading captivity captive and had planted his banner in the land of glory. He has prepared it by carrying our names with him as our High Priest into the holy of holies and making angels ready to receive us. They that enter heaven will find they are neither unknown nor unexpected.

Another cheering word is this: 'I will come again and receive you unto myself.' Christ will not wait for believers to come up to him, but will come down to them, to raise them from their graves and escort them to their heavenly home. As Joseph came to meet Jacob, so will Jesus come to call his people together and guide them to their inheritance. The second advent ought never to be forgotten. Great is the blessedness of looking back to Christ coming the first time to suffer for us, but no less great is the comfort of looking forward to Christ coming the second time, to raise and reward his saints.

—

For meditation: *Do you love Christ's appearing? (2 Tim. 4:8.)*

Suggested further reading: Psalm 119:97-104

How much better Jesus speaks of believers than they speak of themselves! He says to his disciples, 'Ye know whither I go, and ye know the way.' And yet Thomas at once breaks in with the remark: 'We know neither the whither nor the way.' The apparent contradiction demands explanation. It is more seeming than real.

Certainly, in one point of view, the knowledge of the disciples was very small. They knew little before the crucifixion and resurrection compared to what they might have known and little compared to what they afterwards knew after the Day of Pentecost. About our Lord's purpose in coming into the world, about his sacrificial death and substitution for us on the cross, their ignorance was glaring and great. It might well be said that they 'knew in part' only and were children in understanding.

And yet, in another point of view, the knowledge of the disciples was very great. They knew far more than the great majority of the Jewish nation and received truths which the scribes and Pharisees entirely rejected. Compared to the world around them, they were in the highest sense enlightened. They knew and believed that their Master was the promised Messiah, the Son of the living God, and to know him was the first step towards heaven. All things go by comparison. Before we lightly esteem the disciples because of their ignorance, let us take care that we do not underrate their knowledge. They knew more precious truth than they were aware of themselves. Their hearts were better than their heads.

The plain truth is that all believers are apt to undervalue the work of the Spirit in their own souls and to fancy they know nothing because they do not know everything.

For meditation: *If you know Christ you know more than the worldly wise (Ps. 119:99,100).*

Suggested further reading: Acts 4:8-12

'I am the way, the truth, and the life.' The fulness of these precious words can probably never be taken in by man. He that attempts to unfold them does little more than scratch the surface of a rich soil.

Christ is 'the way' — the way to heaven and peace with God. He is not only the guide and teacher and lawgiver, like Moses; he is himself the door, the ladder and the road through whom we must draw near to God. He has opened the way to the tree of life, which was closed when Adam and Eve fell, by the satisfaction he made for us on the cross. Through his blood we may draw near with boldness and have access with confidence into God's presence.

Christ is 'the truth' — the whole substance of true religion which the mind of man requires. Without him the wisest heathen groped in gross darkness and knew nothing about God. Before he came even the Jews saw 'through a glass darkly' and discerned nothing distinctly under the types, figures and ceremonies of the Mosaic law. Christ is the whole truth and meets and satisfies every desire of the human mind.

Christ is 'the life' — the sinner's title to eternal life and pardon, the believer's root of spiritual life and holiness, the surety of the Christian's resurrection life. He that believeth on Christ hath everlasting life. He that abideth in him, as the branch abides in the vine, shall bring forth much fruit. He that believeth on him, though he were dead, yet shall he live. The root of all life, for soul and for body, is Christ.

Forever let us grasp and hold fast these truths. To use Christ daily as the way, to believe Christ daily as the truth, to live on Christ daily as the life — this is to be a well-informed, a thoroughly furnished and an established Christian.

For meditation: *'If I have Christ, what need I more?'*

Suggested further reading: *Revelation 20:11-15*

The Lord Jesus shuts out all ways of salvation but himself. 'No man,' he declares, 'no man cometh unto the Father but by me.'
'Coming to the Father' in this place means coming to him in a friendly relation for peace and comfort now in this life. 'By me' is literally 'through me, as a door, a gate, a road, a path, an entrance. It is an expression which would be peculiarly expressive to the Jews, taught from their childhood to draw near to God only through the priests.
It avails nothing that a man is clever, learned, highly gifted, amiable, charitable, kind-hearted and zealous about some sort of religion. All this will not save his soul if he does not draw near to God by Christ's atonement and make use of God's own Son as his Mediator and Saviour. God is so holy that all men are guilty and debtors in his sight. Sin is so sinful that no mortal man can make satisfaction for it. There must be a mediator, a ransom-payer, a redeemer, between ourselves and God, or else we can never be saved. There is only one door, one bridge, one ladder, between earth and heaven — the crucified Son of God. Whosoever will enter in by that door may be saved, but to him who refuses to use that door the Bible holds out no hope at all. Without shedding of blood there is no remission.
Let us beware, if we love life, of supposing that mere earnestness will take a man to heaven, though he know nothing of Christ. The idea is a deadly and ruinous error. Sincerity will never wipe away our sins. It is not true that every man will be saved by his own religion, no matter what he believes, so long as he is diligent and sincere. We must not pretend to be wiser than God. Christ has said, and Christ will stand to it, 'No man cometh unto the Father but by me.'

For meditation: *Is your name in the Lamb's book of life?*

Suggested further reading: Isaiah 9:1-7

The seventh verse contains a deep saying, like every saying which handles the mysterious union of the Father and the Son in St John's Gospel. The meaning seems to be, 'If you had rightly, properly and perfectly known me, as the divine Messiah, in all the fulness of my nature, you would then have known more of that Father to whom I am inseparably united. No one can rightly know me without knowing the Father, because I and the Father are one.'

'Understand from this time forward that in knowing me you know the Father and in seeing me see the Father, so far as the Father can be seen and known by man.'

Sayings like these are full of deep mystery. We have no eyes to see their meaning fully, no line to fathom it, no language to express it, no mind to take it in. We must be content to believe when we cannot explain and to admire and revere when we cannot interpret. Let it suffice us to know and hold that the Father is God and the Son is God and yet that they are one in essence though two distinct persons — ineffably one and yet ineffably distinct. These are high things and we cannot attain to a full comprehension of them.

Let us, however, take comfort in the simple truth that Christ is very God of very God, equal with the Father in all things and one with him. He who loved us and shed his blood for us on the cross and bids us trust him for pardon is no mere man like ourselves. He is 'God over all, blessed for ever' and able to save to the uttermost the chief of sinners. Though our sins be as scarlet, he can make them white as snow. He that casts his soul on Christ has an almighty Friend — a Friend who is one with the Father and very God.

For meditation: *Christ is Emmanuel, 'God with us' (Matt. 1:23). He is not far off but near.*

Suggested further reading: Exodus 33:12-34:9

We are not told Philip's motive in making this request. Perhaps, like Moses, he and the other disciples had a pious desire to see a more full vision and revelation of God's glory, as an authentication of their Master's divine mission. 'Show me thy glory' (Exod. 33:18). Perhaps Philip's petition is recorded to show how little clear knowledge the apostles yet had of their Master's nature and how little they realized that he and the Father were one: 'If we could only see once for all the divine being whom thou dost call the Father, it would be sufficient. We should be satisfied and our doubts would be removed.' At any rate we have no right to think that Philip spoke like the unbelieving Jews, who always pretended to want signs and wonders. Whatever sense we put on the words, we must carefully remember not to judge Philip too harshly. Living as we do in the twentieth century, amidst light and creeds and knowledge, we can have faint ideas of the extreme difficulty that must have been felt by the disciples in fully realizing their Master's nature, in the days when he was 'in the form of a servant' and under a veil of poverty, weakness and humiliation.

Melancthon remarks that Philip's petition represents the natural wish of man in every age. Men feel an inward craving everywhere to see God.

Our Lord's answer is undoubtedly a gentle rebuke. The expression 'so long time' is noteworthy when we remember that Philip was one of the very first disciples whom Jesus called (see John 1:43). The meaning seems to be 'After three long years, Philip, dost thou not yet thoroughly know and understand who I am?'

Our Lord's reply can only mean, 'He that hath thoroughly seen me with the eye of faith and realized that I am the eternal Son, the divine Messiah, hath seen as much of my Father, whose express image I am, as mortal man can comprehend.' There is so close and intimate a union between persons in the Trinity that he who sees the Son sees the Father.

For meditation: *We can know no more of God than is seen in the Lord Jesus.*

Suggested further reading: Mark 6:1-6

Verse 10 means, 'The words that I speak to you, I speak not independently of the Father, and the works that I do, I do not do them independently of the Father. The Father, who dwells in me, speaks in me and works in me. My words are words given me to speak and my works are works given me to do in the eternal counsel between the Father and the Son. Both in speaking and working, I and my Father are one. What I speak he speaks and what I work he works.'

The whole difficulty of the verse arises from forgetting the close and mysterious and indissoluble union between the persons of the Trinity. How little we realize the fulness of the expression, 'The Father dwelleth in me'!

Direct instruction follows the rebuke of the preceding verse. Our Lord repeats for the benefit not of Philip only, but of all the eleven, the great doctrine he had so often taught them: 'Once more, I say, Believe, all of you, my words, when I say that I and the Father are so closely united that I am in him and he in me.' The word rendered 'believe' in this verse is in the plural number. Our Lord does not address Philip only, but the whole company of the apostles.

What an example we have here of the necessity of repeating instruction over and over again! Our Lord had evidently taught these things before to the eleven and yet they had either not understood or not remembered.

Our Lord condescends to the weakness of the disciples. 'If you will not believe the close union of myself and the Father because of my word, believe it because of the works I work. They are such works as no one could work of himself and without the Father.'

Let us carefully observe how our Lord here, as elsewhere, specially names his works, or miracles, as testimonies of his nature and divine mission. To leave out miracles in the list of the evidences of Christianity is a great mistake.

For meditation: *Only one thing is more amazing than the miraculous – the unbelief of those who see it.*

Suggested further reading: Colossians 1:19-23

Our Lord says, 'He that believeth on me, the works that I do
shall he do also; and greater works than these shall he do;
because I go unto my Father.'
    The full meaning of this promise is not to be sought in the
miracles which the apostles wrought after Christ left the world.
Such a notion seems hardly borne out by facts. We read of no
apostle walking on the water, or raising a person four days
dead, like Lazarus. What our Lord has in view seems to be the
far greater number of conversions, the far wider spread of the
gospel, which would take place under the ministry of the
apostles than under his own teaching. This was the case, we
know from the Acts of the Apostles. We read of no sermon
preached by Christ under which three thousand were converted in one day, as they were on the Day of Pentecost. In short,
'greater works' mean more conversions. There is no greater
work possible than the conversion of a soul.
    Let us admire the condescension of our Master in allowing to
the ministry of his weak servants more success than to his own.
Let us learn that his visible presence is not absolutely necessary
to the progress of his kingdom. He can help forward his cause
on earth quite as much by sitting at the right hand of the Father
and sending forth the Holy Ghost, as by walking to and fro in
the world. Let us believe that there is nothing too hard or too
great for believers to do, so long as their Lord intercedes for
them in heaven. Let us work on in faith and expect great things,
though we feel weak and lonely, like the disciples. Our Lord is
working with us and for us, though we cannot see him. It was
not so much the sword of Joshua that defeated Amalek as the
intercession of Moses on the hill (Exod. 17:11).

For meditation: *Our Lord taught a few people with limited success. In one generation after him the whole world had heard the
gospel (Col. 1:23).*

Suggested further reading: *1 John 5:10-15*

'Whatsoever ye shall ask in my name, that will I do . . . If ye shall ask anything in my name, I will do it.'

These words are a direct encouragement to the simple, yet great, duty of praying. Everyone who kneels daily before God and from his heart 'says his prayers' has a right to take comfort in these words. Weak and imperfect as his supplications may be, so long as they are put in Christ's hands and offered in Christ's name, they shall not be in vain. We have a Friend at court, an Advocate with the Father, and if we honour him by sending all our petitions through him, he pledges his word that they shall succeed. Of course, it is taken for granted that the things we ask are for our souls' good and not mere temporal benefits. 'Anything' and 'whatsoever' do not include wealth and money and worldly prosperity. These things are not always good for us and our Lord loves us too well to let us have them. But whatever is really good for our souls, we need not doubt we shall have, if we ask in Christ's name.

How is it that many true Christians have so little? How is it that they go halting and mourning on the way to heaven and enjoy so little peace and show so little strength in Christ's service? The answer is simple and plain. 'They have not, because they ask not.' They have little because they ask little. They are no better than they are, because they do not ask their Lord to make them better. Our languid desires are the reason of our languid performances. We are not straitened in our Lord, but in ourselves. Happy are they who never forget the words: 'Open thy mouth wide, and I will fill it' (Ps.81:10). He that does much for Christ and leaves his mark in the world will always prove to be one who prays much.

For meditation: *What do you not have because you do not ask, or because you ask with wrong motives? (James 4:2,3.)*

Suggested further reading:　　*Galatians 5:16-26*

Here we have a direct practical exhortation: 'If ye really love me, prove your love not by weeping and lamenting at my departure, but by striving to do my will when I am gone. Doing, and not crying, is the best proof of love.' The commandments here mentioned must include all the Lord's moral teaching while on earth and specially such rules and laws as he had laid down in the 'Sermon on the Mount.'

In this verse our Lord had in view the disposition of his disciples to give way to grief and distress at his leaving them and to forget that the true test of love was not useless and barren lamentation, but practical obedience to their Master's commands.

Let us notice how our Lord speaks of 'my commandments'. We never read of Moses or any other servant of God using such an expression. It is the language of one who was one with God the Father and had power to lay down laws and make statutes for his church.

Our Lord says, 'I will pray the Father, and he shall give you another Comforter . . . even the Spirit of truth.'

This is the first time that the Holy Ghost is mentioned as Christ's special gift to his people. Of course, we are not to suppose that he did not dwell in the hearts of all the Old Testament saints.

No one ever served God acceptably, from Abel downwards, without the grace of the Holy Ghost. John the Baptist was 'filled' with him. But he was given with peculiar influence and power to believers when the New Testament dispensation came in and this is the special promise of the passage before us.

It can only mean that he shall come with more fulness, influence, grace and manifestation than he did before.

One principal point is the mention of all the three persons in the blessed Trinity, the Son praying, the Father giving, the Spirit comforting.

For meditation: *We are not only commanded to obey; we are also given the Holy Spirit to equip us to obey.*

Suggested further reading: 1 John 1:5-2:1

The word 'Comforter' is the same that is translated 'Advocate' and applied to Christ himself in 1 John 2:1. This word aptly expresses the office of the Spirit as pleading our cause and making intercession for the saints and helping them in prayer and preaching (see Rom. 8:26; Matt. 10:19,20).

The Holy Ghost is spoken of as 'a person'. To apply the language before us to a mere influence or inward feeling is an unreasonable strain of words.

We should never speak of him as a mere 'influence', or dishonour him by calling him 'it'.

The Holy Ghost is given to the church of the elect, 'to abide with them' until Christ comes the second time. He is meant to supply all the needs of believers and to fill up all that is wanting while Christ's visible presence is removed. He is sent to abide with and help them until Christ returns.

The Holy Ghost is called 'the Spirit of truth'. It is his special office to apply truth to the hearts of Christians, to guide them into all truth and to sanctify them by the truth.

The Holy Ghost is said to be one whom 'the world cannot receive and does not know'. His operations are in the strongest sense foolishness to the natural man. The inward feelings of conviction, repentance, faith, hope, fear and love, which he always produces, are precisely that part of religion which the world cannot understand.

The Holy Ghost is said to 'dwell in' believers and to be known of them. They know the feelings that he creates and the fruits that he produces, though they may not be able to explain them, or see at first whence they come. But they all are what they are — new men, new creatures, light and salt in the earth, compared to the worldly — by the indwelling of the Holy Ghost.

Let us never rest till we feel and know that he dwells in us. 'If any man have not the Spirit of Christ, he is none of his' (Rom. 8:9).

For meditation: *Is the fruit of the Spirit in evidence in your life? (Gal. 5:22,23.)*

Suggested further reading: Titus 2:11-15

Now what is the 'coming' here spoken of? It is only fair to say that this is a disputed point among Christians. Many refer it to our Lord's coming to his disciples after his resurrection. Many refer it to his invisible coming into the hearts of his people by the grace of the Holy Spirit. Many refer it to his coming by the outpouring of the Holy Ghost on the Day of Pentecost. It may well be doubted, however, whether any one of these three views conveys the full meaning of our Lord's words: 'I will come.'

The true sense of the expression appears to be the second personal coming of Christ at the end of the world. It is a wide, broad, sweeping promise, intended for all believers, in every age, and not for the apostles alone: 'I will not stay always in heaven. I will one day come back to you.' It is like the message which the angels brought to the disciples after the ascension: 'This same Jesus shall come in like manner as ye have seen him go' (Acts 1:11). It is like the last promise which winds up the book of Revelation: 'Surely I come quickly' (Rev. 22:20). Just in the same way, the parting consolation held out to believers the night before the crucifixion is a personal return: 'I will come.'

Let us settle it in our minds that all believers are comparatively 'orphans' and children in their minority, until the second advent. Our best things are yet to come. Faith has yet to be exchanged for sight and hope for certainty. Our peace and joy are at present very imperfect. They are as nothing to what we shall have when Christ returns. For the return let us look and long and pray. Let us place it in the forefront of all our doctrinal system, next to the atoning death and the interceding life of our Lord. The highest style of Christians are the men who look for and love the Lord's appearing (2 Tim. 4:8).

For meditation: *'Absence makes the heart grow fonder.' Does each year of waiting for our Lord's second coming make him dearer to you?*

Suggested further reading: Colossians 3:1-4

Christ's life secures the life of his believing people. He says, 'Because I live ye shall live also.' There is a mysterious and indissoluble union between Christ and every true Christian. The man that is once joined to him by faith is as closely united as a member of the body is united to the head. So long as Christ, his Head, lives, so long he will live. He cannot die unless Christ can be plucked from heaven and Christ's life destroyed. But this, since Christ is very God, is totally impossible! 'Christ being raised from the dead, dieth no more: death hath no more dominion over him' (Rom.6:9). That which is divine, in the very nature of things, cannot die.

Christ's life secures the continuance of spiritual life to his people. They shall not fall away. They shall persevere unto the end. The divine nature of which they are partakers shall not perish. The incorruptible seed within them shall not be destroyed by the devil and the world. Weak as they are in themselves, they are closely knit to an immortal Head and not one member of his mystical body shall ever perish.

Christ's life secures the resurrection life of his people. Just as he rose again from the grave, because death could not hold him one moment beyond the appointed time, so shall all his believing members rise again in the day when he calls them from the tomb. The victory that Jesus won, when he rolled the stone away and came forth from the tomb, was a victory not only for himself, but for his people. If the Head rose, much more shall the members.

Truths like these ought to be often pondered by true Christians. The careless world knows little of a believer's privileges. It sees little but the outside of him. It does not understand the secret of his present strength and of his strong hope of good things to come. And what is that secret? Invisible union with an invisible Saviour in heaven! Each child of God is invisibly linked to the throne of the Rock of Ages. When that throne can be shaken, and not till then, we may despair. But Christ lives and we shall live also.

For meditation: *The believer is secure as long as Christ lives.*

Suggested further reading:　*1 Corinthians 13:8-12*

Full and perfect knowledge of divine things will never be attained by believers until the second advent. Our Lord says, 'At that day,' the day of my coming, 'ye shall know that I am in my Father, and ye in me, and I in you.'

The best of saints knows but little so long as he is in the body. The fall of our father Adam has corrupted our understandings, as well as our consciences, hearts and wills. Even after conversion we see through a glass darkly and on no point do we see so dimly as on the nature of our own union with Christ and the Father. These are matters in which we must be content to believe humbly and like little children, to receive on trust the things which we cannot explain.

But it is a blessed and cheering thought that when Christ comes again, the remains of ignorance shall be rolled away. Raised from the dead, freed from the darkness of this world, no longer tempted by the devil and tried by the flesh, believers shall see as they have been seen and know as they have been known. We shall have light enough one day. What we know not now, we shall know hereafter.

Let us rest our souls on this comfortable thought, when we see the mournful divisions which rend the church of Christ. Let us remember that a large portion of them arise from ignorance. We know in part and therefore misunderstand one another. A day comes when Lutherans shall no longer wrangle with Zwinglians, nor Calvinist with Arminian, nor churchman with dissenter. That day is the day of Christ's second coming. Then and then only will the promise receive its complete fulfilment: 'At that day ye shall know.'

For meditation:　*The most knowledgeable Christian on earth is still only in the nursery school of knowledge.*

Suggested further reading: *1 John 1:8-2:6*

Keeping Christ's commandments is the best test of love to Christ. Burgon observes, 'This amounts to a declaration that the sad hearts and weeping eyes of the apostles would not be accepted by their Lord as any proof of their love. Obedience was the test he chose.'

This is a lesson of vast importance and one that needs continually pressing on the attention of Christians. It is not talking about religion, and talking fluently and well too, but steadily doing Christ's will and walking in Christ's ways, that is the proof of our being true believers. Good feelings and desires are useless if they are not accompanied by action. They may even become mischievous to the soul, induce hardness of conscience and do positive harm. Passive impressions which do not lead to action gradually deaden and paralyse the heart. Living and doing are the only real evidence of grace. Where the Holy Spirit is, there will always be a holy life. A jealous watchfulness over tempers, words and deeds, a constant endeavour to live by the rule of the Sermon on the Mount — this is the best proof that we love Christ.

Of course, such maxims as these must not be wrested and misunderstood. We are not to suppose for a moment that 'keeping Christ's commandments' can save us. Our best works are full of imperfection. When we have done all we can, we are feeble and unprofitable servants. 'By grace are ye saved through faith . . . not of works' (Eph. 2:8). But while we hold one class of truths, we must not forget another. Faith in the blood of Christ must always be attended by loving obedience to the will of Christ. What the Master has joined together, the disciple must not put asunder. Do we profess to love Christ? Then let us show it by our lives. The apostle who said, 'Thou knowest that I love thee!' received the charge: 'Feed my lambs.' That meant, 'Do something. Be useful; follow my example' (John 21:17).

For meditation: *It takes little effort to talk about religion, but to live it is another matter.*

Suggested further reading: Romans 9:14-26

There is a special love of God the Father which is peculiarly set
on believers, over and above the general love of pity and compassion with which he regards all mankind. In the highest sense
God is a 'Father' to none but those who love Christ.

Verse 21 is another encouragement to the man who strives to
keep Christ's commandments. Christ will specially love that
man and will give him special manifestations of his grace and
favour, invisibly and spiritually. He shall feel and know in his
own heart comforts and joys that wicked men and inconsistent
professors know nothing of. That the 'manifesting' of himself
here spoken of is a purely unseen and spiritual thing is self-
evident. It is one of those things which can only be known by
experience and is only known by holy and consistent
Christians.

We should carefully observe here that Christ does more for
the comfort of some of his people than he does for others.
Those who follow Christ most closely and obediently will
always follow him most comfortably and feel most of his
inward presence. It is one thing, as St John says, to know
Christ, another to know that we know him (1 John 2:3).

In verse 24 the same great principle already taught is laid
down again from the negative side. Where there is no
obedience to Christ, there is no love. Nothing can be more
plain than our Lord's repeated warnings that practical
obedience, keeping his commandments and sayings, doing his
will, is the only sure test of love to him. Without this obedience,
profession, talk,knowledge, churchmanship, yea, even feeling,
conviction, weeping and crying are all worthless things.

Verse 24 is to remind the disciples of the authority and dignity of our Lord's sayings and commandments. They are not
his words only, but his Father's. He that despises them despises
the Father and he that honours them by obedience honours the
Father.

For meditation: *It is a believer's privilege to say, 'He loved me'
(Gal. 2:20).*

Suggested further reading: *Genesis 22:15-18*

There are special comforts laid up for those who love Christ and prove it by keeping his words. This, at any rate, seems the general sense of our Lord's language: 'My Father will love him and we will come unto him and make our abode with him.'
    The full meaning of this promise, no doubt, is a deep thing. We have no line to fathom it. It is a thing which no man can understand except he that receives and experiences it. But we need not shrink from believing that eminent holiness brings eminent comfort with it and that no man has such sensible enjoyment of his religion as the man who, like Enoch and Abraham, walks closely with God. There is more of heaven on earth to be obtained than most Christians are aware of. 'The secret of the Lord is with them that fear him, and he will show thm his covenant.' 'If any man hear my voice and open the door, I will come in to him, and sup with him, and he with me' (Ps. 25:14; Rev. 3:20). Promises like these, we may be sure, mean something, and were not written in vain.
    How is it, people often ask, that so many professing believers have so little happiness in their religion? How is it that so many know little of 'joy and peace in believing' and go mourning and heavy-hearted towards heaven? The answer to these questions is a sorrowful one, but it must be given. Few believers attend as strictly as they should to Christ's practical sayings and words. There is far too much loose and careless obedience to Christ's commandments. There is far too much forgetfulness that, while good works cannot justify us, they are not to be despised. Let these things sink down into our hearts. If we want to be eminently happy, we must strive to be eminently holy.
    Let us note the condescension of the Father and the Son and the high privileges of a believer. No matter how poor and lowly a man may be, if he has faith and grace, he has the best of company and friends. Christ and the Father dwell in his heart and he is never alone and cannot be poor. He is the temple of Father, Son and Holy Ghost.

For meditation: *Does God bless you because you have obeyed?*
(Gen. 22:16.)

Suggested further reading: 1 Corinthians 2:9-15

Let us note how distinctly the Holy Spirit is spoken of here as a person and not an influence. Let us note how the Father sends the Spirit, but also sends him in Christ's name and with a special reference to Christ's work.

One part of the Holy Ghost's work is to teach and to bring things to remembrance. It is written: 'The Comforter shall teach you all things, and bring all things to your remembrance.'

To confine this promise to the eleven apostles, as some do, seems a narrow and unsatisfactory mode of interpreting Scripture. It appears to reach far beyond the Day of Pentecost and the gift of writing inspired books of God's holy Word. It is safer, wiser and more consistent with the whole tone of our Lord's last discourse to regard the promise as the common property of all believers, in every age of the world. Our Lord knows the ignorance and forgetfulness of our nature in spiritual things. He graciously declares that when he leaves the world, his people shall have a Teacher and Remembrancer.

Are we sensible of spiritual ignorance? Do we feel that at best we know in part and see in part? Do we desire to understand more clearly the doctrines of the gospel? Let us pray daily for the help of the 'teaching' Spirit. It is his office to illuminate the soul, to open the eyes of the understanding and to guide us into all truth. He can make dark places light and rough places smooth.

Do we find our memory of spiritual things defective? Do we complain that, though we read and hear, we seem to lose as fast as we gain? Let us pray daily for the help of the Holy Ghost. He can bring things to our remembrance. He can make us remember 'old things and new'. He can keep in our minds the whole system of truth and duty and make us ready for every good word and work.

For meditation: *Are you confident of your own understanding of Scripture, or do you seek God's help?*

Suggested further reading: *Isaiah 26:3-12*

Let us notice Christ's last legacy to his people. We find him saying, 'Peace I leave with you, my peace I give unto you; not as the world giveth give I unto you.'

Peace is Christ's peculiar gift — not money, not worldly ease, not temporal prosperity. These are at best very questionable possessions. They often do more harm than good to the soul. They act as clogs and weights to our spiritual life. Inward peace of conscience, arising from a sense of pardoned sin and reconciliation with God, is a far greater blessing. This peace is the property of all believers, whether high or low, rich or poor.

The peace which Christ gives he calls 'my peace'. It is specially his own to give, because he bought it by his own blood, purchased it by his own substitution and is appointed by the Father to dispense it to a perishing world. Just as Joseph was sealed and commissioned to give corn to the starving Egyptians, so is Christ specially commissioned, in the counsels of the eternal Trinity, to give peace to mankind.

The peace that Christ gives is not given as the world gives. What he gives, the world cannot give at all, and what he gives is given neither unwillingly, nor sparingly, nor for a little time. Christ is far more willing to give than the world is to receive. What he gives, he gives to all eternity and never takes away. He is ready to give abundantly above all that we can ask or think. 'Open thy mouth wide,' he says, 'and I will fill it' (Ps. 81:10).

Who can wonder that a legacy like this should be backed by the renewed emphatic charge: 'Let not your heart be troubled, neither let it be afraid'? There is nothing lacking on Christ's part for our comfort, if we will only come to him, believe and receive. The chief of sinners has no cause to be afraid. If we will only look to the one true Saviour, there is medicine for every trouble of heart. Half our doubts and fears arise from dim perceptions of the real nature of Christ's gospel.

For meditation: *The condition attached to the promise of Philippians 4:7 is found in Philippians 4:6.*

Suggested further reading: *Philippians 2:5-11*

Verse 28 presents two difficulties.

    a. What did our Lord mean by saying, 'My Father is greater than I'? I answer that the words of the Athanasian Creed contain the best reply. Christ is no doubt 'equal to the Father as touching his Godhead and inferior to the Father as touching his manhood'. The enemies of the doctrine of Christ's divinity forget that Trinitarians maintain the humanity of Christ as strongly as his divinity and never shrink from admitting that, while Christ as God is equal to the Father, as man he is inferior to the Father. And it is in this sense that he here says truly, 'My Father is greater than I.' It was specially spoken of the time of his incarnation and humiliation. When the Word was 'made flesh', he took on him 'the form of a servant' (Phil. 2:7). This was temporary inferiority.

    b. But what did our Lord mean by saying that the disciples ought to rejoice at his going to the Father *because* 'The Father is greater than I'? This is a hard knot to untie and has received different solutions. My own impression is that the meaning must be something of this kind: 'Ye ought to rejoice at my going to the Father, because in so going I shall resume that glory which I had with him before the world was and which I laid aside on becoming incarnate. Here on earth, during the thirty-three years of my incarnation, I have been in the form of a servant and dwelling in a body as one inferior to my Father. In leaving this world I go to take up again the equal glory and honour which I had with the Father before my incarnation and to lay aside the position of inferiority in which I have tabernacled here below. I go to be once more almighty with the Almighty and to share once more my Father's throne, as a person in that Trinity in which "none is afore or after other, none is greater or less than another". I go to receive the kingdom and honour which in eternal counsels the Father has prepared for the Son, and on this account, if you really knew and understood all, you would rejoice at my going.'

For meditation: *2 Corinthians 8:9.*

Suggested further reading: 1 Peter 1:15-19

Let us observe Christ's perfect holiness. We find him saying, 'The prince of this world cometh and hath nothing in me.' The meaning of these remarkable words admits of only one interpretation. Our Lord would have his disciples know that Satan, 'the prince of this world', was about to make his last and most violent attack on him. He was mustering all his strength for one more tremendous onset. He was coming up with his utmost malice to try the second Adam in the garden of Gethsemane and on the cross of Calvary. But our blessed Master declares, 'He hath nothing in me.' 'There is nothing he can lay hold on. There is no weak and defective point in me. I have kept my Father's commandment and finished the work he gave me to do. Satan, therefore, cannot overthrow me. He can lay nothing to my charge. He cannot condemn me. I shall come forth from the trial more than conqueror.'

Let us mark the difference between Christ and all others who have been born of woman. He is the only one in whom Satan has found 'nothing'. He came to Adam and Eve and found weakness. He came to Noah, Abraham, Moses, David and all the saints and found imperfection. He came to Christ and found 'nothing' at all. He was a Lamb 'without blemish and without spot', a suitable sacrifice for a world of sinners, a suitable head for a redeemed race.

Let us thank God that we have such a perfect, sinless Saviour, that his righteousness is a perfect righteousness and his life a blameless life. In ourselves and our doings we shall find everything imperfect and if we had no other hope than our own goodness we might well despair. But in Christ we have a perfect, sinless Representative and Substitute. Well may we say, with the triumphant apostle, 'Who shall lay anything to our charge?' (Rom. 8:33.) Christ hath died for us and suffered in our stead. In him Satan can find nothing. We are hidden in him. The Father sees us in him, unworthy as we are, and for his sake is well pleased.

For meditation: *Hebrews 7:26.*

Suggested further reading: Matthew 11:25-27

Verse 31 is a somewhat dark and obscure passage. The meaning is probably something of this kind: 'I do all I am doing now and go to the cross voluntarily, though innocent, that the world may have full proof that I love the Father who sent me to die, and am willing to go through everything which he has commanded me to go through. Innocent as I am, and without one spot of sin that Satan can lay to my charge, I willingly go forward to the cross, to show how I love the Father's will and am determined to do it by dying for sinners.'

We ought not to leave the closing portion of this wonderful chapter without noticing one striking feature in it. That feature is the singular frequency with which our Lord uses the expression: 'My Father', and 'the Father'. In the last five verses we find it four times. In the whole chapter it occurs no fewer than twenty-two times. In this respect the chapter stands alone in the Bible.

The reason of this frequent use of the expression is a deep subject. Perhaps the less we speculate and dogmatize about it the better. Our Lord was one who never spoke a word without a meaning and we need not doubt there was a meaning here. Yet may we not reverently suppose that he desired to leave on the minds of his disciples a strong impression of his entire unity with the Father? Seldom does our Lord lay claim to such high dignity and such power of giving and supplying comfort to his church as in this discourse. Was there not, then, a fitness in his continually reminding his disciples that in all his giving he was one with the Father and did nothing without the Father? This, at any rate, seems a fair conjecture. Let it be taken for what it is worth.

For meditation: *Thoroughness of knowledge is a key to intimacy in relationships.*

Suggested further reading: Ephesians 5:25-33

The general lesson of each parable is the main thing to be noticed. The minor details must not be tortured and pressed to an excess in order to extract a meaning from them. The mistakes into which Christians have fallen by neglecting this rule are neither few nor small.

We are meant to learn from these verses that the union between Christ and believers is very close. He is 'the Vine' and they are 'the branches'. The union between the branch of a vine and the main stem is the closest that can be conceived. It is the whole secret of the branch's life, strength, vigour, beauty and fertility. Separate from the parent stem, it has no life of its own. The sap and juice that flow from the stem are the origin and maintaining power of all its leaves, buds, blossoms and fruit. Cut off from the stem, it must soon wither and die.

The union between Christ and believers is just as close and just as real. In themselves believers have no life or strength or spiritual power. All that they have of vital religion comes from Christ. They are what they are and feel what they feel and do what they do, because they draw out of Jesus a continual supply of grace, help and ability. Joined to the Lord by faith and united in mysterious union with him by the Spirit, they stand and walk and continue and run the Christian race. But every jot of good about them is drawn from their spiritual Head, Jesus Christ.

The thought before us is both comfortable and instructive. Believers have no cause to despair of their own salvation and to think they will never reach heaven. Let them consider that they are not left to themselves and their own strength. Their root is Christ and all that there is in the root is for the benefit of the branches. Because he lives, they shall live also. Worldly people have no cause to wonder at the continuance and perseverance of believers. Weak as they are in themselves, their Root is in heaven and never dies. 'When I am weak,' said Paul, 'then am I strong' (2 Cor. 12:10).

For meditation: *1 Corinthians 6:17.*

Suggested further reading: Matthew 7:15-23

There are false Christians as well as true ones. There are 'branches in the vine' which appear to be joined to the parent stem and yet bear no fruit. There are men and women who appear to be members of Christ and yet will prove finally to have had no vital union with him.

There are myriads of professing Christians in every church whose union with Christ is only outward and formal. Some of them are joined to Christ by baptism and church membership. Some of them go even further than this and are regular communicants and loud talkers about religion. But they all lack the one thing needful. Notwithstanding services and sermons and sacrament, they have no grace in their hearts, no faith, no inward work of the Holy Spirit. They are not one with Christ and Christ in them. Their union with him is only nominal and not real. They have 'a name to live', but in the sight of God they are dead.

Christians of this stamp are aptly represented by branches in a vine which bear no fruit. Useless and unsightly, such branches are only fit to be cut off and burned. They draw nothing out of the parent stem and make no return for the place they occupy. Just so will it be at the last day with false professors and nominal Christians. Their end, except they repent, will be destruction. They will be separated from the company of true believers and cast out, as withered, useless branches, into everlasting fire. They will find at last, whatever they thought in this world, that there is a worm that never dies and a fire that is not quenched.

The fruits of the Spirit are the only satisfactory evidence of a man being a true Christian. The disciple that 'abides in Christ', like a branch abiding in the vine, will always bear fruit. Repentance towards God, faith towards our Lord Jesus Christ, holiness of life and conduct — these are what the New Testament calls 'fruit'. Where these things are wanting, it is vain to talk of possessing dormant grace and spiritual life.

For meditation: *Galatians 5:22,23.*

Suggested further reading: Hebrews 12:4-13

God will often increase the holiness of true Christians by his providential dealings with them. 'Every branch,' it is written, 'that beareth fruit, he purgeth it, that it may bear more fruit.'

The meaning of this language is clear and plain. Just as the vine-dresser prunes and cuts back the branches of a fruitful vine, in order to make them more fruitful, so does God purify and sanctify believers by the circumstances of life in which he places them.

Trial, to speak plainly, is the instrument by which our Father in heaven makes Christians more holy. By trial he calls out their passive graces and proves whether they can suffer his will as well as do it. By trial he weans them from the world, draws them to Christ, drives them to the Bible and prayer, shows them their own hearts and makes them humble. This is the process by which he 'purges' them and makes them more fruitful. The lives of the saints in every age are the best and truest comment on the text. Never, hardly, do we find an eminent saint, either in the Old Testament or the New, who was not purifed by suffering and, like his Master, a 'man of sorrows'.

Clement of Alexandria and many writers in all ages remark on this verse that the vine branch which is not sharply pruned is peculiarly liable to run to wood and bear no fruit.

Let us learn to be patient in the days of darkness, if we know anything of vital union with Christ. Let us remember the doctrine of the passage before us and not murmur and complain because of trials. Our trials are not meant to do us harm, but good. God chastens us 'for our profit, that we may be partakers of his holiness' (Heb. 12:10). Fruit is the thing that our Master desires to see in us and he will not spare the pruning-knife if he sees we need it. In the last day we shall see that all was well done.

For meditation: *The cleansing of a wound may be painful but it is necessary for health.*

Suggested further reading: Hebrews 6:4-12

In verse 5 our Lord gives encouragement to the disciples to keep up the habit of close union with him. This is the secret of bearing 'much fruit' and being an eminently holy and useful Christian. The experience of every age of the church proves the truth of this saying. The greatest saints have always lived nearest to Christ.

Do we not see here that there is a difference in the degrees of fruitfulness to which Christians attain? Is there not a tacit distinction here between 'fruit' and 'much fruit'?

With regard to the closing words of verse 5, the marginal rendering gives our Lord's meaning more completely: 'Severed from me, separate from me, you have no strength and can do nothing. You are lifeless as a branch cut off from the parent stem.'

In verse 6 the consequences of not abiding in Christ, of refusing to live the life of faith in Christ, are here described under a terrible figure. The end of such false professors will be like the end of fruitless and dead branches of a vine. Sooner of later they are cast out of the vineyard as withered, useless things and gathered as firewood to be burned. Such will be the last end of professing Christians who turn their backs on Jesus and bear no fruit to God's glory. They will finally come to the fire that is never quenched in hell.

These are awful words. They seem, however, to apply specially to backsliders and apostates, like Judas Iscariot. There must be about a man some appearance of professed faith in Christ, before he can come to the state described here. Doubtless there are those who seem to depart from grace and to go back from union with Christ, but we need not doubt in such cases that the grace was not real, but seeming, and the union was not true, but fictitious.

For meditation: *'I'm a believer and can live as I like' is the philosophy of the presumptuous, not the words of the assured.*

Suggested further reading: Psalm 91

Our Lord declares, 'If ye abide in me, and my words abide in you, ye shall ask what ye will, and it shall be done unto you.' This is a distinct promise of power and success in prayer. And what does it turn upon? We must 'abide in Christ' and Christ's words must 'abide in us'.

To abide in Christ means to keep up a habit of constant close communion with him, to be always leaning on him, resting on him, pouring out our hearts to him and using him as our Fountain of life and strength, as our chief Companion and best Friend. To have his words abiding in us is to keep his sayings and precepts continually before our memories and minds and to make them the guide of our actions and the rule of our daily conduct and behaviour.

Christians of this stamp, we are told, shall not pray in vain. Whatever they ask they shall obtain, so long as they ask things according to God's mind. No work shall be found too hard and no difficulty insurmountable. Asking they shall receive and seeking they shall find. Such men were Martin Luther, the German Reformer, and our own martyr, Bishop Latimer. Such a man was John Knox, of whom Queen Mary said that she feared his prayers more than an army of twenty thousand men. It is written in a certain place: 'The effectual fervent prayer of a righteous man availeth much' (James 5:16).

Now, why is there so little power of prayer like this in our own time? Simply because there is so little close communion with Christ and so little strict conformity to his will. Men do not 'abide in Christ' and therefore pray in vain. Christ's words do not abide in them, as their standard of practice, and therefore their prayers seem not to be heard. They ask and receive not, because they ask amiss. Let this lesson sink down into our hearts. He that would have answers to his prayers must carefully remember Christ's directions. We must keep up intimate friendship with the great Advocate in heaven, if our petitions are to prosper.

For meditation: *Do you have not because you ask not? (James 4:2.)*

Suggested further reading: *1 John 3:21-24*

Our Lord declares, 'Herein is my Father glorified, that ye bear
much fruit; so shall ye be my disciples.' The meaning of this
promise seems to be that fruitfulness in Christian practice will
not only bring glory to God, but will supply the best evidence
to our own hearts that we are real disciples of Christ.

Assurance of our own interest in Christ and our consequent
eternal safety is one of the highest privileges in religion. To be
always doubting and fearing is miserable work. Nothing is
worse than suspense in any matter of importance and above all
in the matter of our souls. He that would know one of the best
receipts for obtaining assurance should diligently study
Christ's words now before us. Let him strive to bear much fruit
in his life, his habits, his temper, his words and his works. So
doing, he shall feel the 'witness of the Spirit' in his heart and
give abundant proof that he is a living branch of the true Vine.
He shall find inward evidence in his own soul that he is a child
of God and shall supply the world with outward evidence that
cannot be disputed.

Would we know why so many professing Christians have
little comfort in their religion and go fearing and doubting
along the road to heaven? The question receives a solution in
the saying of our Lord we are now considering. Men are
content with a little Christianity and a little fruit of the Spirit
and do not labour to be holy in all manner of conversation.
They must not wonder if they enjoy little peace, feel little hope
and leave behind them little evidence. The fault lies with themselves. God has linked together holiness and happiness and
what God has joined together we must not think to put
asunder.

The feeling of one eternal person in the Trinity to another
person is a thing into which we cannot enter. Yet even such is
the love of Christ towards those who believe in him — a vast,
wide, deep, unmeasurable love that passeth knowledge and can
never be fully comprehended by man (v.9).

For meditation: *Where there is little real holiness there can be
little real happiness.*

Suggested further reading: Deuteronomy 8:1-10

Our Lord declares, 'If ye keep my commandments, ye shall abide in my love.' The meaning of this promise is near akin to that of the preceding one. The man who makes conscience of diligently observing Christ's precepts is the man who shall continually enjoy a sense of Christ's love in his soul.

Of course, we must not misunderstand our Lord's words when he speaks of 'keeping his commandments'. There is a sense in which no one can keep them. Our best works are imperfect and defective and when we have done our best we may well cry, 'God be merciful to me a sinner.' Yet we must not run into the other extreme and give way to the lazy idea that we can do nothing at all. By the grace of God we may make Christ's laws our rule of life and show daily that we desire to please him. So doing,our gracious Master will give us a constant sense of his favour and make us feel his face smiling on us, like the sun shining on a fine day. 'The secret of the Lord is with them that fear him and he will show them his covenant' (Ps. 25:14).

Lessons like these may be legal to some and bring down much blame on those who advocate them. Such is the narrow-mindedness of human nature that few can look on more than one side of truth! Let the servant of Christ call no man his master. Let him hold on his way and never be ashamed of diligence, fruitfulness and jealous watchfulness, in his obedience to Christ's commands. These things are perfectly consistent with salvation by grace and justification by faith, whatever anyone may say to the contrary.

Let us hear the conclusion of the whole matter. The Christian who is careful over his words and tempers and works will generally be the most happy Christian. 'Joy and peace in believing' will never accompany an inconsistent life. It is not for nothing that our Lord concludes the passage: 'These things have I spoken unto you that you joy might be full.'

For meditation: *Do you delight yourself in God's commandments? (Ps. 119:47.)*

Suggested further reading: 1 Corinthians 13:1-7

We should observe how our Lord speaks of the grace of brotherly love. He returns to it a second time, though he has already spoken of it in the former part of his discourse. He would have us know that we can never think too highly of love, attach too much weight to it, labour too much to practise it. Truths which our Master thinks it needful to enforce on us by repetition must needs be of first-class importance.

He commands us to love one another. 'This is my commandment.' It is a positive duty laid on our consciences to practise this grace. We have no more right to neglect it than any of the ten precepts given on Mount Sinai.

He supplies the highest standard of love: 'Love one another, as I have loved you.' No lower measure must content us. The weakest, the lowest, the most ignorant, the most defective disciple is not to be despised. All are to be loved with an active, self-denying, self-sacrificing love. He that cannot do this, or will not try to do it, is disobeying the command of his Master.

A precept like this should stir up in us great searchings of heart. It condemns the selfish, ill-natured, jealous, ill-tempered spirit of many professing Christians with a sweeping condemnation. Sound views of doctrine and knowledge of controversy will avail us nothing at last, if we have known nothing of love. Without charity we may pass muster very well as churchmen but without charity we are no better, says St Paul, than 'sounding brass and tinkling cymbal' (1 Cor. 13:1). Where there is no Christ-like love, there is no grace, no work of the Spirit and no reality in our religion. Blessed are they that do not forget Christ's commandment! They are those who shall have right to the tree of life and enter the celestial city. The unloving Christian is unmeet for heaven.

For meditation: *The Christian has a responsibility of love towards all men, but especially towards his fellow believers.*

Suggested further reading: 1 John 3:11-18

The frequent repetition of this command teaches the vast importance of Christian charity and the great rarity of it. How anyone can pretend to Christian hope who is ignorant of Christian love, it is hard to understand. He that supposes he is right in the sight of God, because his doctrinal views are correct, while he is unloving in his temper and sharp, cross, snappish and ill-natured in the use of his tongue, exhibits wretched ignorance of the first principles of Christ's gospel. The crossness, spitefulness, jealousy, maliciousness and general disagreeableness of many high professors of 'sound doctrine' are a positive scandal to Christianity. Where there is little love there can be little grace.

In verse 13 our Lord teaches what should be the measure and degree of the love which Christians should have to one another. It should be a self-sacrificing love, even to death, as his was. He proved the greatness of his love by dying for his friends and even for his enemies (Rom. 5:6-8). It would be impossible for love to go further. There is no greater love than willingness to lay down life for those we love. Christ did this and Christians should be willing to do the same.

Let us note here that our Lord clearly speaks of his own death as a sacrificial and propitiatory death. Even his friends need a substitute to die for them.

Verse 14 seems closely connected with the preceding one. 'You are the friends for whom I lay down my life, if you do whatever things I command you.' We are not to dream that we are Christ's friends, if we do not habitually practise his commands. Very striking is it to observe how frequently our Lord returns to this great principle, that obedience is the great test of vital Christianity and doing the real mark of saving faith. Men who talk of being 'the Lord's people', while they live in sin and neglect Christ's plain commands, are in the broad way that leads to destruction.

For meditation: *What evidence have your fellow Christians that you have passed from death to life? (1 John 3:14.)*

Suggested further reading: James 2:14-24

Having used the word 'friends', our Lord tells his disciples that he has used that word purposely to cheer and encourage them. 'Observe that I call you friends. I do so intentionally. I no longer call you servants, because the servant from his position knows not all his master's mind and is not in his confidence. But to you I have revealed all the truths which my Father sent me to teach the world and have kept nothing back. I may therefore justly call you friends.'

This is indeed a glorious privilege. To know Christ, serve Christ, follow Christ, obey Christ, work in Christ's vineyard, fight Christ's battles — all this is no small matter. But for sinful men and women like ourselves to be called 'friends of Christ' is something that our weak minds can hardly grasp and take in. The King of kings and Lord of lords not only pities and saves all them that believe in him, but actually calls them his 'friends'. We need not wonder, in the face of such language as this, that St Paul should say, 'The love of Christ . . . passeth knowledge' (Eph. 3:19).

Let the expression before us encourage Christians to deal familiarly with Christ in prayer. Why should we be afraid to pour out all our hearts and unbosom all our secrets, in speaking to one who calls us his 'friends'? Let it cheer us in all the troubles and sorrows of life and increase our confidence in our Lord. 'He that hath friends,' says Solomon, 'will show himself friendly' (Prov. 18:24). Certainly our great Master in heaven will never forsake his 'friends'. Poor and unworthy as we are, he will not cast us off, but will stand by us and keep us to the end. David never forgot Jonathan and the Son of David will never forget his people. None so rich, so strong, so independent, so well off, so thoroughly provided for as the man of whom Christ says, 'This is my friend!'

For meditation:
> *And will this sovereign King of glory condescend,*
> *And will he write his name my Father and my Friend?*

Suggested further reading: 2 Timothy 1:8-12

Our Lord speaks of the doctrine of election. He says, 'Ye have not chosen me, but I have chosen you . . . that ye should go and bring forth fruit.' The choosing here mentioned is evidently twofold. It includes not only the election to the apostolic office, which was peculiar to the eleven, but the election to eternal life, which is the privilege of all believers. To this last 'choosing', as it specially concerns ourselves, we may profitably direct our attention.

Election to eternal life is a truth of Scripture which we must receive humbly and believe implicitly. Why the Lord Jesus calls some and does not call others, quickens whom he will and leaves others alone in their sins, these are deep things which we cannot explain. Let it suffice us to know that it is a fact. God must begin the work of grace in a man's heart, or else a man will never be saved. Christ must first choose us and call us by his Spirit, or else we shall never choose Christ. Beyond doubt, if not saved, we shall have none to blame but ourselves. But if saved, we certainly trace up the beginning of our salvation to the choosing grace of Christ. Our song to all eternity will be that which fell from the lips of Jonah: 'Salvation is of the Lord' (Jonah 2:9).

Election is always to sanctification. Those whom Christ chooses out of mankind, he chooses not only that they may be saved, but that they may bear fruit, and fruit that can be seen. All other election beside this is a mere vain delusion and a miserable invention of man. It was the faith and hope and love of the Thessalonians which made St Paul say, 'I know your election of God' (1 Thess. 1:4). Where there is no visible fruit of sanctification, we may be sure there is no election.

Armed with such principles as these, we have no cause to be afraid of the doctrine of election. Like any other truth of the gospel, it is liable to be abused and perverted. But to a pious mind it is a doctrine 'full of sweet, pleasant and unspeakable comfort'.

For meditation: *We are Christians not by chance but by divine choice.*

Suggested further reading: *Hebrews 11:32-38*

We are shown in this passage what true Christians must expect to meet in this world — hatred and persecution. If the disciples looked for kindness and gratitude from man, they would be painfully disappointed. They must lay their account to be ill-treated like their Master. 'The world hateth you. Be not moved or surprised. It they have persecuted me, they will also persecute you; if they have kept my saying, they will keep yours also.'

Facts, painful facts in every age, supply abundant proof that our Lord's warning was not without cause. Persecution was the lot of the apostles and their companions wherever they went. Not more than one or two of them died quietly in his bed. Persecution has been the lot of true believers throughout the twenty Christian centuries of history. The doings of Roman emperors and Roman popes, the Spanish Inquisition, the martyrdoms of Queen Mary's reign — all tell the same story. Persecution is the lot of all really godly people at this very day. Ridicule, mockery, slander, misrepresentation still show the feelings of unconverted people against the true Christian. As it was in St Paul's day, so it is now. In public and in private, at school and at college, at home and abroad, 'All that will live godly in Christ Jesus shall suffer persecution' (2 Tim.3:12). Mere churchmanship and outward profession are a cheap religion, of course, and cost a man nothing. But real vital Christianity will always bring with it a cross.

To know and understand these things is of the utmost importance to our comfort. Nothing is so mischievous as the habit of indulging false expectations. Let us realize that human nature never changes, that 'the carnal mind is enmity against God' and against God's image in his people. Let us settle it in our minds that no holiness of life or consistency of conduct will ever prevent wicked people hating the servants of Christ, just as they hated their blameless Master. Let us remember these things and then we shall not be disappointed.

For meditation: *Expect nothing from men but great things from God.*

Suggested further reading: Matthew 10:16-25

We are shown in this passage two reasons for patience under the persecution of this world. Each is weighty and supplies matter for much thought.

For one thing, persecution is the cup of which Christ himself drank. Faultless as he was in everything, in temper, word and deed, unwearied as he was in works of kindness, always going about doing good, never was anyone so hated as Jesus was to the last day of his earthly ministry. Scribes and high priests, Pharisees and Sadducees, Jews and Gentiles united in pouring contempt on him and opposing him and never rested till he was put to death.

Surely this simple fact alone should sustain our spirits and prevent our being cast down by the hatred of man. Let us consider that we are only walking in our Master's footsteps and sharing our Master's portion. Do we deserve to be better treated? Are we better than he? Let us fight against these murmuring thoughts. Let us drink quietly the cup which our Father gives us. Above all, let us often call to mind the saying: 'Remember the word that I spake unto you, The servant is not greater than his Master.'

For another thing, persecution helps to prove that we are children of God and have treasure in heaven. It supplies evidence that we are really born again, that we have grace in our hearts and are heirs of glory: 'If ye were of the world, the world would love his own: but because ye are not of the world, therefore the world hateth you.' Persecution, in short, is like the goldsmith's hallmark on real silver and gold; it is one of the marks of a converted man.

Let us nerve our minds with this cheering thought, when we feel ready to faint and give way under the world's hatred. No doubt it is hard to bear and the more hard when our conscience tells us we are innocent. But, after all, let us never forget that it is a token for good. It is a symptom of a work begun within us by the Holy Ghost, which can never be overthrown.

For meditation: *Men only persecute what they fear.*

Suggested further reading: 2 Thessalonians 2:5-12

Our Lord reminds the eleven of the things he had said before, when he first sent them out to preach (Matt. 10:24; Luke 6:40). He had always told them that they must not expect to be better treated than he had been himself. He quotes the proverbial saying that 'A servant must not expect to fare better than his master.' 'Did they persecute me? Then they will persecute you. Did they keep, mind and attend to my teaching? As a rule the greater part did not, and you must expect the same.' Wrong expectations are one great cause of Christians feeling troubled and perplexed.

Our Lord here tells his disciples that he himself was the cause of all the enmity and hatred they would meet with. They would be hated on account of their Master, more than on account of themselves.

It may be some comfort to a persecuted Christian to think that it is for his Master's sake that he is ill used. He is 'filling up that which is behind of the afflictions of Christ' (Col. 1:24). He is bearing the reproach of Christ' (Heb. 11:26).

Dark ignorance was the great cause of the conduct of the unbelieving Jews. They did not rightly know God the Father who had sent Christ into the world. They did not know that Christ was the Messiah whom the Father had promised to send. In this state of ignorance they blindly persecuted Christ and his disciples.

This judicial blindness and hardness of the Jewish nation in the time of our Lord and his apostles is a thing that ought to be carefully observed by all Bible readers (see Acts 3:17; 13:27; 28:25-27; 1 Cor. 2:8; 2 Cor. 3:14). It was a peculiar judicial blindness, we must remember, to which the whole nation was given over, like Pharaoh, as a final punishment for many centuries of idolatry, wickedness and unbelief. Nothing but this seems thoroughly to account for the extraordinary unbelief of many of our Lord's hearers.

For meditation: *When we toy with unbelief God may leave us to sink in it.*

Suggested further reading: Amos 9:7-10

We should observe how our Lord speaks of the misuse of religious privileges. It intensifies man's guilt and will increase his condemnation. He tells his disciples that if he had not 'spoken' and 'done' among the Jews things which none ever spoke or did before, 'they had not had sin'. By this, we must remember, he means, 'They had not been so sinful and so guilty as they are now.' But now they were utterly without excuse. They had seen Christ's works and heard Christ's teaching and yet remained unbelieving. What more could be done for them? Nothing — absolutely nothing! They wilfully sinned against the clearest possible light and were of all men most guilty.

Let us settle it down as a first principle in our religion that religious privileges are in a certain sense very dangerous things. If they do not help us towards heaven, they will only sink us deeper into hell. They add to our responsibility. 'To whomsoever much is given, of him shall much be required' (Luke 12:48). He that dwells in a land of open Bibles and preached gospel and yet dreams that he will stand in the judgement day on the same level with an untaught Chinese is fearfully deceived. He will find to his own cost, except he repents, that his judgement will be according to his light. The mere fact that he had knowledge and did not improve it will of itself prove one of his greatest sins. 'He that knew his Master's will and did it not, shall be beaten with many stripes' (Luke 12:47).

Well would it be for all professing Christians in England, if this point was more thoroughly considered! Nothing is more common then to hear men taking comfort in the thought that they 'know what is right', while at the same time they are evidently unconverted and unfit to die. They rest in that unhappy phrase, 'We know it, we know it,' as if knowledge could wash away all their sins, forgetting that the devil has more knowledge than any of us and yet is no better for it. Let the burning words of our Lord in the passage now before us sink down into our hearts and never be forgotten.

For meditation: *If ignorance does not excuse sin, then knowledge makes it worse.*

Suggested further reading: Acts 5:1-11

We should observe in these verses how our Lord speaks of the Holy Ghost.

He speaks of him as a person. He is 'the Comforter' who is to come; he is one sent and 'proceeding'; he is one whose office it is to 'testify'. These are not words that can be used of a mere influence or inward feeling. So to interpret them is to contradict common sense and to strain the meaning of plain language. Reason and fairness require us to understand that it is a personal being who is here mentioned, even he whom we are justly taught to adore as the third person in the blessed Trinity.

Again, our Lord speaks of the Holy Ghost as one whom he 'will send from the Father' and one 'who proceedeth from the Father'. These are deep sayings, no doubt, so deep that we have no line to fathom them. The mere fact that for centuries the Eastern and Western churches of Christendom have been divided about their meaning should teach us to handle them with modesty and reverence. One thing, at all events, is very clear and plain. There is a close and intimate connection between the Spirit, the Father and the Son. Why the Holy Ghost should be said in this verse to be *sent* by the Son and to *proceed* from the Father, we cannot tell. But we may quietly repose our minds in the thought expressed in an ancient creed that 'In this Trinity none is afore or after other: none is greater or less than another.' 'Such as the Father is, such is the Son and such is the Holy Ghost.' Above all, we may rest in the comfortable truth that in the salvation of our souls all three persons in the Trinity equally co-operate. It was God in Trinity who said, 'Let us create,' and it is God in Trinity who says, 'Let us save.'

Forever let us take heed to our doctrine about the Holy Spirit. Let us make sure that we hold sound and scriptural views of his nature, his person and his operations. A religion which entirely leaves him out and gives him no place is far from uncommon. Let us beware that such a religion is not ours.

For meditation: *Our religion is to be Christ-centred but it is not to despise the Father or the Spirit.*

Suggested further reading: Acts 10:39-43

We should observe how our Lord speaks of the special office of
the apostles. They were to be his witnesses in the world: 'Ye also
shall bear witness.'
    The expression is singularly instructive and full of meaning.
It taught the eleven what they must expect their portion to be,
so long as they lived. They would have to bear testimony to
facts which many would not believe and to truths which the
natural heart would dislike. They would often have to stand
alone, a few against many, a little flock against a great multitude. None of these things must move them. They must count it
no strange thing to be persecuted, hated, opposed and dis-
credited. They must not mind it. To witness was their grand
duty, whether men believed them or not. So witnessing, their
record would be on high, in God's book of remembrance, and
so witnessing, sooner or later, the Judge of all would give them
a crown of glory that fadeth not away.
    Let us never forget, as we leave this passage, that the position
of the apostles is that which, in a certain sense, every true
Christian must fill, as long as the world stands. We must all be
witnesses for Christ. We must not be ashamed to stand up for
Christ's cause, to speak out for Christ and to persist in
maintaining the truth of Christ's gospel. Wherever we live, in
town or in country, in public or in private, abroad or at home,
we must boldly confess our Master on every opportunity. So
doing, we shall walk in the steps of the apostles, though at a
long interval. So doing, we shall please our Master and may
hope at last that we shall receive the apostles' reward.

For meditation: *Enthusiasm for politics and false religion soon
opens men's mouths. Shall love for Christ shut ours?*

Suggested further reading: Luke 14:25-33

In leaving chapter 15 let us not fail to note how systematically our blessed Master gave his disciples instruction on three most important points. The first was their relation to himself. They were to abide in close union with him, like branches in a vine. The second was their relation to one another. They were to love one another with a deep, self-sacrificing love, like their Master's. The third was their relation to the world. They were to expect its hatred, not be surprised at it; to bear it patiently and not be afraid of it.

Chapter 16 is a direct continuation of the last chapter, without break or pause. Our Lord's object in this first verse is to cheer and revive the minds of the apostles and to prevent them being discouraged by the persecution of the unbelieving Jews. 'I have spoken the things which I have just been speaking, in order to obviate the depressing effect of the treatment you will receive. Lest you should be stumbled and offended by the conduct of your enemies, I have told you the things you have just heard.'

Stier remarks that 'these things' include both the warning of the world's hatred and the promise of the witnessing Spirit. Foreknowledge of the world's hatred would prevent the disciples being surprised and disappointed. The promise of the Spirit would cheer and encourage.

How great a stumbling-block it often is to young and unestablished Christians to find themselves persecuted and illused for their religion, it is needless to point out. Our Lord knew this and took care to arm the eleven apostles with warnings. He never kept back the cross, or concealed the difficulties in the way to heaven.

For meditation: *No one and nothing is to have a greater call on our allegiance than our Lord.*

Suggested further reading: Hebrews 10:32-39

We find our Lord explaining his special reason for delivering the prophecy just referred to, as well as all his discourse. 'These things,' he says, 'I have spoken unto you, that ye should not be offended.'

Well did our Lord know that nothing is so dangerous to our comfort as to indulge false expectations. He therefore prepared his disciples for what they must expect to meet with in his service. Forewarned, forearmed! They must not look for a smooth course and a peaceful journey. They must make up their minds to battles, conflicts, wounds, opposition, persecution and perhaps even death. Like a wise general, he did not conceal from his soldiers the nature of the campaign they were beginning. He told them all that was before them, in faithfulness and love, that when the time of trial came, they might remember his words and not be disappointed and offended. He wisely forewarned them that the cross was the way to the crown.

To count the cost is one of the first duties that ought to be pressed on Christians in every age. It is no kindness to young beginners to paint the service of Christ in false colours and to keep back from them the old truth: 'Through much tribulation we must enter the kingdom of God.' By prophesying smooth things and crying 'Peace', we may easily fill the ranks of Christ's army with professing soldiers. But they are just the soldiers, who, like the stony-ground hearers, in time of tribulation will fall away and turn back in the day of battle. No Christian is in healthy state of mind who is not prepared for trouble and persecution. He that expects to cross the troubled waters of this world and to reach heaven with wind and tide always in his favour knows nothing yet as he ought to know. We never can tell what is before us in life. But of one thing we may be very sure: we must carry the cross if we would wear the crown. Let us grasp this principle firmly and never forget it. Then, when the hour of trial comes, we shall 'not be offended'.

For meditation: *When Christianity costs little, its truths are held to lightly and its practices treated without seriousness.*

Suggested further reading: Acts 5:27-42

We find our Lord delivering a remarkable prophecy. He tells his disciples that they will be cast out of the Jewish church and persecuted even unto death: 'They shall put you out of the synagogues: yea, the time cometh, that whosoever killeth you will think that he doeth God service.'

How strange that seems at first sight! Excommunication, suffering and death are the portion that the Prince of peace predicts to his disciples. So far from receiving them and their message with gratitude, the world would hate them, despitefully use them and put them to death. And, worst of all, their persecutors would actually persuade themselves that it was right to persecute and would inflict the cruellest injuries in the sacred name of religion.

How true the prediction has turned out! Like every other prophecy of Scripture, it has been fulfilled to the very letter. The Acts of the Apostles show us how the unbelieving Jews persecuted the early Christians. The pages of history tell us what horrible crimes have been committed by the popish Inquisition. The annals of our own country inform us how our holy Reformers were burned at the stake for their religion by men who professed to do all they did from zeal for pure Christianity. Unlikely and incredible as it might seem at the time, the great Prophet of the church has been found in this, as in everything else, to have predicted nothing but literal truth.

Let it never surprise us to hear of true Christians being persecuted, in one way or another, even in our own day. Human nature never changes. Grace is never really popular. The quantity of persecution which God's children have to suffer in every rank of life, even now, if they confess their Master, is far greater than the thoughtless world supposes. They only know it who go through it, at school, at college, in the counting-house, in the barrack-room, on board the ship. Those words shall always be found true: 'All that will live godly in Christ Jesus shall suffer persecution' (2 Tim. 3:12).

For meditation: *Men may put Christians out of their societies but God preserves them for his new universe.*

Suggested further reading: Luke 6:17-26

We find our Lord explaining his special reason for delivering the prophecy just referred to, as well as all his discourse. 'These things,' he says, 'I have spoken unto you, that ye should not be offended.'

Well did our Lord know that nothing is so dangerous to our comfort as to indulge false expectations. He therefore prepared his disciples for what they must expect to meet with in his service. Forewarned, forearmed! They must not look for a smooth course and a peaceful journey. They must make up their minds to battles, conflicts, wounds, opposition, persecution and perhaps even death. Like a wise general, he did not conceal from his soldiers the nature of the campaign they were beginning. He told them all that was before them, in faithfulness and love, that when the time of trial came, they might remember his words and not be disappointed and offended. He wisely forewarned them that the cross was the way to the crown.

To count the cost is one of the first duties that ought to be pressed on Christians in every age. It is no kindness to young beginners to paint the service of Christ in false colours and to keep back from them the old truth: 'Through much tribulation we must enter the kingdom of God.' By prophesying smooth things and crying, 'Peace,' we may easily fill the ranks of Christ's army with professing soldiers. But they are just the soldiers who, like the stony-ground hearers, in time of tribulation will fall away and turn back in the day of battle. No Christian is in a healthy state of mind who is not prepared for trouble and persecution. He that expects to cross the troubled waters of this world and to reach heaven with wind and tide always in his favour knows nothing yet as he ought to know. We never can tell what is before us in life. But of one thing we may be very sure: we must carry the cross if we would wear the crown. Let us grasp this principle firmly and never forget it. Then, when the hour of trial comes, we shall 'not be offended'.

For meditation: *If everyone speaks well of us, it probably indicates that our version of the gospel has little to say about their sin.*

Suggested further reading: *Genesis 50:15-20*

Our Lord's words seem to convey a reproof to the disciples for not inquiring more earnestly about the heavenly home to which their Master was going. Peter, no doubt, had said with vague curiosity, 'Whither goest thou?' (John 13:36); but his question had not originated in a desire to know the place, so much as in surprise that his Lord was going at all. Our Lord seems here to say, 'If your hearts were in a right frame, you would seek to understand the nature of my going and the place to which I go.'

Let us observe that the disciples, with all their grace, were slow to use their opportunities and to seek the knowledge which they might have obtained. They had not because they asked not.

The minds of the eleven were absorbed and overwhelmed with sorrow at the thought of their Master going and they could think of nothing else. Instead of seizing the little time that was left, in order to learn more from his lips about his place and work in heaven, they were completely taken up with sorrow and could think of nothing else but their Master's departure.

We should do well to mark how mischievous overmuch sorrow is and to seek grace to keep it in proper control. No affection, if uncontrolled, so disarranges the order of men's minds and unfits them for the duties of their calling.

We can well suppose that our gracious Lord saw the minds of his disciples crushed at the idea of his leaving them. Little as they realized his full meaning, on this, as well as on other occasions, they evidently had a vague notion that they were about to be left, like orphans, in a cold and unkind world, by their almighty Friend. Their hearts quailed and shrunk back at the thought. Most graciously does our Lord cheer them by words of deep and mysterious meaning. He tells them that his departure, however painful it might seem, was not an evil, but a good. They would actually find it was not a loss, but a gain. His bodily absence would be more useful than his presence.

For meditation: *We do not always see the wisdom of God's ways.*

Suggested further reading: Isaiah 44:1-5

If Christ had not died, risen again and ascended up into heaven, it is plain that the Holy Ghost could not have come down with special power on the Day of Pentecost and bestowed his manifold gifts on the church. Mysterious as it may be, there was a connection in the eternal counsels of God between the ascension of Christ and the outpouring of the Spirit.

If Christ had remained bodily with the disciples, he could not have been in more places than one at the same time. The presence of the Spirit whom he sent down would fill every place where believers were assembled in his name, in every part of the world.

If Christ had remained upon earth and not gone up into heaven, he could not have become a high priest for his people in the same full and perfect manner that he became after his ascension. He went away to sit down at the right hand of God and to appear for us in our human nature glorified, as our Advocate with the Father.

Finally, if Christ had always remained bodily with his disciples, there would have been far less room for the exercise of their faith and hope and trust than there was when he went away. Their graces would not have been called into such active exercise and they would have had less opportunity of glorifying God and exhibiting his power in the world.

After all there remains the broad fact that after the Lord Jesus went away and the Comforter came down on the Day of Pentecost, the religion of the disciples became a new thing altogether. The growth of their knowledge and faith and hope and zeal and courage was so remarkable that they were twice the men they were before. They did far more for Christ when he was absent than they had ever done when he was present. What stronger proof can we require that it was expedient for them that their Master should go away?

For meditation: *A world without a Calvary and a world without a Pentecost are now equally inconceivable.*

Suggested further reading: Isaiah 32:14-20

When our Lord in this passage speaks of the Holy Spirit 'coming', we must take care that we do not misunderstand his meaning. On the one hand, we must remember that the Holy Ghost was in all believers in the Old Testament days, from the very beginning. No man was ever saved from the power of sin and made a saint, except by the renewing of the Holy Ghost. Abraham and Isaac and Samuel and David and the prophets were made what they were by the operation of the Holy Ghost. On the other hand, we must never forget that after Christ's ascension the Holy Ghost was poured down on men with far greater energy as individuals and with far wider influence on the nations of the world at large than he was ever poured out before. It is this increased energy and influence that our Lord has in view in the verses before us. He meant that after his own ascension the Holy Ghost would 'come' down into the world with such a vastly increased power that it would seem as if he had 'come' for the first time and had never been in the world before.

The difficulty of rightly explaining the wondrous sayings of our Lord in this place is undeniably very great. It may well be doubted whether the full meaning of his words has ever been entirely grasped by man and whether there is not something at the bottom which has not been completely unfolded. The common, superficial explanation that our Lord only meant that the work of the Spirit in saving individual believers is to convince them of their own sins, of Christ's righteousness and of the certainty of judgement at last will hardly satisfy thinking minds. It is a short-cut and superficial way of getting over Scripture difficulties. It contains excellent and sound doctrine, no doubt, but it does not meet the full meaning of our Lord's words. It is truth, but not the truth of the text. It is not individuals here and there whom he says the Spirit is to convince, but the world.

For meditation: *The Spirit strives even with those who ultimately are condemned (Gen. 6:3).*

Suggested further reading: Acts 2:37-47

Our Lord probably meant to show us what the Holy Ghost would do to the world of unbelieving Jews. He would convince them 'of sin and righteousness and judgement'.

He would convince the Jews 'of *sin*'. He would compel them to feel and acknowledge in their own minds that in rejecting Jesus of Nazareth they had committed a great sin and were guilty of gross unbelief.

He would convince the Jews of '*righteousness*'. He would press home on their consciences that Jesus of Nazareth was not an impostor and a deceiver, as they had said, but a holy, just and blameless person, whom God had owned by receiving up into heaven.

He would convince the Jews of '*judgement*'. He would oblige them to see that Jesus of Nazareth had conquered, overcome and judged the devil and all his host and was exalted to be a Prince and a Saviour at the right hand of God.

That the Holy Ghost did actually so convince the Jewish nation after the Day of Pentecost is clearly shown by the Acts of the Apostles. It was he who gave the humble fishermen of Galilee such grace and might in testifying of Christ that their adversaries were put to silence. It was his reproving and convincing power which enabled them to 'fill Jerusalem with their doctrine'. Not a few of the nation, we know, were savingly convinced, like St Paul, and 'a great company of priests' became obedient to the faith. Myriads more, we have every reason to believe, were mentally convinced, if they had not courage to come out and take up the cross. The whole tone of the Jewish people towards the end of the Acts of the Apostles is unlike what it is at the beginning. A vast reproving and convincing influence, even where not saving, seems to have gone over their minds. Surely this was partly what our Lord had in view on these verses when he said, 'The Holy Ghost shall reprove and convince.'

For meditation: *By the means of a single sermon the Holy Spirit converted 3 000 unbelieving Jews. His power has not changed.*

Suggested further reading: Ephesians 2:11-22

Our Lord probably meant to foretell what the Holy Ghost would do for the whole of mankind, both Gentiles as well as Jews.

He would reprove in every part of the earth the current ideas of men about sin, righteousness, judgement and convince people of some far higher ideas on these points than they had before acknowledged. He would make men see more clearly the nature of sin, the need of righteousness, the certainty of judgement. In a word, he would insensibly be an Advocate and convincing pleader for God throughout the whole world and raise up a standard of morality, purity and knowledge, of which formerly men had no conception.

That the Holy Ghost actually did so in every part of the earth, after the Day of Pentecost, is a simple matter of fact. The unlearned and lowly Jews, whom he sent forth and strengthened to preach the gospel after our Lord's ascension, 'turned the world upside down' and in two or three centuries altered the habits, tastes and practices of the whole civilized world. The power of the devil received a decided check. Even infidels dare not deny that the doctrines of Christianity had an enormous effect on men's ways, lives and opinions, when they were first preached and that there were no special graces or eloquence in the preachers that can account for it. In truth, the world was 'reproved and convinced' in spite of itself, and even those who did not become believers became better men. Surely this also was partly what our Lord had in view when he said to his disciples, 'When the Holy Ghost comes, he shall convince the world of sin, and righteousness, and judgement.'

For meditation: *Through the work of Christ and the Holy Spirit the Jews and the Gentiles have found salvation.*

Suggested further reading: Psalm 119:17-24

'The Spirit of truth,' says our Lord to his weak and half-informed followers, 'shall guide you into all truth.' That promise was for our sakes, no doubt, as well as for theirs. Whatever we need to know for our present peace and sanctification, the Holy Ghost is ready to teach us. All truth in science, nature and philosophy, of course, is not included in this promise. But into all spiritual truth that is really profitable and that our minds can comprehend and bear, the Holy Spirit is ready and willing to guide us. Then let us never forget, in reading the Bible, to pray for the teaching of the Holy Ghost. We must not wonder if we find the Bible a dark and difficult book, if we do not regularly seek light from him by whom it was first inspired. In this, as in many other things, 'we have not because we ask not'.

Verse 13 is meant to show the close and intimate union existing between the Spirit and the two other persons in the blessed Trinity. 'He shall not speak from himself, independently of me and my Father. He shall only speak such things as he shall hear from us.'

The phrases 'speak' and 'hear' are both accommodations to man's weakness. The Spirit does not literally 'speak' or literally 'hear'. It must mean, 'His teachings and guidings shall be those of one who is in the closest union with the Father and the Son.'

He shall 'glorify Christ'. He shall continually teach and lead and guide disciples to make much of Christ. Any religious teaching which does not tend to exalt Christ has a fatal defect about it. It cannot be from the Spirit.

The object of verse 15 seems to be to show the entire unity between Father, Son and Holy Spirit in the revelation of truth made to man. 'The Holy Spirit shall show you things concerning me, and yet things at the same time concerning the Father because all things that the Father hath are mine.'

For meditation: *Are your prayers for God's help in reading the Scriptures formal or real?*

Suggested further reading:　*Song of Solomon 5:2-6*

Christ's absence from the earth will be a time of sorrow to believers, but of joy to the world. It is written: 'Ye shall weep and lament, but the world shall rejoice.' To confine these words to the single point of Christ's approaching death and burial appears a narrow view of their meaning. Like many of our Lord's sayings on the last evening of his earthly ministry, they seem to extend over the whole period of time between his first and second advents.

Christ's personal absence must needs be a sorrow to all true-hearted believers. 'The children of the bridechamber cannot but fast when the bridegroom is taken from them.' Faith is not sight. Hope is not certainty. Reading and hearing are not the same as beholding. Praying is not the same as speaking face to face. There is something, even in the hearts of the most eminent saints, that will never be fully satisfied as long as they are on earth and Christ is in heaven. So long as they dwell in a body of corruption and see through a glass darkly, so long as they behold creation groaning under the power of sin and all things not put under Christ — so long their happiness and peace must needs be incomplete.

Yet this same personal absence of Christ is no cause of sorrow to the children of this world. It was not to the unbelieving Jews, we may be sure. When Christ was condemned and crucified, they rejoiced and were glad. They thought that the hated reprover of their sins and false teaching was silenced for ever. It is not to the careless and the wicked of our day, we may be sure. The longer Christ keeps away from this earth and lets them alone, the better will they be pleased. 'We do not want this Christ to reign over us' is the feeling of the world. His absence causes them no pain. Their so-called happiness is complete without him. All this may sound very painful and startling. But where is the thinking reader of the Bible who can deny that it is true? The world does not want Christ back again and thinks that it does very well without him. What a fearful waking up there will be by and by!

For meditation:　*Do you feel the loss of Christ's presence?*

Suggested further reading: 2 Thessalonians 1:3-10

Christ's personal return shall be a source of boundless joy to his believing people. It is written: 'I will see you again, and your heart shall rejoice, and your joy no man taketh from you.' Once more we must take care that we do not narrow the meaning of these words by tying them down to our Lord's resurrection. They surely reach much further than this. The joy of the disciples when they saw Christ risen from the dead was a joy soon obscured by his ascension and withdrawal into heaven. The true joy, the perfect joy, the joy that can never be taken away, will be the joy which Christ's people will feel when Christ returns the second time, at the end of this world.

The second personal advent of Christ, to speak plainly, is the one grand object on which our Lord, both here and elsewhere, teaches all believers to fix their eyes. We ought to be always looking for and 'loving his appearing', as the perfection of our happiness and the consummation of all our hopes (2 Peter 3:12; 2 Tim. 4:8). That same Jesus who was taken up visibly into heaven shall also come again visibly, even as he went. Let the eyes of our faith be always fixed on this coming. It is not enough that we look *backwards* to the cross and rejoice in Christ dying for our sins, and *upwards* to the right hand of God and rejoice in Christ's interceding for every believer. We must do more than this. We must look *forwards* to Christ's return from heaven to bless his people and to wind up the work of redemption. Then, and then only, will the prayer of twenty centuries receive its complete answer: 'Thy kingdom come. Thy will be done on earth as it is in heaven.' Well may our Lord say that in that day of resurrection and reunion our 'hearts shall rejoice'. 'When we awake up after his likeness we shall be satisfied' (Ps. 17:15).

For meditation: *Are you looking forward to the Lord's second coming?*

Suggested further reading: Isaiah 64:1-8

We learn in these verses that while Christ is absent believers must ask much in prayer. It is written: 'Hitherto have ye asked nothing in my name: ask and ye shall receive, that your joy may be full.'

We may well believe that up to this time the disciples had never realized their Master's full dignity. They had certainly never understood that he was the one Mediator between God and man, in whose name and for whose sake they were to put up their prayers. Here they are distinctly told that henceforward they are to 'ask in his name'. Nor can we doubt that our Lord would have all his people, in every age, understand that the secret of comfort during his absence is to be instant in prayer. He would have us know that if we cannot see him with our bodily eyes any longer, we can talk with him and through him have special access to God. 'Ask, and ye shall receive,' he proclaims to all his people in every age, 'and your joy shall be full.'

Let the lesson sink down deeply into our hearts. Of all the list of Christian duties there is none to which there is such abounding encouragement as prayer. It is a duty which concerns all. High and low, rich and poor, learned and unlearned — all must pray. It is a duty for which all are accountable. All cannot read, or hear, or sing, but all who have the Spirit of adoption can pray. Above all, it is a duty in which everything depends on the heart and motive within. Our words may be feeble and ill-chosen and our language broken and ungrammatical and unworthy to be written down. But if the heart be right, it matters not. He that sits in heaven can spell out the meaning of every petition sent up in the name of Jesus and can make the asker know and feel that he receives.

'If we know these things, happy are we if we do them.' Let prayer in the name of Jesus be a daily habit with us every morning and evening of our lives. Keeping up that habit, we shall find strength for duty, comfort in trouble, guidance in perplexity, hope in sickness and support in death.

For meditation: *Does Isaiah 64 reflect your prayer life?*

Suggested further reading: Matthew 7:7-11

Clear knowledge of God the Father is one of the foundations of the Christian religion. Our Lord says to his disciples, 'The time cometh when I shall show you plainly of the Father.' He does not say, we should mark, 'I will show you plainly about myself.' It is the Father whom he promises to show.

The wisdom of this remarkable saying is very deep. There are few subjects of which men know so little in reality as the character and attributes of God the Father. It is not for nothing that it is written: 'No man knoweth the Father save the Son, and he to whomsoever the Son shall reveal him' (Matt. 11:27). 'The only begotten Son which is in the bosom of the Father, he hath declared him' (John 1:18). Thousands fancy they know the Father because they think of him as great and almighty and all-hearing and wise and eternal, but they think no further. To think of him as just and yet the justifier of the sinner who believes in Jesus, as the God who sent his Son to suffer and die, as God in Christ reconciling the world unto himself, as God specially well-pleased with the atoning sacrifice of his Son, whereby his law is honoured — to think of God the Father in this way is not given to most men. No wonder that our Master says, 'I will show you plainly of the Father.'

Let it be part of our daily prayers that we may know more of 'the only true God', as well as of Jesus Christ whom he has sent. Let us beware alike of the mistakes which some make, who speak of God as if there was no Christ, and of the mistakes which others make, who speak of Christ as if there was no God. Let us seek to know all three persons in the blessed Trinity and give to each one the honour due to him.

For meditation: *Christianity is no mere Jesus cult. The Son has come to make the Father known (John 1:18).*

Suggested further reading: *Hebrews 6:9-12*

Anton paraphrases, 'Ye need not so think of my intercession as if the Father were not himself well disposed, but must first be coerced into kindness. No! He himself loveth you and himself ordained my intercession.'

We should notice here how graciously our Lord acknowledges the grace there was in the disciples, with all their weakness. When myriads of Jews regarded Jesus as an impostor, the eleven loved him and believed in him. Jesus never forgets to honour grace, however much it may be mingled with infirmity.

How weak was the faith and love of the apostles! How soon, in a very few hours, they were buried under a cloud of unbelief and cowardice! These very men whom Jesus commends for loving and believing, before the morning sun arose forsook him and fled. Yet, weak as their graces were, they were real and true and genuine. They were graces which hundreds of learned priests and scribes and Pharisees never attained and, not attaining, died miserably in their sins.

Let us take great comfort in this blessed truth. The Saviour of sinners will not cast off them that believe in him, because they are babes in faith and knowledge. He will not break the bruised reed or quench the smoking flax. He can see reality under much infirmity and where he sees it, he is graciously pleased. The followers of such a Saviour may well be bold and confident. They have a Friend who despises not the least member of his flock and casts out none who come to him, however weak and feeble, if they are only true.

For meditation: *God never forgets anything that we do, however insignificant it is.*

Suggested further reading: Luke 8:11-15

'When Christ came forth from the Father, he so came into the world as never to leave the Father, and he so left the world and went unto the Father as never to leave the world' (see v.28).

The words of the disciples seem to be a reference to our Lord's statement in the twenty-fifth verse, that the time was coming when he would no more speak in proverbs, but show them plainly concerning the Father. The eleven appear to catch at that promise. 'Even now thou art speaking to us more plainly than we have ever heard thee speaking before, and not in figurative language.'

Verse 29 is a peculiar verse. It is hard to see what there was in our Lord's statement in verse 28 to carry such conviction to the minds of the eleven and to make them see things about their Master so much more clearly than they had seen them before. But the precise reason why words affect men's minds and lay hold on their attention at one time and not at another is a deep mystery and hard to explain. The very same truths which a man hears from one mouth and is utterly unimpressed come home to him with such power from another mouth that he will declare he never heard them before! Nay, more, the very same speaker who is heard without attention one day is heard another day teaching the very same things with the deepest interest by the same hearers and they will tell you they never heard them before!

Our Lord warns the eleven of their self-ignorance. They thought they believed. They did not doubt their own faith. Let them not be too confident. They would soon find they had an evil root of unbelief within. Never do we find our Lord flattering his disciples. Warnings against self-confidence need to be continually pressed on believers. Nothing is so deceptive as feeling and excitement in religion. We know not the weakness of our hearts.

For meditation: *We should never confuse religious enthusiasm with religious conviction.*

Suggested further reading: *Isaiah 43:1-7*

In this sentence our Lord reveals to his confident hearers the amazing fact that they, even they, would in a very short time forsake him, desert him, run away and fail in faith altogether. 'Behold!' he begins, to denote how wonderful it was, 'the hour cometh, yea, is now come. This very night, before the sun rises, the thing is immediately going to take place. Ye shall be scattered, like sheep fleeing from a wolf, one running one way and another another, every man going off to his own things, his own friends, or his own house, or his own place of refuge. Ye shall leave me alone. You will actually allow me to be taken off by myself as a prisoner to the high priests and to Pontius Pilate and not so much as one of you will stand by me.'

How little the best of believers know of their own hearts, or understand how they may behave in times of trial! If any men were ever fully and fairly warned of their coming failure, the disciples were. We can only suppose that they did not understand our Lord, or did not realize the magnitude of the trial coming on them, or fancied that he would work some miracle at the last moment for his deliverance.

Our Lord reminds his disciples that their desertion would not deprive him of all comfort: 'And yet, when you are scattered, and have left me, I am not entirely alone, because the Father is always with me.'

We need not doubt that one great need of the sentence was to teach the disciples where they must look themselves in their own future trials. They must never forget that God the Father would always be near them and with them, even in the darkest times. A sense of God's presence is one great source of the comfort of believers. The last promise in Matthew before the ascension was 'I am with you alway, even unto the end of the world' (Matt. 28:20).

For meditation: *Even in his darkest and loneliest times the believer has the promises of Hebrews 13:5,6.*

Suggested further reading: Psalm 42

Christ is the true source of peace. We read that our Lord winds up all his discourse with these soothing words: 'These things have I spoken unto you, that ye might have peace.' The end and scope of his parting address, he would have us know, is to draw us nearer to himself as the only fountain of comfort. He does not tell us that we shall have no trouble in the world. He holds out no promise of freedom from tribulation while we are in the body. But he bids us rest in the thought that he has fought our battle and won a victory for us. Though tried and troubled and vexed with things here below, we shall not be destroyed. 'Be of good cheer,' is his parting charge, 'Be of good cheer; I have overcome the world.'

John Huss, the famous martyr who was burned at Constance, is said to have drawn special comfort from this passage during the lonely imprisonment which preceded his death.

Let us lean back our souls on these comfortable words and take courage. The storms of trial and persecution may sometimes beat heavily on us, but let them only drive us closer to Christ. The sorrows and losses and crosses and disappointments of our life may often make us feel sorely cast down, but let them only make us tighten our hold on Christ. Armed with this very promise let us, under every cross, come boldly to the throne of grace that we may obtain mercy and find grace to help in time of need. Let us often say to our souls, 'Why art thou cast down, and why art thou disquieted?' And let us often say to our gracious Master, 'Lord, didst not thou say, Be of good cheer? Lord, do as thou hast said, and cheer us to the end.'

For meditation: *Meditation upon the character of God is a great cure for depression.*

Suggested further reading: Hebrews 5:7-10

Henry remarks that this was a prayer after sermon, a prayer after sacrament, a family prayer, a parting prayer, a prayer before a sacrifice, a prayer which was a specimen of Christ's intercession.

We have here the only long prayer of the Lord Jesus which the Holy Ghost has thought good to record for our learning. That he often prayed we know well; but this is the only prayer reported. We have many of his sermons, parables and conversations, but only this prayer.

We have here the prayer of one who spake as never man spake and prayed as never man prayed, the prayer of the second person in the Trinity to the Father, the prayer of one whose office it is, as our High Priest, to make intercession for his people.

We have a prayer offered up by the Lord Jesus on a specially interesting occasion, just after the Lord's Supper, just after a most striking discourse, just before his betrayal and crucifixion, just before the disciples forsook him and fled, just at the end of his earthly ministry.

We have here a prayer which is singularly full of deep and profound expressions, so deep, indeed, that we have no line to fathom them. The wisest Christian will always confess that there are things here which he cannot fully explain.

The Bible reader who attaches no weight to such considerations as these must be in a very strange state of mind.

Augustine remarks, 'The prayer which Christ made for us, he hath also made known to us. Being so great a Master, not only what he saith in discoursing to the disciples, but also what he saith to the Father in praying for them is their edification.'

Calvin remarks, 'Doctrine has no power, unless efficacy is imparted to it from above. Christ holds out an example to teachers, not to employ themselves only in sowing the Word, but by mingling prayers with it to implore the assistance of God, that his blessing may render their labour fruitful.'

For meditation: *If Christ needed to pray, how much more do you?*

Suggested further reading: Philippians 2:5-11

The 'hour' here named is the hour appointed in God's eternal counsels for the sacrifice of the death of Christ and the final accomplishment of his atonement. That time, which had been promised by God and expected by saints for 4000 years ever since Adam's fall, had at length arrived and the seed of the woman was actually about to bruise the serpent's head by dying as man's Substitute and Redeemer. Up to this night 'the hour was not yet come' (John 7:30; 8:20); and till it had come, our Lord's enemies could not hurt him. Now, at last, the hour had come and the sacrifice was ready.

Let us remember, though in a far lower sense, that believers are all immortal till their hour is come, and till then they are safe and cannot be harmed by death.

The glory of God and his attributes is the grand end of all creation and of all God's arrangements and providences. Nothing brings such glory to God as the completion of the redeeming work of Christ, by his death, resurrection and ascension into heaven. Our Lord seems to me to ask that his death may at once take place, that he through death may be taken up to glory and that there the justice, holiness, mercy and faithfulness of the Father may be glorified and exhibited to all creation and many souls be at once saved and glorify the divine wisdom and power.

Augustine remarks, 'Some take the Father's glorifying the Son to consist in this, that he spared him not, but delivered him up for us all. But if he be said to be glorified by passion, how much more by resurrection? For in the passion it is more his humility than his glory that is shown forth, as the apostle says in Philippians 2:7-11.'

For meditation: *All that God does he does for his own glory, for there is no greater motive than this, even for him!*

Suggested further reading: *Ephesians 1:3-14*

We have a glorious account of our Lord Jesus Christ's office and dignity. We read that the Father has 'given him power over all flesh, that he should give eternal life'. The keys of heaven are in Christ's hands. The salvation of every soul of mankind is at his disposal.

There is a twofold giving of men to the Son by the Father. One is eternal, in the purpose of his grace, and this is mainly meant here. The other is in time, when the Father by his Spirit draws men to Christ (John 6:44). All the elect are given from eternity to the Son, to be redeemed by his blood, and all the redeemed are in due time drawn by the Father to the Son, to be kept to eternal life.

The Son gives 'eternal life' to none but those who are 'given to him', in the everlasting counsels of the Trinity, from all eternity. Who these are man cannot say. 'Many of the given ones,' says Traill, 'do not for a long time know it.' All are invited to repent and believe, without distinction. No one is warranted in saying, 'I was not given to Christ and cannot be saved.' But that the last day will prove that none are saved except those given to Christ by the Father is clear and plain.

The phrase 'eternal life' includes everything that is necessary to the complete salvation of a soul — the life of justification, sanctification and final glory.

Poole remarks, 'We need not ascend up to heaven to search the rolls of the eternal counsels. All whom the Father hath given to Christ shall come to Christ and not only receive him as Priest, but give themselves up to be ruled and quickened by him. By such a receiving of Christ we shall know whether we are of the number of those that are given to Christ.'

For meditation: *Every believer is a love gift to Christ from the Father from all eternity.*

Suggested further reading: Hebrews 8:7-12

Verse 3 is mercifully given to us by our Lord as a description of saved souls. 'The secret of possessing eternal life, of being justified and sanctified now and glorified hereafter, consists simply in this: in having a right saving knowledge of the one true God and of that Jesus Christ whom he has sent to save sinners.' In short, our Lord declares that he who rightly knows God and Christ is the man who possesses eternal life.

Of course, we must distinctly understand that mere head-knowledge, like that of the devil, is not meant by our Lord in this verse. The knowledge he means is a knowledge which dwells in the heart and influences the life. A true saint is one who 'knows the Lord'. To know God on the one hand — his holiness, his purity, his hatred of sin — and to know Christ on the other hand — his redemption, his mediatorial office, his love to sinners — are the two grand foundations of saving religion.

Right knowledge, after all, lies at the root of all vital Christianity, as light was the beginning of creation. We need to be 'renewed in knowledge' (Col. 3:10). We must know what we believe and we cannot properly worship an unknown God. 'Do we know God?' and 'Do we know Christ aright?' are the two great questions to be considered. God known out of Christ is a consuming fire and will fill us with fear only. Christ known without God will not be truly valued; we shall see no meaning in his cross and passion. To see clearly at the same time a holy, pure, sin-hating God and a loving, merciful, sin-atoning Christ is the very ABC of comfortable religion. In short, it is life eternal to know rightly God and Christ. 'To know God without Christ,' says Newton, 'is not to know him savingly.'

God out of Christ is a consuming fire; God not worshipped in Christ is an idol; all hopes of acceptance out of Christ are vain dreams.

For meditation: *To have eternal life after death is the consequence of having eternal life now.*

Suggested further reading: Hebrews 10:11-14

The meaning of these words I take to be this: 'I have now glorified thee during my life on earth by keeping thy law perfectly,
so that Satan can find no defect or blemish in me, by witnessing
faithfully to thy truth in opposition to the sins and false
teaching of the Jews, by showing thee and thy mind towards
man in a way that was never known before.'

Christ alone, of all born of woman, could say literally, 'I
have finished the work thou gavest me to do.' He did what the
first Adam failed to do and all the saints in every age fail to do:
he kept the law perfectly and by so keeping it brought in everlasting righteousness for all them that believe. Yet here is the
model we ought to keep before our eyes continually. We must
aim to finish the work our Father appoints for us, whether
great or small.

Musculus remarks that true godly obedience is to be seen not
merely in doing such work as we arbitrarily take up, but in
doing such work as God appoints us to do.

The glory which the Son had with the Father, in the time
before the creation of the world, is a matter passing our com-
prehension. But the pre-existence of Christ, the doctrine that
Father and Son are two distinct persons and the equal glory of
the Father and the Son are at any rate taught here very plainly.
It seems perfectly impossible to reconcile the verse with the
Socinian theory that Christ was a mere man, like David or
Paul, and did not exist before he was born at Bethlehem.

Let us also learn the practical lesson that a prayer for glory
comes best from those who have done work upon earth for
God. A lazy wish to go to glory without working is not
according to Christ's example.

For meditation: *The crown follows the race. It is not for the
non-starter or the person who gives up (Heb. 10:35).*

Suggested further reading: *Revelation 7:1-8*

Believers are 'given' to Christ by the Father, according to an everlasting covenant made and sealed long before they were born and taken out from the world by the calling of the Spirit in due time. They are the Father's peculiar property, as well as the property of the Son. They were of the world and nowise better than others. Their calling and election out of the world to be Christ's people, and not any foreseen merit of their own, is the real foundation of their character.

These are deep things, things to be read with peculiar reverence, because they are the words of the Son addressed to the Father and handling matter about believers which the eternal Trinity alone can handle with positiveness and certainty. Who those are who are given to Christ by the Father we can only certainly know by outward evidences. But that all believers are so given by the Father, predestined, elect, chosen, called by an everlasting covenant and their names and exact number known from all eternity, is truth which we must reverently believe and never hesitate to receive. So long as we are on earth, we have to do with invitations, promises, commands, evidences and faith, and God's election never destroys our responsibility. But all true believers, who really repent and believe and have the Spirit, may fairly take comfort in the thought that they were known and cared for and given to Christ by an eternal covenant, long before they knew Christ or cared for him. It is an unspeakable comfort to remember that Christ cares for that which the Father had given him.

Our Lord continues the description of his disciples and names things about them which may be seen by men as well as God. He says, 'They have kept, or observed, or attended to, the word of the gospel, which thou didst send them by me. While others would not attend to or keep that word, these eleven men had hearing ears and attentive hearts and diligently obeyed thy message.' Practical obedience is the first great test of genuine discipleship.

For meditation: *Romans 8:29,30.*

Suggested further reading: Luke 21:1-4

What a gracious account we have of our Lord Jesus Christ's
disciples! We find our Lord himself saying of them, 'They have
kept thy word . . . they have known that all things thou hast
given me are of thee . . . they have received thy words . . . they
have known surely that I came out from thee . . . they have
believed that thou didst send me.'

These are wonderful words when we consider the character
of the eleven men to whom they were applied. How weak was
their faith! How slender their knowledge! How shallow their
spiritual attainments! How faint their hearts in the hour of
danger! Yet a very little time after Jesus spoke these words they
all forsook him and fled and one of them denied him three
times with an oath. No one, in short, can read the four Gospels
with attention and fail to see that never had a great master such
weak servants as Jesus had in the eleven apostles. Yet these very
weak servants were the men of whom the gracious Head of the
church speaks here in high and honourable terms.

The lesson before us is full of comfort and instruction. It is
evident that Jesus sees far more in his believing people than
they see in themselves, or than others see in them. The least
degree of faith is very precious in his sight. Though it be no
bigger than a grain of mustard seed, it is a plant of heavenly
growth and makes a boundless difference between the possessor of it and the man of the world. Wherever the gracious
Saviour of sinners sees true faith in himself, however feeble, he
looks with compassion on many infirmities and passes by
many defects. It was even so with the eleven apostles. They
were weak and unstable as water, but they believed and loved
their Master when millions refused to own him.

For meditation: *Our Lord loves to praise his children.*

Suggested further reading: Deuteronomy 4:5-8

In verse 9 our Lord begins that part of his prayer which is specially intercessory and proceeds to name things which he asks for his disciples, from this point down to the end of the chapter. It may be convenient to remember that the things he asks may be divided under four heads. He prays that his disciples may be kept, sanctified, united and be with him in glory. Four more important things cannot be desired for believers.

The Lord Jesus does things for his believing people which he does not do for the wicked and unbelieving. He helps their souls by special intercession. He says, 'I pray for them: I pray not for the world, but for them which thou hast given me.'

The doctrine before us is one which is specially hated by the world. Nothing gives such offence and stirs up such bitter feeling among the wicked as the idea of God making any distinction between man and man and loving one person more than another. Yet the world's objections to the doctrine are, as usual, weak and unreasonable. Surely a little reflection might show us that a God who regarded good and bad, holy and unholy, righteous and unrighteous, with equal complacency and favour would be a very strange kind of God!

Of course, like every other gospel truth, the doctrine before us needs careful statement and scriptural guarding. On the one hand, we must not narrow the love of Christ to sinners and on the other we must not make it too broad. It is true that Christ loves all sinners and invites all to be saved, but it is also true that he specially loves the 'blessed company of all faithful people', whom he sanctifies and glorifies. It is true that he has wrought out a redemption *sufficient* for all mankind and offers it freely to all, but it is also true that his redemption is *effectual* only to them that believe.

For meditation: *As the husband has a special love reserved exclusively for his wife, so Christ has a special love for his people.*

Suggested further reading: 1 Timothy 2:1-6

Christ is the Mediator between God and man, but it is also true that he intercedes actively for none but those that come unto God by him. Hence it is written: 'I pray for them: I pray not for the world.'

This special intercession of the Lord Jesus is one grand secret of the believer's safety. He is daily watched and thought for and provided for with unfailing care by one whose eye never slumbers and never sleeps. Jesus is 'able to save them to the uttermost who come unto God by him, because he ever liveth to make intercession for them' (Heb. 7:25). They never perish, because he never ceases to pray for them and his prayer must prevail. They stand and persevere to the end, not because of their own strength and goodness, but because Jesus intercedes for them. When Judas fell never to rise again, while Peter fell but repented and was restored, the reason of the difference lay under those words of Christ to Peter: 'I have prayed for thee, that thy faith fail not' (Luke 22:32).

The true servant of Christ ought to lean back his soul on the truth before us and take comfort in it. It is one of the peculiar privileges and treasures of a believer and ought to be well known. However much it may be wrested and abused by false professors and hypocrites, it is one which those who really feel in themselves the workings of the Spirit should hold firmly and never let go. Well says the judicious Hooker, 'No man's condition so safe as ours: the prayer of Christ is more than sufficient both to strengthen us, be we never so weak; and to overthrow all adversary power, be it never so strong and potent.'

For meditation: *John 11:41,42.*

Suggested further reading: Philippians 1:1-6

The 'son of perdition', of course, refers to Judas Iscariot, the traitor, the only one of the apostles who was lost and cast away in hell. The name given to Judas is a strong Hebraism and means 'a person worthy of perdition, or only fit to be lost and cast away, by reason of his wickedness'. David says to Saul's servants, 'Ye are worthy to die,' or, as the margin says, 'sons of death' (1 Sam. 26:16). Again he says to Nathan, 'The man that hath done this thing shall surely die,' or, 'is a son of death' (2 Sam. 12:5; see also Ps. 79:11; Matt. 13:38; Luke 16:8). It is a tremendously strong expression to come from the lips of our merciful and loving Saviour. It shows the desperate helplessness of anyone who, living in great light and privileges like Judas, misuses his opportunities and deliberately follows the bent of his own sinful inclinations. He becomes the 'child of hell' (Matt. 23:15).

A question of very grave importance arises out of the words before us. Did our Lord mean that Judas was originally one of those that the Father 'gave to him' and was primarily a true believer? Did he therefore fall away from grace?

I maintain that the 'but' in the text is not an 'exceptive' word, but an 'adversative' one. I hold the right meaning to be 'Those whom thou gavest me I have kept, and out of them not one is lost. But there is one man who is lost, even Judas, the son of perdition; not one who was ever given to me, but one whom I declared long ago to be a 'devil', a man whose hardened heart fitted him for destruction.

Our Lord does not mean, 'No one of those given to me is lost *except* the son of perdition.' What he does mean is 'Not one of those given to me is lost. On the other hand, and in contrast, Judas, a man not given to me, a graceless man, is lost.'

For meditation:
> *The work that his goodness began,*
> *The arm of his strength will complete*
> (Toplady).

Suggested further reading: 1 Kings 19:1-9

Christ does not wish his believing people to be taken out of the world, but to be kept from the evil of it.

We need not doubt that our Lord's all-seeing eye detected in the hearts of his disciples an impatient desire to get away from this troubled world. Few in number and weak in strength, surrounded on every side by enemies and persecutors, they might well long to be released from the scene of conflict and to go home. Even David had said in a certain place, 'Oh, that I had wings like a dove, then would I flee away and be at rest!' (Ps. 55:6.) Seeing all this, our Lord has wisely placed on record this part of his prayer for the perpetual benefit of his church. He has taught us the great lesson that he thinks it better for his people to remain in the world and be kept from its evil than to be taken out of the world and removed from the presence of evil altogether.

Nor is it difficult on reflection to see the wisdom of our Lord's mind about his people, in this as in everything else. Pleasant as it might be to flesh and blood to be snatched away from conflict and temptation, we may easily see that it would not be profitable. How could Christ's people do any good in the world, if taken away from it immediately after conversion? How could they exhibit the power of grace and make proof of faith and courage and patience, as good soldiers of a crucified Lord? How could they be duly trained for heaven and taught to value the blood and intercession and patience of their Redeemer, unless they purchased their experience by suffering? Questions like these admit of only one kind of answer. To abide here in this vale of tears, tried, tempted, assaulted and yet kept from falling into sin, is the surest plan to promote the sanctification of Christians and to glorify Christ.

For meditation: _The Lord does not promise to preserve us **from** trouble, but **through** troubles._

Suggested further reading: 1 Thessalonians 4:1-8

In verse 17 our Lord proceeds to name the second thing he asks for his disciples in prayer. Preservation was the first thing and sanctification the second. He asks his Father to make the disciples more holy, to lead them on to higher degrees of holiness and purity. He asks him to do it 'through the truth', by bringing truth to bear more effectually and powerfully on their hearts and consciences and inner man. And to prevent mistake as to what he meant by truth, he adds, 'Thy Word, thy revealed Word, is the truth that I mean.'

No doubt the word 'sanctify' originally and primarily means 'set apart, separate for religious uses'; and it might be used of a vessel, a house, or an animal. But inasmuch as in human beings this separation is principally evidenced by holiness and godliness of life and character, the secondary sense of 'sanctify' is 'to make holy', and holy and godly people are 'sanctified'. This I hold to be the meaning here most decidedly. It is a prayer for the increased holiness and practical godliness of Christ's people. In short, the petition comes to this: 'Separate them more and more from sin and sinners, by making them more pure, more spiritually-minded and more like thyself.'

It is a prayer that the Father would make his people more holy, more spiritual, more pure, more saintly in thought and word and deed, in life and character. Grace had done something for the disciples already — called, converted, renewed and changed them. The great Head of the church prays that the work of grace may be carried higher and further and that his people may be more thoroughly sanctified and made holy in body, soul and spirit — in fact, more like himself.

Surely we need not say much to show the matchless wisdom of this prayer. More holiness is the very thing to be desired for all servants of Christ. Holy living is the great proof of the reality of Christianity.

For meditation: *2 Corinthians 7:1.*

Suggested further reading: *2 Peter 1:3-11*

Four great principles may be gathered from verse 17.

a. The importance of sanctification and practical godliness. Our Lord specially asks it for his people. Those that despise Christian life and character and think it of no importance, so long as they are sound in doctrine, know very little of the mind of Christ. Our Christianity is worth nothing, if it does not make us value and seek practical sanctification.

b. The wide difference between justification and sanctification. Justification is a perfect and complete work obtained for us by Christ, imputed to us and external to us, as perfect and complete the moment we believe as it can ever be, and admitting of no degrees. Sanctification is an inward work wrought in our hearts by the Holy Spirit and never quite perfect so long as we live in this body of sin. The disciples needed no prayer for justification; they were completely justified already. They did need prayer for their sanctification, for they were not completely sanctified.

c. Sanctification is a thing that admits of growth; else why should our Lord pray, 'Sanctify them'? The doctrine of imputed sanctification is one that I can find nowhere in the Word of God. Christ's imputed righteousness I see clearly, but not an imputed holiness. Holiness is a thing imparted and inwrought, but not imputed.

d. The Word is the great instrument by which the Holy Ghost carries forward the work of inward sanctification. By bringing that Word to bear more forcibly on mind and will and conscience and affection, we make the character grow more holy. Sanctification from without by bodily austerities and asceticism and a round of forms, ceremonies and outward means is a delusion. True sanctification begins from within. Here lies the immense importance of regularly reading the written Word and hearing the preached Word. It surely, though insensibly, promotes our sanctification. Believers who neglect the Word will not grow in holiness and victory over sin.

For meditation: *The life of holiness is a walking tract able to be read by all.*

Suggested further reading: Ephesians 5:25-33

Calvin remarks, 'As the apostles were not destitute of grace, we ought to infer from Christ's words that sanctification is not instantly completed in us on the first day, but that we make progress in it through the whole course of our life.'

The connection between verse 18 and the preceding one seems to me to be this: 'I ask for the increased sanctification of my disciples, because of the position they have to occupy on earth. Just as thou didst send me to be thy Messenger to this sinful world, so have I now sent them to be my messengers to the world. It is therefore of the utmost importance that they should be holy — the holy messengers of a holy Master — and so stop the mouths of their accusers.' Believers are Christ's witnesses and the character of a witness should be spotless and blameless. For this reason our Lord specially prays that his disciples may be 'sanctified'.

Verse 19 is a rather hard passage. In one sense, of course, our Lord needed no sanctification. He was always perfectly holy and without sin. I believe, with Chrysostom, the meaning must be 'I consecrate myself and offer myself up as a sacrifice and a priest, for one special reason, to say nothing of others: in order that these my disciples may be sanctified by the truth and made a holy people.' Is it not as good as saying, 'The sanctification no less than the justification of my people is the end of my sacrifice? I want to have a people who are sanctified as well as justified. So much importance do I attach to this that this is one principal reason why I now offer myself to die as a sacrifice.' The same idea seems to lie in the text: 'He gave himself for us that he might redeem us from all iniquity, and purify unto himself a peculiar people.' And again: 'Christ loved the church and gave himself for it, that he might sanctify it' (Titus 2:14; Eph. 5:26; 1 Peter 2:24).

For meditation: *There was no limit to Christ's self-giving for the church. How can the church hold back anything from him?*

Suggested further reading: Ephesians 4:1-6

In verse 20 and the three following verses our Lord proceeds to name another thing that he prays for his people. He asks that they may be 'one'. He had already named this on behalf of the eleven apostles. But he takes occasion now to enlarge the prayer and to include others besides the eleven — the whole company of future believers. 'I now pray also for all who shall believe on me through the preaching of my disciples in all future time, and not for my eleven apostles only.' All believers needed preservation and sanctification in every age, but none so much as the eleven, because they were the first to attack the world and bear the brunt of the battle. In some respects it was more easy to be 'one' at the first beginnings of the church, and harder to be kept and 'sanctified'. As the church grew, it would be more difficult to keep unity. The want of unity and consequent strife among English Christians in the last 300 years has been a miserable example of the enormous damage that believers may do their Master's cause.

Let us mark how wide was the scope of our Lord's intercessory prayer. He prayed not only for present, but for future believers. So should it be with our prayers. We may look forward and pray for believers yet to be born, though we may not look back and pray for believers who are dead.

George Newton observes what an encouragement it should be to us in praying for others, for a child or a friend, to remember that perhaps Christ is asking him or her of God too. He here prays for those who did not yet believe, but were to believe one day.

Let us mark how the 'word' preached is mentioned as the means of making men believe. Faith cometh by hearing. The church which places sacraments above the preaching of the Word will have no blessing of God, because it rejects God's order.

For meditation: *Do you attempt in any way to show your unity with other true believers or are you an isolated island of self-satisfaction?*

Suggested further reading: 1 John 2:28-3:3

Jesus prays that his people may at last be with him and behold his glory. 'I will,' he says, 'that those whom thou hast given me, be with me where I am: that they may behold my glory.'

This is a singularly beautiful and touching conclusion to our Lord's remarkable prayer. We may well believe that it was meant to cheer and comfort those who heard it and to strengthen them for the parting scene which was fast drawing near. But for all who read it even now, this part of his prayer is full of sweet and unspeakable comfort.

We do not see Christ now. We read of him, hear of him, believe in him and rest our souls in his finished work. But even the best of us, at our best, walk by faith and not by sight and our poor halting faith often makes us walk very feebly in the way to heaven. There shall be an end of all this state of things one day. We shall at length see Christ as he is and know as we have been known. We shall behold him face to face and not through a glass darkly. We shall actually be in his presence and company and go out no more. If faith has been pleasant, much more will sight be, and if hope has been sweet, much more will certainty be. No wonder that when St Paul has written, 'We shall ever be with the Lord,' he adds, 'Comfort one another with these words' (1 Thess. 4:17,18).

We know little of heaven now. Our thoughts are all confounded when we try to form an idea of a future state in which pardoned sinners shall be perfectly happy. 'It does not yet appear what we shall be' (1 John 3:2). But we may rest ourselves on the blessed thought that after death we shall be 'with Christ'.

For meditation: *How much of your desire for heaven is a longing to be free from trouble and how much is it a desire for the presence of Christ?*

Suggested further reading: *1 Corinthians 1:10-17*

We can ask no stronger proof of the value of unity among Christians and the sinfulness of division than the great prominence which our Master assigns to the subject in this passage. How painfully true it is that in every age divisions have been the scandal of religion and the weakness of the church of Christ! How often Christians have wasted their strength in contending against their brethren, instead of contending against sin and the devil! How repeatedly they have given occasion to the world to say, 'When you have settled your own internal differences we will believe!' All this, we need not doubt, the Lord Jesus foresaw with prophetic eye. It was the foresight of it which made him pray so earnestly that believers might be 'one'.

Let the recollection of this part of Christ's prayer abide in our minds and exercise a constant influence on our behaviour as Christians. Let no man think lightly, as some men seem to do, of schism, or count it a small thing to multiply sects, parties and denominations. These very things, we may depend, only help the devil and damage the cause of Christ. 'If it be possible, as much as lieth in us, let us live peaceably with all men' (Rom. 12:18). Let us bear much, concede much and put up with much, before we plunge into secessions and separations. They are movements in which there is often much false fire. Let rabid zealots who delight in sect-making and party-forming rail at us and denounce us if they please. We need not mind them. So long as we have Christ and a good conscience, let us patiently hold on our way, follow the things that make for peace and strive to promote unity. It was not for nothing that our Lord prayed so fervently that his people might be 'one'.

For meditation: *Let us make every effort to be in harmony with our fellow believers. Are we not members of one spiritual family?*

Suggested further reading: *Ephesians 3:14-21*

It is well to remember that the church, whose unity the Lord desires and prays for, is not any particular or visible church, but the church which is his body, the church of the elect, the church which is made up of true believers and saints alone.

The unity which our Lord prays for is not unity of forms, discipline, government and the like, but unity of heart and will and doctrine and practice. Those who make uniformity the chief subject of this part of Christ's prayer entirely miss the mark. There may be uniformity without unity, as in many visible churches on earth now. There may be unity without uniformity, as between godly Episcopalians and godly Presbyterians. Uniformity no doubt may be a great help to unity, but it is not unity itself.

The unity which our Lord prays about here is that true, substantial, spiritual, internal heart unity which undoubtedly exists among all members of Christ of every church and denomination. It is the unity which results from one Holy Ghost having made the members of Christ what they are. It is unity which makes them feel more of one mind with one another than with mere professors of their own party. It is unity which is the truest freemasonry on earth. It is unity which shakes the world and obliges it to confess the truth of Christianity. For the continued maintenance of this unity and an increase of it, our Lord seems to me in this prayer specially to pray. And we need not wonder. The divisions of mere worldly professors are of little moment. The divisions of real true believers are the greatest possible injury to the cause of the gospel. If all believers at this moment were of one mind and would work together, they might soon turn the world upside down. No wonder the Lord prayed for unity.

For meditation: *It is easy to confuse schemes for church union which unite heretics and believers with the true unity of all true believers.*

Suggested further reading: *Genesis 3:1-7*

Henry observes, 'The office of the priest was to teach and pray and offer sacrifice. Christ, after teaching and praying, applies himself to make atonement. He had said all he had to say as a prophet. He now addresses himself to his work as a priest.'

The Cedron here mentioned is the same as the Kidron named more than once in the Old Testament. The word 'brook' means, literally, a 'winter torrent', and this, according to all travellers, is precisely what the Kidron is. Excepting in winter, or after rains, it is merely the dry bed of a watercourse. It lies on the east side of Jerusalem, between the city and the Mount of Olives. It is the same Kidron which David passed over weeping when obliged to flee from Jerusalem by the rebellion of Absalom (2 Sam. 15:23). It is the same Kidron by the side of which Asa burnt the idol of his mother Maachah (2 Chron. 15:16), and into which Josiah cast the dust of the idolatrous altars which he destroyed (2 Kings 23:12).

Lampe says that the way by which our Lord left the city was the way by which the scapegoat, Azazel, was annually sent out into the wilderness on the great Day of Atonement.

Bishop Andrews says that 'The first breach made by the Romans, when Titus took Jerusalem, was at the brook Cedron, where they took Christ.'

There can be little doubt that this garden is the same as the 'place called Gethsemane'.

Almost all commentators notice the curious fact that the fall of Adam and Eve took place in a garden and Christ's passion also began in a garden and the sepulchre where Christ was laid was in a garden and the place where he was crucified was in a garden (John 19:41).

Augustine remarks, 'It was fitting that the blood of the Physician should there be poured out, where the disease of the sick man first commenced.'

For meditation: *Even the new universe will contain a river in a garden (Rev. 22:1,2).*

Suggested further reading: *Daniel 6:10,11*

Verse 2 tells us that this garden was a place where our Lord and his disciples were in the habit of assembling together when they went up to Jerusalem at the great Jewish feasts. At such seasons the crowd of worshippers was very great, and many had to content themselves with such shelter as they could find under trees, or rocks, in the open air. This is what Luke means when he says, 'At night he went out and abode in the mount that is called the Mount of Olives' (Luke 21:37). Excepting at the celebration of the first Lord's Supper, we have no mention of our Lord ever being in any *house* in Jerusalem.

The fact that the traitor Judas 'knew the place', while our Lord deliberately went there, shows three things. One is that our Lord went to his death willingly and voluntarily; he went to the 'garden', knowing well that Judas was acquainted with the place. Another thing is that our Lord was in the habit of going to this garden so 'often' that Judas felt sure he would be found there. Another thing is that the heart of Judas must have been desperately hard, when, after so many seasons of spiritual refreshment as he must have seen in this garden, he could use his knowledge for the purpose of betraying his Master. He 'knew the place', because he had often heard his Master teaching and praying there. He knew it from spiritual associations and yet turned his knowledge to wicked ends!

May we not learn from this verse that there is nothing to be ashamed of, nothing wrong, in loving one place more than another and choosing one place more than another for communion wtih God? Even our blessed Lord had one special place near Jerusalem, more than other places, to which he often resorted. The common idea of some that it matters not where or in what place we worship and that it is unspiritual and wrong to care for one seat in church more than another can hardly be reconciled with this verse.

For meditation: *To have special places and times for prayer is not wrong as long as we avoid superstition.*

Suggested further reading: Matthew 16:13-23

Verse 4 shows our Lord's perfect foreknowledge of everything that was about to happen to him. Never was there a more willing, deliberate and voluntary sufferer than our Lord. The best of martyrs, like Ridley and Latimer, did not know for certain up to the moment of their deaths that something might not occur to alter the mind of their persecutors and save their lives. Our Lord knew perfectly well that his death was sure, by the determinate counsel and foreknowledge of God.

Ford quotes a saying of Pinart that 'What rendered Christ's sufferings most terrible was the perfect foreknowledge he had of the torments he should endure. From the first moment of his life he had present to his mind the scourge, the thorns, the cross and the agonizing death which awaited him. Saw he a lamb in the meadow or a victim in the temple, the sight reminded him that he was the Lamb of God and that he was to be offered up a sacrifice.'

Our Lord came forward from that part of the garden where he was and did not wait for the party of Judas to find him. On the contrary, he suddenly showed himself and met them face to face. The effect of this action alone must have been startling to the soldiers. They would feel at once that they had to do with no common person.

Henry remarks, 'When the people would have forced him to take a crown and wished to make him a king, he withdrew and hid himself (John 6:15). But when they came to force him to his cross he offered himself. He came to this world to suffer and went to the other world to reign.'

Jesus himself was the first to speak and did not wait to be challenged or commanded to surrender. This sudden question no doubt would take the party of Judas by surprise and prepare the way for the mighty miracle which followed. The soldiers must needs have felt, 'This is not the language or manner of a malefactor or a guilty man.'

For meditation: *The terror of the cross for Christ included knowing what would happen. The mercy of God to us is to hide the future from us.*

Suggested further reading: 1 Corinthians 10:1-13

We should notice in these verses the exceeding hardness of heart to which a backsliding professor may attain. We are told that Judas, one of the twelve apostles, became guide to them that took Jesus. We are told that he used his knowledge of the place of our Lord's retirement, in order to bring his deadly enemies upon him, and we are told that when the band of men and officers approached his Master in order to make him prisoner, Judas 'stood with them'. Yet this was a man who for three years had been a constant companion of Christ, had seen his miracles, had heard his sermons, had enjoyed the benefit of his private instruction, had professed himself a believer, had even worked and preached in Christ's name! 'Lord,' we may well say, 'what is man?' From the highest degree of privilege down to the lowest depth of sin, there is but a succession of steps. Privileges misused seem to paralyse the conscience. The same fire that melts wax will harden clay.

Let us beware of resting our hopes of salvation on religious knowledge, however great, or religious advantages, however many. We may know all doctrinal truth and be able to teach others and yet prove rotten at heart and go down to the pit with Judas. We may bask in the full sunshine of spiritual privileges and hear the best of Christian teaching and yet bear no fruit to God's glory and be found withered branches of the vine, only fit to be burned. 'Let him that thinketh he standeth take heed lest he fall' (1 Cor. 10:12). Above all, let us beware of cherishing within our hearts any secret besetting sin, such as love of money or love of the world. One faulty link in a chain-cable may cause a shipwreck. One little leak may sink a ship. One allowed and unmortified sin may ruin a professing Christian. Let him that is tempted to be a careless man in his religious life consider these things and take care. Let him remember Judas Iscariot. His history is meant to be a lesson.

For meditation: *The higher we rise, the greater our privileges and the further our fall.*

Suggested further reading: 1 Corinthians 9:15-23

We should notice in these verses the entire voluntariness of Christ's sufferings. We are told that the first time that our Lord said to the soldiers, 'I am he, they went backward, and fell to the ground.' A secret invisible power, no doubt, accompanied the words. In no other way can we account for a band of hardy Roman soldiers falling prostrate before a single unarmed man. A real miracle was wrought, though few had eyes to see it. At the moment when our Lord seemed weak, he showed that he was strong.

Let us carefully remember that our blessed Lord suffered and died of his own free will. He did not die because he could not help it; he did not suffer because he could not escape. All the soldiers of Pilate's army could not have taken him, if he had not been willing to be taken. They could not have hurt a hair of his head, if he had not given them permission. But here, as in all his earthly ministry, Jesus was a willing sufferer. He had set his heart on accomplishing our redemption. He loved us and gave himself for us, cheerfully, willingly, gladly, in order to make atonement for our sins. It was 'the joy set before him' which made him endure the cross and despise the shame and yield himself up without reluctance into the hands of his enemies.

We should notice in these verses our Lord's tender care for his disciples' safety. Even at this critical moment, when his own unspeakable sufferings were about to begin, he did not forget the little band of believers who stood around him. He remembered their weakness. He knew how little fit they were to go into the fiery furnace of the high priest's palace and Pilate's judgement hall. He mercifully makes for them a way of escape: 'If ye seek me, let these go their way.' It seems most probable that here also a miraculous influence accompanied his words. At any rate, not a hair of the disciples' heads was touched. While the Shepherd was taken, the sheep were allowed to flee away unharmed.

For meditation: _It is better to serve God voluntarily than out of necessity._

Suggested further reading: Matthew 5:38-48

Peter's impetuous temperament comes out in the action before us. Impulsive, earnest, zealous and inconsiderate of consequences, he acted hastily and his zeal soon cooled down and was changed into fear. It in not those who are for a time most demonstrative and fervent whose religion is deepest. John never smote with the sword, but John never denied his Lord and was at the foot of the cross when Christ died.

Whether the ear was cut off entirely, or only so cut as to hang down by the skin, may be left to conjecture. In any case we know that it gave occasion for the last miracle of bodily cure which our Lord ever wrought. Luke tells us that he 'touched' the ear and it was instantaneously healed. To the very end of his ministry our Lord did good to his enemies and gave proof of his divine power. But his hardened enemies gave no heed. Miracles alone convert no one. As in the case of Pharaoh, they only seem to make some men harder and more wicked.

We cannot doubt that Peter meant to kill Malchus with this blow, which was probably aimed at his head. His own agitation probably and the special interposition of God alone prevented him taking away the life of another and endangering his own life and that of his fellow disciples.

Musculus remarks how entirely Peter seems to have forgotten all his Master's frequent predictions that he would be delivered to the Gentiles and be condemned to death and acts as if he could prevent what was coming. It was clearly an impulsive act, done without reflection. Zeal not according to knowledge often drives a man into foolish actions and makes work for repentance.

The gospel is not to be propagated or maintained by carnal weapons, or by smiting and violence. Matthew adds the solemn words: 'All they that take the sword shall perish with the sword.' How needful the rebuke and how true the comment have often been proved by the history of the church of Christ. The appeal to the sword can rarely be justified and has often recoiled on the head of its promoters.

For meditation: *Matthew 26:52.*

Suggested further reading: Exodus 9:27-35

We should mark, for one thing, the amazing hardness of unconverted men. We see this in the conduct of the men by whom our Lord was taken prisoner. Some of them most probably were Roman soldiers and some of them were Jewish servants of the priests and Pharisees. But in one respect they were all alike. Both parties saw our Lord's divine power exhibited when they 'went backward, and fell to the ground'. Both saw a miracle, according to St Luke's Gospel, when Jesus touched the ear of Malchus and healed him. Yet both remained unmoved, cold, indifferent and insensible, as if they had seen nothing out of the common way.

The degree of hardness and insensibility of conscience to which men may attain, when they live twenty or thirty years without the slightest contact with religion, is something awful and appalling. God and the things of God seem to sink out of sight and disappear from the mind's eye. The world and the things of the world seem to absorb the whole attention. In such cases we may well believe miracles would produce little or no effect, as in the case before us. The eye would gaze on them, like the eye of a beast looking at a romantic landscape, without any impression being made on the heart. He who thinks that seeing a miracle would convert him into a thorough Christian has got much to learn.

Let us not wonder if we see cases of hardness and unbelief in our own day and generation. Such cases will continually be found among those classes of mankind who, from their profession or position, are completely cut off from means of grace. Twenty or thirty years of total irreligion, without the influence of Sunday, Bible or Christian teaching, will make a man's heart hard as the nether millstone. His conscience at last will seem dead, buried and gone. He will appear past feeling. Painful as these cases are, we must not think them peculiar to our own times. They existed under Christ's own eyes and they will exist until Christ returns.

For meditation: *Jeremiah 17:9.*

Suggested further reading: Isaiah 45:1-6

In the time when our Lord Jesus was on earth, the office of the high priest among the Jews was filled up with the utmost disorder and irregularity. Instead of the high priest being high priest for life, he was often elected for a year or two and then deposed and his office given to another. There were often living at one time several priests who had served the office of high priest and then ceased to hold it, like sheriffs or mayors among ourselves. In the case before us Annas appears, after ceasing to be high priest himself, to have lived in the same palace with his son-in-law Caiaphas and to have assisted him as an assessor and adviser in the discharge of his duties, which from his age and official experience he would be well qualified to do. Remembering this, we may understand our Lord being 'led away to Annas first', and then passed on by him to Caiaphas.

The gross inconsistency of the Jews in making such ado about the law of Moses, while they permitted and tolerated such entire departures from its regulations about the high priest's office, is a curious example of what blindness unconverted men may exhibit.

Henry remarks, 'It was the ruin of Caiaphas that he was high priest that year, and so became a ringleader in putting Christ to death. Many a man's advancement has lost him his reputation, and he would not have been dishonoured if he had not been preferred and promoted.'

Let us not forget that this was the very Caiaphas who, after the raising of Lazarus, had said publicly that it was expedient that one man should die for the people. Behold how he is made the unconscious instrument of bringing that saying to pass, though in a widely different sense from that which he intended!

Let us note how the great wicked men of this world — the Sennacheribs and Neros and Bloody Marys and Napoleons — are used by God as his saws and axes and hammers to do his work and carry out the building of his church, though they are not themselves in the least aware of it. Indeed Caiaphas helps forward the one great sacrifice for the sins of the world!

For meditation: *Romans 8:28.*

Suggested further reading: Isaiah 53

We see the Son of God taken prisoner and led away bound like a malefactor, arraigned before wicked and unjust judges, insulted and treated with contempt. And yet this unresisting prisoner had only to will his deliverance and he would at once have been free. He had only to command the confusion of his enemies, and they would at once have been confounded. He knew all these things, and yet condescended to be treated as a malefactor without resisting.

To suffer for those whom we love and who are in some sense worthy of our affections is suffering that we can understand. To submit to ill-treatment quietly when we have no power to resist is submission that is both graceful and wise. But to suffer voluntarily when we have the power to prevent it, and to suffer for a world of unbelieving and ungodly sinners, unasked and unthanked — this is a line of conduct which passes man's understanding. Never let us forget that this is the peculiar beauty of Christ's sufferings, when we read the wondrous story of his cross and passion. He was led away captive and dragged before the high priest's bar, not because he could not help himself, but because he had set his whole heart on saving sinners, by bearing their sins, by being treated as a sinner and by being punished in their stead. He was a willing prisoner, that we might be set free. He was willingly arraigned and condemned, that we might be absolved and declared innocent. 'He suffered for sins, the just for the unjust, that he might bring us unto God' (1 Peter 3:18). 'Though he was rich, yet for our sakes he became poor, that we through his poverty might be rich' (2 Cor. 8:9). 'He was made sin for us who knew no sin, that we might be made the righteousness of God in him' (2 Cor. 5:21). Surely if there is any doctrine of the gospel which needs to be clearly known, it is the doctrine of Christ's voluntary substitution. He suffered and died willingly and unresistingly, because he knew that he had come to be our Substitute and by substitution to purchase our salvation.

For meditation: *1 Peter 2:24.*

Suggested further reading:　1 Kings 13:7-24

The first flight and running away of the disciples is passed over entirely by John. He simply mentions that Peter followed his Master, though at a distance, lovingly anxious to see what was done to him, yet not bold enough to keep near him like a disciple. Anyone can see that the unhappy disciple was under the influence of very mixed feelings. Love made him ashamed to run away and hide himself. Cowardice made him afraid to show his colours and stick by his Lord's side. Hence he chose a middle course — the worst, as it happened, that he could have followed. After being self-confident when he should have been humble and sleeping when he ought to have been praying, he could not have done a more foolish thing than to flutter round the fire and place himself within reach of temptation. It teaches the foolishness of man when his grace is weak. No prayer is more useful than the familiar one: 'Lead us not into temptation.' Peter forgot it here.

At first Peter stood outside the door of the palace, not daring to go in. It is a little detail in the story of his fall which the three other Gospel writers omit to mention. Again we see in him the mixture of good and bad feelings, cowardice and love contending for the mastery. Happy would it have been for him if he had stayed outside the door!

Rollock remarks that when Peter found the door shut, he ought not to have stood there, but to have gone away. 'It was by God's providence the door was shut. He got a warning then to leave off, but would not. These impediments, cast in our way when we purpose to do a thing, should not be idly looked at, but should make us carefully try the deed, whether it be lawful.'

Let us mark what mistakes even the best believers make in dealing with their brethren. John thought it would be a kind and useful thing to bring Peter into the high priest's house. He was perfectly mistaken and was unintentionally one link in the chain of causes which led to his fall. People may harm each other with the best intention.

For meditation:　*Beware of causing others to sin.*

Suggested further reading: James 5:1-6

Verse 19 describes the first judicial examination that our Lord underwent. He was questioned concerning 'his disciples' — that is, who they were, how many, what position they occupied and what were their names. And concerning 'his doctrine' — that is, what were the principal points or truths of his creed, what were the peculiar things he called on man to believe. The object of this preliminary inquiry seems manifest. It was meant to elicit some admission from our Lord's mouth, on which some formal charge of heresy and blasphemy before the Sanhedrin might be founded.

Verse 20 contains a calm, dignified statement from our Lord of the general course of his ministry. He had done nothing in a clandestine or underhand way. He had always spoken openly 'to the world' and not confined his teaching to any one class. He had always taught publicly in synagogues and in the temple where the Jews resorted. He had said nothing privately and secretly, as if he had any cause to be ashamed of it.

The verse is mainly remarkable for the strong light it throws on our Lord's habit of teaching throughout the three years of his ministry. It shows that he was eminently a public teacher, kept back no part of his message from any class of the population and proclaimed it with equal boldness in every place. There was nothing whatever of reserve about his gospel. This is his own account and we therefore know that it is correct. 'I have spoken in the most public manner and taught in the most public places and done nothing in a corner.'

The boldness and dignity of our Lord's reply to Annas in verse 23 are very noteworthy. They are an example to all Christians of the courageous and unflinching tone which an innocent defendant may justly adopt before the bar of an unrighteous judge. 'The righteous is bold as a lion.'

For meditation: *In the face of abuse and hostility, we have our Lord's example to follow.*

Suggested further reading: Acts 23:1-5

One of the attendants standing by rudely interrupts our Lord by striking him and coarsely taxing him with impertinence and disrespect in so speaking as he had spoken to the high priest.

Stier remarks that this was the first blow which the holy body of Jesus received from the hands of sinners.

We may learn from this circumstance what a low, degraded and disorderly condition the Jewish courts of ecclesiastical law must have been in at this period, when such a thing as publicly striking a prisoner could take place and when violence could be shown to a prisoner in a full court of justice for answering boldly for himself. It supplies strong evidence of the miserably fallen state of the whole Jewish nation, when such an act could be done under the very eyes of a judge. Nothing is a surer index of the real condition of a nation than the conduct of its courts of justice and its just or unjust treatment of prisoners. The sceptre had clearly fallen from Judah and rottenness was at the core of the nation, when the thing mentioned in this verse could happen. Our Lord's assailant evidently held that a prisoner must never reply to his judge, however unjust or corrupt the judge might be.

Our Lord's reply to him who smote is a calm and dignified reproof: 'If I have spoken wickedly, bear witness in a just and orderly way becoming a court of law, but do not strike me. If, on the contrary, I have spoken well, what reasonable cause canst thou allege for striking me, either here or out of court?'

Let us note that our Lord's conduct at this point teaches that his maxim, 'If anyone smite thee on thy right cheek, turn to him the other also' (Matt. 5:39), is a maxim which must be taken with reserve and is not of unlimited application. There may be times when, in defence of truth and for the honour of justice, a Christian must firmly protest against violence and publicly refuse to countenance it by tame submission.

For meditation: *Is there not an interesting contrast between our Lord and Paul on trial? (John 18:23; Acts 23:3.)*

Suggested further reading: *Galatians 2:11-16*

The apostle stood among the crowd of his Master's enemies and warmed himself like one of them, as if he had nothing to think of but his bodily comfort, while his beloved Master stood in a distant part of the hall, cold and a prisoner. Who can doubt that Peter, in his miserable cowardice, wished to appear one of the party who hated his Master and thought to conceal his real character by doing as they did? And who can doubt that while he warmed his hands he felt cold, wretched and comfortless in his own soul? 'The backslider in heart is filled with his own ways.'

How many do as others do and go with the crowd, while they know inwardly they are wrong!

A second time we find the unhappy apostle telling a lie and this time it is added emphatically: 'He denied it.' The further a backslider goes, the worse he becomes. The first time he seems to have said quietly, 'I am not.' The second time he flatly 'denied'. Even an apostle can fall into being a liar!

The third denial, we know from the other Gospels, was more loud and emphatic than any and was made with cursing and swearing! The further à man falls, the heavier his fall.

Calvin remarks on the course of a backslider, 'At first the fault will not be very great; next, it becomes habitual; and at last, after the conscience has been laid asleep, he who has accustomed himself to despise God will think nothing unlawful, but will dare to commit the greatest wickedness.'

As long as the world stands, Peter's fall will be an instructive example of what even a great saint may come to if he neglects to work and pray, of the mercy of Christ in restoring such a backslider and of the honesty of the Gospel writers in recording such a history.

For meditation:
>   *Prone to wander, Lord, I feel it;*
>   *Prone to leave the God I love*
>   (Robinson).

Suggested further reading: Matthew 23:23-28

We should notice the false conscientiousness of our Lord's wicked enemies. We are told that the Jews who brought Christ before Pilate would not go into 'the judgement hall, lest they should be defiled, but that they might eat the passover'. That was scrupulosity indeed! These hardened men were actually engaged in doing the wickedest act that mortal man ever did. They wanted to kill their own Messiah. And yet at this very time they talked of being 'defiled' and were very particular about the Passover!

The conscience of unconverted men is a very curious part of their moral nature. While in some cases it becomes hardened, seared and dead, until it feels nothing, in others it becomes morbidly scrupulous about the lesser matters of religion.

Let us pray that our consciences may always be enlightened by the Holy Ghost and that we may be kept from a one-sided and deformed Christianity. A religion that makes a man neglect the weightier matters of daily holiness and separation from the world and concentrate his whole attention on forms, sacraments, ceremonies and public services is, to say the least, very suspicious. It may be accompanied by immense zeal and show of earnestness, but it is not sound in the sight of God. The Pharisees paid tithe of mint, anise and cummin, and compassed sea and land to make proselytes, while they neglected 'judgement, mercy and faith' (Matt. 23:23). The very Jews who thirsted for Christ's blood were the Jews who feared the defilement of a Roman judgement hall and made much ado about keeping the Passover! Let their conduct be a beacon to Christians as long as the world stands. That religion is worth little which does not make us say, 'I esteem all thy commandments concerning all things to be right, and I hate every false way' (Ps.119:128). That Christianity is worthless which makes us compound for the neglect of heart religion and practical holiness by an extravagant zeal for man-made ceremonies or outward forms.

For meditation: *Christianity is more than keeping a set of minor rules.*

Suggested further reading: Romans 13:1-7

Our Lord's main object in saying, 'My kingdom is not of this world,' was to inform Pilate's mind concerning the true nature of his kingdom and to correct any false impression he might have received from the Jews. He tells him that he did not come to set up a kingdom which would interfere with the Roman government. He did not aim at establishing a temporal power, to be supported by armies and maintained by taxes. The only dominion he exercised was over men's hearts and the only weapons that his subjects employed were spiritual weapons. A kingdom which required neither money nor servants for its support was one of which the Roman emperors need not be afraid. In the highest sense it was a kingdom 'not of this world'.

But our Lord did not intend to teach that the kings of this world have nothing to do with religion and ought to ignore God altogether in the government of their subjects. No such idea, we may be sure, was in his mind. He knew perfectly well that it was written, 'By me kings reign' (Prov. 8:15), and that kings are as much required to use their influence for God as the meanest of their subjects. He knew that the prosperity of kingdoms is wholly dependent on the blessing of God and that kings are as much bound to encourage righteousness and godliness as to punish unrighteousness and immorality. To suppose that he meant to teach Pilate that, in his judgement, an infidel might be as good a king as a Christian, and a man like Gallio as good a ruler as David or Solomon, is simply absurd.

Let us carefully hold fast the true meaning of our Lord's words in these latter days. Let us never be ashamed to maintain that no government can expect to prosper which refuses to recognize religion, which deals with its subjects as if they had no souls and cares not whether they serve God, or Baal, or no god at all. Such a government will find, sooner or later, that its line of policy is suicidal and damaging to its best interests. No doubt the kings of this world cannot make men Christians by laws and statutes. But they can encourage and support Christianity and they will do so if they are wise.

For meditation: *1 Timothy 2:1,2.*

Suggested further reading: *Proverbs 8:1-11*

We are told that when our Lord spoke of the truth, the Roman governor replied, 'What is truth?' We are not told with what motive this question was asked, nor does it appear on the face of the narrative that he who asked it waited for an answer. It seems far more likely that the saying was the sarcastic, sneering exclamation of one who did not believe that there was any such thing as 'truth'. It sounds like the language of one who had heard, from his earliest youth, so many barren speculations about 'truth' among Roman and Greek philosophers that he doubted its very existence. 'Truth indeed! What is truth?'

There are multitudes in every Christian land whose state of mind is just like that of Pilate. Hundreds are continually excusing their own irreligion by the specious plea that, like the Roman governor, they cannot find out 'what is truth'. They point to the endless controversies of Romanists and Protestants, of High Churchmen and Low Churchmen, of churchmen and dissenters, and pretend to say that they do not understand who is right and who is wrong. Sheltered under this favourite excuse, they pass through life without any decided religion and in this wretched, comfortless state, too often die.

But is it really true that truth cannot be discovered? Nothing of the kind! God never left any honest diligent inquirer without light and guidance. Pride is one reason why many cannot discover truth. They do not humbly go down on their knees and earnestly ask God to teach them. Laziness is another reason. They do not honestly take pains and search the Scriptures. The followers of unhappy Pilate, as a rule, do not deal fairly and honestly with their consciences. Their favourite question, 'What is truth?' is nothing better than a pretence and an excuse. The words of Solomon will be found true as long as the world stands: 'If thou criest after knowledge, and liftest up thy voice for understanding; if thou seekest her as silver, and searchest for her as for hid treasures; then shalt thou understand the fear of the Lord, and find the knowledge of God' (Prov. 2:4,5). No man ever followed that advice and missed the way to heaven.

For meditation: *John 14:6.*

Suggested further reading: *2 Corinthians 10:1-5*

We should notice in these verses the account that our Lord gives of his own mission. He says, 'To this end was I born, and for this cause came I into the world, that I should bear witness unto the truth.'

Of course, we are not to suppose our Lord meant that this was the only end of his mission. No doubt he spoke with special reference to what he knew was passing through Pilate's mind. He did not come to win a kingdom with the sword and to gather adherents and followers by force. He came armed with no other weapon but 'truth'. To testify to fallen man the truth about God, about sin, about the need of a Redeemer, about the nature of holiness, to declare and lift up before man's eyes this long lost and buried 'truth' was one great purpose of his ministry. He came to be God's witness to a lost and corrupt world. That the world needed such a testimony, he does not shrink from telling the proud Roman governor. And this is what St Paul had in view when he tells Timothy that 'Before Pontius Pilate Christ witnessed a good confession' (1 Tim. 6:13).

The servants of Christ in every age must remember that our Lord's conduct in this place is meant to be their example. Like him, we are to be witnesses to God's truth, salt in the midst of corruption, light in the midst of darkness, men and women not afraid to stand alone and to testify for God against the ways of sin and the world. To do so may entail on us much trouble and even persecution. But the duty is clear and plain. If we love life, if we would keep a good conscience and be owned by Christ at the last day, we must be 'witnesses'. It is written: 'Whosoever shall be ashamed of me and of my words in this adulterous and sinful generation, of him also shall the Son of man be ashamed, when he cometh in the glory of his Father with the holy angels' (Mark 8:38).

For meditation: *The old saying, 'The truth will out,' is as true of real Christianity as of hidden sin.*

Suggested further reading: 2 Timothy 1:1-7

It is quite possible that the fame and character of Jesus had reached Pilate's ears long before he was brought before him. It is hard to suppose that such miracles as our Lord wrought would never be talked of within the palace of the chief ruler of Judæa. The raising of Lazarus must surely have been reported among his servants. Our Lord's triumphal entry into Jerusalem, attended by myriads of people shouting, 'Blessed is the King,' must surely have been noted by the soldiers and officers of Pilate's guard. Can we wonder that all this made him regard our Lord with something like awe? Wicked men are often very superstitious.

The pitiable and miserable character of Pilate, the Roman governor, begins to come into clear light from this point. We see him a man utterly destitute of moral courage, knowing what was right and just in the case before him, yet afraid to act on his knowledge, knowing that our Lord was innocent, yet not daring to displease the Jews by acquitting him, knowing that he was doing wrong and yet afraid to do right. 'The fear of man bringeth a snare' (Prov. 29:25). Wretched and contemptible are those rulers and statesmen whose first principle is to please the people, even at the expense of their own consciences, and who are ready to do what they know to be wrong rather than offend the mob! Wretched are those nations which for their sins are given over to be governed by such statesmen! True godly rulers should lead the people and not be led by them, should do what is right and leave consequences to God. A base determination to keep in with the world at any price and a slavish fear of man's opinion were leading principles in Pilate's character. There are many like him. Nothing is more common than to see statesmen evading the plain line of duty and trying to shuffle responsibility on others, rather than give offence to the mob. This is precisely what Pilate did here. The spirit of his reply to the Jews is 'I had rather not be troubled with the case. Cannot you settle it yourselves, without asking me to interfere?'

For meditation: *Christians are not called to be timid, but bold in the Spirit (Acts 4:31).*

Suggested further reading: 2 Corinthians 5:14-21

Verse 40 describes the complete failure of Pilate's notable plan, by which he hoped to satisfy the Jews and yet release Jesus. The fierce and bigoted party of Caiaphas would not listen to his proposal for a moment. They declared they would rather have Barabbas, a notorious prisoner in the hands of the Romans, released than Jesus. Nothing would content them but our Lord's death. Barabbas, we know from St Luke (23:19), was a murderer as well as a robber. The Jews were asked to decide whether the holy Jesus or the vile criminal should be let go free and released from prison. Such was their utter hardness, bitterness, cruelty and hatred of our Lord that they actually declare they would rather have Barabbas set free than Jesus! Nothing in short would satisfy them but Christ's blood. Thus they committed the great sin which Peter charges home on them not long after: 'Ye denied Jesus in the presence of Pilate, when he was determined to let him go . . . Ye denied the Holy One and the Just, and desired a murderer to be granted unto you' (Acts 3:13,14). They publicly declared that they liked a robber and a murderer better than Christ!

We have here a lively illustration of the great Christian doctrine of substitution. Barabbas, the real criminal, is acquitted and let go free. Jesus, innocent and guiltless, is condemned and sentenced to death. So is it in the salvation of our souls. We are all by nature like Barabbas and deserve God's wrath and condemnation; yet he was accounted righteous and set free. The Lord Jesus Christ is perfectly innocent and yet he is counted a sinner, punished as a sinner and put to death that we may live. Christ suffers, though guiltless, that we may be pardoned. We are pardoned, though guilty, because of what Christ does for us. We are sinners and yet counted righteous. Christ is righteous and yet counted a sinner. Happy is that man who understands this doctrine and has laid hold on it by faith for the salvation of his own soul.

For meditation: *Because the sinless Saviour died,*
                       My sinful soul is counted free
                                                    (Bancroft).

Suggested further reading: Leviticus 16:18-22

The cruel injury inflicted on our Lord's body was a punishment sometimes so painful and violent that the sufferer died under it. As to Pilate's reason for inflicting this punishment on our Lord, there seems little doubt. He secretly hoped that this tremendous scourging in the Roman fashion would satisfy the Jews and that after seeing Jesus beaten, bleeding and torn with rods, they would be content to let him go free. As usual he was double-minded, cruel and deceitful. He tried to please the Jews by ill-treating our Lord as much as possible and at the same time he hoped to please his own conscience a little by not putting him to death. He told the Jews, indeed, according to Luke's account, what he wanted: 'I will chastise him and release him' (Luke 23:16). How entirely this weak design failed we shall see by and by.

The importance of this particular portion of our Lord's sufferings is strongly shown by the fact that Isaiah specially says, 'By his stripes we are healed,' and that St Peter specially quotes that text in his first epistle (Isa. 53:5; 1 Peter 2:24). Our Lord himself particularly foretold that he would be scourged (Luke 18:33).

We see his complete and perfect substitution for sinners. He, the innocent sin-bearer, wore the crown of thorns, that we, the guilty, might wear a crown of glory. Vast is the contrast which there will be between the crown of glory that Christ will wear at his second advent and the crown of thorns which he wore at this first coming.

It was, moreover, a striking symbol of the consequences of the Fall being laid on the head of our divine Substitute. In Leviticus it is written that Aaron shall lay his hands 'upon the head of the live goat, and confess over him all the iniquities of the children of Israel, and all their transgression in all their sins, putting them upon the head of the goat' (Lev. 16:21).

For meditation:
> *The head that once was crowned with thorns,*
> *Is crowned with glory now*
>   (Kelly).

Suggested further reading: *2 Corinthians 11:23-29*

A mock royal robe was thrown over our Lord's shoulders in order to show how ridiculous and contemptible was the idea of his kingdom. The colour 'purple' was doubtless meant to be a derisive imitation of the well-known imperial purple, the colour worn by emperors and kings. Some have thought that this robe was only an old soldier's cape, such as a guardhouse would easily furnish. Some, with more show of probability, have thought that this 'robe' must be the 'gorgeous robe' which Herod put on our Lord, mentioned by St Luke when he sent him back to Pilate (Luke 23:11), a circumstance which John has not recorded. In any case we need not doubt that the 'robe' was some shabby, cast-off garment. It is worth remembering that this brilliant colour, scarlet or purple, would make our blessed Lord a most conspicuous object to every eye, when he was led through the streets from Herod, or brought forth from Pilate's house to the assembled multitude of Jews. Once more we should call to mind the symbolical nature of this transaction also. Our Lord was clothed with a robe of shame and contempt, that we might be clothed with a spotless garment of righteousness and stand in white robes before the throne of God.

The words of the soldiers were spoken in contemptuous imitation of the words addressed to a Roman emperor, on his assuming imperial power: 'Hail, Emperor! *Ave Imperator!* Let us not fail to remark at this point that ridicule, scorn and contempt were one prominent portion of our blessed Master's sufferings. Anyone who knows human nature must know that few things are more difficult to bear than ridicule, especially when we know that it is undeserved and when it is for religion's sake. Those who have to endure such ridicule may take comfort in the thought that Christ can sympathize with them, for it is a cup which he himself drank to the very dregs. Here again he was our Substitute. He bore contempt that we might receive praise and glory at the last day.

For meditation: *Psalm 22:6-8.*

Suggested further reading: 1 Peter 2:21-25

The Roman governor went forth outside the palace where he lived to the Jews, who were waiting to hear the result of his private interview with our Lord. We must remember that, under the influence of hypocritical scrupulosity, they would not go inside the Gentile governor's house, lest they should be 'defiled', and were therefore waiting in the court outside. Now Pilate comes out of his palace and speaks to them. The words of the verse seem to show that Pilate came out first and that our Lord was led out behind him. 'Behold I am bringing him outside again, that you may know that I can find no fault or cause of condemnation in him, and no ground for your charge that he is a stirrer up of sedition and a rebel king. He is only a weak, harmless fanatic, who lays claim to no kingdom of this world, and I bring him forth to you as a poor, contemptible person worthy of scorn, but not one that I can pronounce worthy of death. I have examined him myself and I inform you that I can see no harm in him.'

It seems to me quite plain that Pilate's private interview with our Lord had completely satisfied the governor that he was a harmless, innocent person and made him feel a strong desire to dismiss him unhurt, and he secretly hoped that the Jews would be satisfied when they saw the prisoner whom they had accused brought out beaten and bruised and treated with scorn and contempt and that they would not press the charge any further. How thoroughly this cowardly double-dealing man was disappointed and what violence he had to do to his own conscience, we shall soon see.

It is very noteworthy that the expression: 'I find no fault in him,' is used three times by Pilate, in the same Greek words, in St John's account of the passion (John 18:38; 19:4-6). It was meet and right that he who had the chief hand in slaying the Lamb of God, the sacrifice for our sins, should three times publicly declare that he found no spot or blemish in him. He was proclaimed a Lamb without spot or fault , after a searching examination, by him that slew him.

For meditation: *Acts 3:14.*

Suggested further reading: Leviticus 24:10-16

The 'law' referred to by the Jews is probably Leviticus 24:16. But it is curious that 'stoning' is the punishment there mentioned and not a word is said of crucifixion. This they do not tell Pilate. There is, perhaps, more fulness in the expression 'a law' than appears at first. It may mean, 'We Jews have a law given us by man from God, which is our rule of faith in religion. It is a law, we know, not binding on Gentiles, but it is a law which we feel bound to obey. One of the articles of that law is that "He that blasphemeth the name of the Lord shall be stoned." We ask that this article may be enforced in the case of this man. He has blasphemed by calling himself the Son of God and he ought to be put to death. We, therefore, demand his life.' There certainly seems an emphasis in the Greek on the word 'we', as if it meant 'we Jews', in contradistinction to Gentiles.

The expression 'Son of God' meant far more to a Jewish mind that it does to us. We see in John 5:18 that the Jews considered that when our Lord said that God was his Father he made himself 'equal with God'. See also John 10:33. One thing at any rate is very clear: whatever Socinians may say, our Lord distinctly laid claim to divinity and the Jews distinctly understood him to mean that he was God as well as man.

Cyril well remarks that if the Jews had dealt justly, they would have told the Gentile ruler that the person before him had not only claimed to be the Son of God, but had also done many miracles in proof of his divinity.

Rollock observes, 'Look, what blinds them! The Word of God, that should make them see, blinds them so that they use it to their ruin. The best things in the world, yea the Word of God itself, serve to wicked men for nothing else but their induration. The more they read, the blinder they are. And why? Because they abuse the Word and make it not a guide to direct their affections and actions.'

For meditation: *Isaiah 9:6.*

Suggested further reading: *Romans 2:12-16*

In verse 8 we see Pilate in a different frame of mind. This new charge of blasphemy against our Lord threw a new light over his feelings. He began to be really frightened and uncomfortable. The thought that the meek and gentle prisoner before him might after all be some superior being, and not a mere common man, filled his weak and ignorant conscience with alarm. What if he had before him some god in human form? What if it should turn out that he was actually inflicting bodily injuries on one of the gods? As a Roman he had doubtless heard and read many stories, drawn from the heathen mythology of Greece and Rome, about gods coming down to earth and appearing in human form. Perhaps the prisoner before him was one! The idea raised new fears in his mind. Already he had been made very uncomfortable about him. Our Lord's calm, dignified and majestic demeanour had doubtless made an impression. His evident innocence of all guilt and the extraordinary malice of his enemies, whose characters Pilate most likely knew well, had produced an effect. His own wife's dream had its influence. Even before the last charge of the Jews, the Roman judge had been awestruck and secretly convinced of our Lord's innocence and anxious to have him set free and actually 'afraid' of his prisoner. But when he heard of his being the 'Son of God', he was made more afraid.

Can we doubt for a moment that he must have heard many accounts of our Lord's ministry and specially of his miracles and astonishing power over the sick and the dead? Can we doubt that he heard of the raising of Lazarus at Bethany within a walk of Jerusalem? Remembering all this, we may well suppose that he regarded the whole case brought before him by the Jews with much anxiety from the very first and we can well understand that when he heard that Jesus was 'the Son of God', he was more than ever alarmed. Unprincipled rulers have an uneasy position.

For meditation: *To suppress conscience is always sinful.*

Suggested further reading: *Ecclesiastes 3:1-8*

Our Lord's silence, when this appeal was made to him by Pilate, is very striking. Hitherto he had spoken freely and replied to questions; now he refused to speak any more. The reason of our Lord's silence must be sought in the state of Pilate's soul. He deserved no answer and therefore got none. He had forfeited his title to any further revelation about his prisoner. He had been told plainly the nature of our Lord's kingdom and the purpose of our Lord's coming into the world and been obliged to confess publicly his innocence. And yet, with all this light and knowledge, he had treated our Lord with flagrant injustice, scourged him, allowed him to be treated with the vilest indignities by his soldiers and held him up to scorn, knowing in his own mind all the time that he was a guiltless person. He had, in short, sinned away his opportunities, forsaken his own mercies and turned a deaf ear to the cries of his own conscience. Hence our Lord would have nothing more to do with him and would tell him nothing more. 'He gave him no answer.'

Here, as in many other cases, we learn that God will not force conviction on men and will not compel obstinate unbelievers to believe and will not always strive with men's consciences. Most men, like Pilate, have a day of grace and an open door put before them. If they refuse to enter in, and choose their own sinful way, the door is often shut and never opened again. There is such a thing as a 'day of visitation', when Christ speaks to men. If they will not hear his voice and open the door of their hearts, they are often let alone, given over to a reprobate mind and left to reap the fruit of their own sins. It was so with Pharaoh and Saul and Ahab, and Pilate's case was like theirs. He had his opportunity and did not choose to use it, but preferred to please the Jews at the expense of his conscience and to do what he knew was wrong. We see the consequence. Our Lord will tell him nothing more.

For meditation: *Matthew 7:6.*

Suggested further reading: Daniel 4:24-27

We see the imperious, fierce, haughty, arrogant temper of the Roman governor breaking out. Accustomed to see prisoners cringing before him and willing to do anything to obtain his favour, he could not understand our Lord's silence. He addresses him in a tone of anger and surprise combined: 'Why dost thou not answer my question? Dost thou know what thou art doing in offending me? Dost thou not know that thou art at my mercy and that I have power to crucify thee or release thee, according as I think right?' I can see no other reasonable construction that can be put on Pilate's words. The idea that the was only persuading our Lord and gently reminding him of his own power seems utterly unreasonable and inconsistent with the following verse.

This high-minded claim to absolute power is one which ungodly great men are fond of making. It is written of Nebuchadnezzar, 'Whom he would he slew, and whom he would he kept alive; and whom he would he set up, and whom he would he put down' (Dan. 5:19). Yet even when such men boast of power, they are often like Pilate, mere slaves and afraid of resisting popular opinion. Pilate talked of 'power to release', but he knew in his own mind that he was afraid and so unable to exercise it.

Our Lord's reply to Pilate may be paraphrased thus: 'Thou speakest of power. Thou dost not know that both thou and the Jews are only tools in the hand of a higher being and that thou couldst have no power whatever against me, if it were not given thee by God. This, however, thou dost not understand and art therefore less guilty than the Jews. The Jews who delivered me into thine hand do know that all power is from God. Thus their knowledge makes them more guilty than thou. Both thou and they are committing a great sin, but their sin is a sin against knowledge and thine is comparatively a sin of ignorance. You are both unconsciously mere instruments in the hand of God and you could do nothing against me, if God did not permit and overrule it.'

For meditation: *Psalm 82:6, 7.*

Suggested further reading: 1 Thessalonians 2:1-6

We see the Jews stopping Pilate short, in his weak efforts to get our Lord released, by an argument which they well knew would weigh heavily on a Roman mind. They tell him plainly that they will accuse him to Cæsar, the Roman emperor, as a governor unfriendly to the imperial interests. 'You are no friend to Cæsar if you let off this prisoner. Everyone who sets himself up as a king, be his kingdom what it may, is usurping part of Cæsar's authority and is a rebel. If you pass over this man's claim to be a king and set him at liberty, we shall complain of you to Cæsar.' This was a settling and clinching argument. Pilate knew well that his own government of Judæa would not bear any investigation. He also knew well the cold, suspicious, cruel character of Tiberius Cæsar, the Emperor of Rome, which is specially mentioned by Tacitus and Suetonius, the Roman historians, and he might well dread the result of any appeal to him from the Jews. From this moment all his hopes of getting rid of this anxious case and letting our Lord go away unharmed were dashed to the ground. He would rather connive at a murder to please the Jews than allow himself to be charged with neglect of imperial interests and unfriendliness to Cæsar.

It is hard to say which was the more wretched and contemptible sight at this point of the history — Pilate trampling on his own conscience to avoid the possible displeasure of an earthly monarch, or the Jews pretending to care for Cæsar's interests and warning Pilate not to do anything unfriendly to him! It was a melancholy exhibition of cowardice on the one side and duplicity on the other and the whole result was a foul murder!

Men like Pontius Pilate, who are always trimming and compromising, led by popular opinion instead of leading popular opinion, afraid of doing right if it gives offence, ready to do wrong if it makes them personally popular — such men are the worst governors that a country can have. They are often God's heavy judgement on a nation because of a nation's sins.

For meditation: *Are you a man-pleaser or a God-pleaser?*

Suggested further reading: 1 Timothy 2:1-7

That our blessed Lord, the eternal Word, should have meekly submitted to be led out after this fashion, as a gazing-stock and an object of scorn, with an old purple robe on his shoulders and a crown of thorns on his head, his back bleeding from scourging and his head from thorns, to feast the eyes of a taunting, howling, bloodthirsty crowd, is indeed a wondrous thought! Truly, 'Though he was rich, yet for our sakes he became poor' (2 Cor. 8:9). Since the world began, the sun never shone on a more surprising spectacle both for angels and men.

'Behold the man.' This famous sentence, so well known as *'Ecce Homo'* in Latin, admits of two views being taken of it. Pilate may have spoken it in contempt: 'Behold the man you accuse of setting himself up as a king! See what a weak, helpless, contemptible creature he is.' Or else Pilate may have spoken it in pity: 'Behold the poor feeble man whom you want me to sentence to death. Surely your demands may be satisfied by what I have done to him. Is he not punished enough?' Perhaps both views are correct. In any case there can be little doubt that the latent feeling of Pilate was the hope that the Jews, on seeing our Lord's miserable condition, would be content and would allow him to be let go. In this hope, again, we shall find he was completely deceived.

Pilate probably threw a strong emphasis on the expression 'man', indicative of contempt. This may have led to the Jews saying so strongly in the seventh verse that the prisoner 'made himself the Son of God' and claimed to be divine and not a mere 'man', as Pilate had said. He probably also meant the Jews to mark that he said, 'Behold the man,' not 'your king', but a mere common man.

We see in verse 15 the complete failure of Pilate's secret scheme for avoiding the condemnation of our Lord. The pitiful sight of the bleeding and despised prisoner had not the effect of softening down the feelings of his cruel enemies. They would not be content with anything but his death and the moment he appeared they raised the fierce cry, 'Crucify him, crucify him.'

For meditation: *'A man of sorrows.'*

Suggested further reading: *Matthew 10:37-39*

Our Lord had to bear his cross when he went forth from the city to Golgotha. We need not doubt that there was a deep meaning in all this circumstance. For one thing, it was part of that depth of humiliation to which our Lord submitted as our Substitute. One portion of the punishment imposed on the vilest criminals was that they should carry their own cross when they went to execution, and this portion was laid upon our Lord. In the fullest sense he was reckoned a sinner and counted a curse for our sakes. For another thing, it was a fulfilment of the great type of the sin-offering of the Mosaic law. It is written that 'The bullock for the sin-offering, and the goat for the sin-offering, whose blood was brought in to make atonement in the holy place, shall one carry forth without the camp' (Lev. 16:27). Little did the blinded Jews imagine, when they madly hounded on the Romans to crucify Jesus outside the gates, that they were unconsciously perfecting the mightiest sin-offering that was ever seen. It is written: 'Jesus, that he might sanctify the people with his own blood, suffered without the gate' (Heb. 13:12).

Like our Master, we must be content to go forth 'without the camp', bearing his reproach. We must come out from the world and be separate and be willing, if need be, to stand alone. Like our Master, we must be willing to take up our cross daily and to be persecuted both for our doctrine and our practice.

To wear material crosses as an ornament, to place material crosses on churches and tombs — all this is cheap and easy work and entails no trouble. But to have Christ's cross in our hearts, to carry Christ's cross in our daily walk, to know the fellowship of his sufferings, to be made conformable to his death, to have crucified affections and live crucified lives — all this needs self-denial and Christians of this stamp are few and far between.

For meditation: *Christianity provides a cross, not a cushion.*

Suggested further reading: Psalm 22:12-18

They crucified him. This famous mode of execution is so well known to everyone that little need be said of it. The common mode of inflicting it, in all probability, was to strip the criminal, to lay him on the cross on his back, to nail his hands to the two extremities of the cross-piece, or fork of the cross, to nail his feet to the upright piece, or principal stem of the cross, then to raise the cross on end and drop it into a hole prepared for it and then to leave the sufferer to a lingering and painful death. It was a death which combined the maximum of pain with the least immediate destruction of life. The agony of having nails driven through parts so full of nerves and sinews as the hands and feet must have been intense. Yet wounds of the hands and feet are not mortal and do not injure any great leading blood-vessel. Hence a crucified person, even in an eastern climate, exposed to the sun, might live two or three days , enduring extreme pain, without being relieved by death, if he was naturally a very strong man and in vigorous health. This is what we must remember our blessed Lord went through, when we read 'they crucified him'. To a sensitive, delicate-minded person, it is hard to imagine any capital punishment more distressing. This is what Jesus endured willingly for us sinners. Hanging, as it were, between earth and heaven, he exactly filled the type of the brazen serpent which Moses lifted up in the wilderness (John 3:14).

When we remember, beside all this, that our Lord's head was crowned with thorns, his back torn with savage scourging and his whole system weighed down by the mental and bodily agony of the sleepless night following the Lord's Supper, we may have some faint idea of the intensity of his sufferings.

There was the inexpressible misery of gradually increasing and lingering anguish.

For meditation: *The incomparable sufferings of our Lord are well captured by the weeping prophet's description of destroyed Jerusalem (Lam. 1:12).*

Suggested further reading: Zechariah 9:9-13

Our Lord was crucified as a king. The title placed over our Lord's head made this plain and unmistakable. The reader of Greek or Latin or Hebrew could not fail to see that he who hung on the central cross of the three on Golgotha had a royal title over his head. The overruling hand of God so ordered matters that the strong will of Pilate overrode for once the wishes of the malicious Jews. In spite of the chief priests, our Lord was crucified as 'the King of the Jews'.

It was meet and right that so it should be. Even before our Lord was born, the angel Gabriel declared to the virgin Mary, 'The Lord God shall give unto him the throne of his father David, and he shall reign over the house of Jacob for ever, and of his kingdom there shall be no end' (Luke 1:32,33). Almost as soon as he was born there came wise men from the East, saying, 'Where is he that is born King of the Jews?' (Matt. 2:2.) The very week before the crucifixion, the multitude who accompanied our Lord at his triumphal entry into Jerusalem had cried, 'Blessed is the King of Israel that cometh in the name of the Lord' (John 12:13). The current belief of all godly Jews was that when Messiah, the Son of David, came he would come as a king. A kingdom of heaven and a kingdom of God was continually proclaimed by our Lord throughout his ministry. A King indeed he was, as he told Pilate, of a kingdom utterly unlike the kingdoms of this world, but for all that a true King of a true kingdom and a Ruler of true subjects. As such he was born. As such he lived. As such he was crucified. And as such he will come again and reign over the whole earth, King of kings and Lord of lords.

Let us take care that we ourselves know Christ as our King and that his kingdom is set up within our hearts. They only will find him their Saviour at the last day who have obeyed him as King in this world. Let us cheerfully pay him that tribute of faith and love and obedience which he prizes far above gold.

For meditation: *The power of Satan was broken by a crucified King (Col. 2:15).*

Suggested further reading: *Genesis 3:8-13*

Verse 21 brings out the feeling which the sight of Pilate's title excited in the minds of the chief priests. They were annoyed and angry. They did not like the idea of this crucified criminal being publicly declared 'the King of the Jews'. They detected the latent scorn and irony which guided Pilate's hands and lay at the bottom of his mind. They did not like so public an announcement that they had crucified their own king and wanted 'no king but Cæsar'. They were vexed at the implied reflection on themselves. Besides this, they were probably uncomfortable in conscience. Hardened and wicked as they were, they had, many of them, we may be sure, a secret conviction, which they vainly tried to keep down, that they were doing a wrong thing and a thing which by and by they would find it hard to defend either to themselves or others. Hence they tried to get Pilate to alter the title and to make it appear that our Lord was only a pretended king — an impostor who 'said that he was king'.

The hard, haughty, imperious character of the wicked Roman governor comes out forcibly in these words. They show his contempt for the Jews. He was glad to hold them up to scorn and contempt, as a people who crucified their own king. It is likely enough that between his wife and his own conscience and the chief priests, the Roman governor was vexed, worried and irritated and savagely resolved not to gratify the Jews any further in any matter. He had gone as far as he chose in allowing them to murder an innocent and just person. He would not go an inch further. He now made a stand and showed that he could be firm and unyielding and unbending when he liked. It is no uncommon thing to see a wicked man, when he has given way to the devil and trampled on his conscience in one direction, trying to make up for it by being firm in another.

For meditation: *Men will go to any lengths to justify themselves, but will shun repentance.*

Suggested further reading: *Zechariah 3:1-5*

The soldiers having now finished their bloody work, having nailed our Lord to the cross, put the title over his head and reared the cross on end, proceeded to do what they probably always did — to divide the clothes of the crucified criminal among themselves. In most countries the clothes of a person put to death by the law are the perquisite of the executioner. So it was with our Lord's clothes. They had most likely first stripped our Lord naked, before nailing his hands and feet to the cross, and had laid his clothes on one side till they had finished their work. They now turned to the clothes and, as they had done many a time on such occasions, proceeded to divide them.

We are told that the conduct of the soldiers was a precise fulfilment of a prophecy delivered a thousand years before (Ps. 22:18). That prophecy foretold not only that Messiah's garments should be parted and distributed, but that men should 'cast lots for his vesture'. Little did the four rough Roman soldiers think that they were actually supplying evidence of the truth of the Scriptures! They only saw that our Lord's 'coat' was a good and serviceable garment, which it was a pity to rend or tear, and therefore they agreed to cast lots who should have it. And yet, in so doing, they added to the great cloud of witnesses who prove the divine authority of the Bible. Men little consider that they are all instruments in God's hand for accomplishing his purposes.

Our Lord was treated, we should observe, just like all common criminals — stripped naked and his clothes sold under his eyes, as one dead already and cast off by man.

It is noteworthy that in this, as in many other things, our Lord was, in striking manner, our Substitute. He was stripped naked and reckoned and dealt with as a guilty sinner, in order that we might be clothed with the garment of his perfect righteousness and reckoned innocent.

For meditation: *God even makes the small malicious acts of man's spite serve him.*

Suggested further reading: Luke 8:1-3

A wonderfully striking incident is recorded in this and the two following verses, which is not found in the other three Gospels. St John tells us that at this awful moment, Mary, the mother of Jesus, and other women — two if not three — stood by the cross on which our Lord hung. 'Love is strong as death' and even amidst the crowd of taunting Jews and rough Roman soldiers these holy women were determined to stand by our Lord to the last and to show their unceasing affection to him. When we remember that our Lord was a condemned criminal, peculiarly hated by the chief priests and executed by Roman soldiers, the faithfulness and courage of these holy women can never be sufficiently admired. As long as the world stands, they supply a glorious proof of what grace can do for the weak and of the strength that love to Christ can supply. When all men but one forsook our Lord, more than one woman boldly confessed him. Women, in short, were the last at the cross and the first at the tomb.

Mary, the mother of our Lord (never called the 'virgin Mary' in Scripture) was there. Who can doubt that when she saw her Son hanging on the cross, she must have realized the truth of old Simeon's prophecy: 'A sword shall pierce through thine own soul also'? (Luke 2:35.)

Why the fierce enemies of our Lord among the Jews and the rough Roman soldiers permitted these holy women to stand undisturbed by the cross is a question we have no means of deciding. Possibly the centurion who superintended the execution may have felt some pity for the little weeping company of weak women. Who can tell but his kindness was a cup of cold water which was repaid him a hundredfold? He said before the day ended, 'Truly this was the Son of God' (Matt. 27:54).

For meditation: *The Scriptures give Christian women much usefulness in supporting roles in the church and home. Their relation to men is one of functional difference, not of inferiority.*

Suggested further reading: Philippians 2:1-4

We are told that even in the awful agonies of body and mind which our Lord endured, he did not forget her of whom he was born. He mercifully remembered her desolate condition and the crushing effect of the sorrowful sight before her. He knew that, holy as she was, she was only a woman and that, as a woman, she must deeply feel the death of such a Son. He therefore commended her to the protection of his best-loved and best-loving disciple in brief and touching words: 'Woman,' he said, 'behold thy son! Then saith he to the disciple, Behold thy mother! And from that hour that disciple took her unto his own home.'

We surely need no stronger proof than we have here that Mary, the mother of Jesus, was never meant to be honoured as divine, or to be prayed to, worshipped and trusted in as the friend and patroness of sinners. Common sense points out that she who needed the care and protection of another was never likely to help men and women to heaven, or to be in any sense a mediator between God and man! It is not too much to say, however painful the assertion, that of all the inventions of the church of Rome, there never was one more utterly devoid of foundation, both in Scripture and reason, than the doctrine of Mary-worship.

Let us turn from points of controversy to a subject of far more practical importance. Let us take comfort in the thought that we have in Jesus a Saviour of matchless tenderness, matchless sympathy, matchless consideration for the condition of his believing people. Let us never forget his words: 'Whosoever shall do the will of God, the same is my brother, and my sister, and my mother' (Mark 3:35). The heart that even on the cross felt for Mary is a heart that never changes. Jesus never forgets any that love him and even in their worst estate remembers their need. No wonder that Peter says, 'Casting all your care upon him, for he careth for you' (1 Peter 5:7).

For meditation: *Even in death our Lord put others first.*

Suggested further reading: Luke 16:19-24

Nothing in the details of our Lord's death, we must always remember, was accidental or by chance. Every part of the great sacrifice for sin was foreordained and arranged in the eternal counsels of the Trinity, even to the words which he was to speak on the cross.

The expression 'I thirst' was chiefly used, I believe, in order to afford a public testimony of the reality and intensity of his bodily sufferings and to prevent anyone supposing, because of his marvellous calmness and patience, that he was miraculously free from suffering. On the contrary, he would have all around him know that he felt what all severely wounded persons and especially what all crucified persons felt — a burning and consuming thirst. So that when we read that 'He suffered for sins,' we are to understand that he really and truly suffered.

Henry observes, 'The torments of hell are represented by a violent thirst in the complaint of the rich man who begged for a drop of water to cool his tongue. To that everlasting thirst we had all been condemned if Christ had not suffered on the cross, and said, "I thirst."'

It is very noteworthy that even in the roughest, hardest kind of men, like these heathen soldiers, there is sometimes a tender and compassionate spot in the breast. According to Matthew's account the cry, 'I thirst,' must have followed soon after the cry, 'My God, my God, why hast thou forsaken me?' This exhibition of great mental and bodily agony combined, in my opinion, touched the feelings of the soldiers and one of them at least ran to give our Lord vinegar. We should remember this in dealing with men. Even the worst have often a soft place, if we can find it out, in their inward nature.

For meditation: *Our Lord entered fully into the deepest experiences of human suffering, so as to be made like us.*

Suggested further reading: Hebrews 10:1-14

Our Lord having now given plain proof that he had endured intense bodily suffering and that, like any other human sufferer, he could appreciate a slight relief of thirst, such as the vinegar afforded, proceeded to utter one of his last and most solemn sayings: 'It is finished.'

This remarkable expression, in the Greek, is one single word in a perfect tense: 'It has been completed.' It stands here in majestic simplicity, without note or comment from St John, and we are left entirely to conjecture what the full meaning of it is. For nineteen hundred years Christians have explained it as they best can and some portion of its meaning in all likelihood has been discovered. Yet it is far from unlikely that such a word, spoken on such an occasion, by such a person, at such a moment, just before death, contains depths which no one has ever completely fathomed. Some meanings there are, which no one perhaps will dispute, belonging to this grand expression which I will briefly mention. No one single meaning, we may be sure, exhausts the whole phrase. It is rich, full and replete with deep truths.

Our Lord meant that his great work of redemption was finished. He had, as Daniel foretold, 'finished transgression, made an end of sin, made reconciliation for iniquity, and brought in everlasting righteousness' (Dan. 9:24). After thirty-three years, since the day when he was born in Bethlehem, he had done all, paid all, performed all, suffered all that was needful to save sinners and satisfy the justice of God. He had fought the battle and won it and in two days would give proof of it by rising again.

Our Lord meant that God's determinate counsel and fore-will concerning his death was now accomplished and finished. All that had been appointed from all eternity that he should suffer, he had now suffered.

For meditation: *We rejoice in an accomplished salvation that needs nothing but to be received.*

Suggested further reading: *Hebrews 9:11-14*

Our Lord meant that he had finished the work of keeping God's holy law. He had kept it to the uttermost, as our Head and Representative, and Satan had found nothing in him. He had magnified the law and made it honourable by doing perfectly all its requirements. 'Woe unto us, ' says Burkitt, 'if Christ had left but one farthing of our debt unpaid. We must have lain in hell insolvent to all eternity.'

Our Lord meant that he had finished the types and figures of the ceremonial law. He had at length offered up the perfect sacrifice, of which every Mosaic sacrifice was a type and symbol, and there remained no more need of offerings for sin. The old covenant was finished.

Our Lord meant that he had finished and fulfilled the prophecies of the Old Testament. At length, as the seed of the woman, he had bruised the serpent's head and accomplished the work which Messiah was engaged by covenant to come and perform.

Our Lord meant that his sufferings were finished. Like his apostle, he had 'finished his course'. His long life of pain and contradiction from sinners, and above all his intense sufferings as bearer of our sins on Gethsemane and Calvary, were at last at an end. The storm was over and the worst was passed. The cup of suffering was at last drained to the very dregs.

Luther remarks, 'In this word, "It is finished," will I comfort myself. I am forced to confess that all *my* finishing of the will of God is imperfect, piecemeal work, while yet the law urges on me that not so much as one tittle of it must remain unaccomplished. Christ is the end of the law. What it requires, Christ has performed.'

For meditation: *He left no work undone that was necessary to our full and eternal salvation.*

Suggested further reading: Hebrews 9:22-28

Above all, let us never forget, as we read of Christ's death, that he died for our sins, as our Substitute. His death is our life. He died that we might live. We who believe on Christ shall live for evermore, sinners as we are, because Christ died for us, the innocent for the guilty. Satan cannot drag us away to ever-lasting death in hell. The second death cannot harm us. We may safely say, 'Who can condemn me, or slay my soul? I know well that I deserve death and that I ought to die because of my sins. But then my blessed Head and Substitute died for me and when he died, I, his poor weak member, was reckoned to die also. Get thee behind me, Satan, for Christ was crucified and died. My debt is paid and thou canst not demand it twice over.' Forever let us bless God that Christ ' gave up the ghost' and really died upon the cross, before myriads of witnesses. That 'giving up the ghost' was the hinge on which all our salvation turned. In vain Christ's life and miracles and preaching, if Christ had not at last died for us! We needed not merely a teacher, but an atonement and the death of a substitute. The mightiest transaction that ever took place on earth since the fall of man was accomplished when Jesus 'gave up the ghost'. The careless crowd around the cross saw nothing but the common death of a common criminal. But in the eyes of God the Father the promised payment for a world's sin was at last effected and the kingdom of heaven was thrown wide open to all believers. The finest pictures of the crucifixion that artists have ever painted give a miserably insufficient idea of what took place when Jesus 'gave up the ghost'. They can show a suffering man on a cross, but they cannot convey the least notion of what was really going on — the satisfaction of God's broken law, the payment of sinners' debt to God and the complete atonement for a world's sin.

For meditation: *God will not require double payment for sin – first from Christ, then from us.*

Suggested further reading: Revelation 1:12-18

The order of the famous seven sayings was as follows:

1. 'Father, forgive them; for they know not what they do.'
2. 'Today shalt thou be with me in paradise.'
3. 'Woman, behold thy son! . . . Behold thy mother.'
4. 'My God, my God, why hast thou forsaken me?'
5. 'I thirst.'
6. 'It is finished.'
7. 'Father, into thy hands I commend my spirit.'

In order to understand verse 30 aright, there is one point concerning our Lord's death which must be carefully remembered. His death was entirely a voluntary act on his part. In this one respect his death was unlike that of a common man, and we need not wonder at it when we consider that he was God and man in one person. The final separation between body and soul in his case could not take place until he willed it and all the power of Jews and Romans together could not have effected it against his will. We die because we cannot help it; Christ died because he willed to die and not until the moment arrived when he saw it best. He said himself, 'No man taketh life from me, but I lay it down of myself. I have power to lay it down, and I have power to take it again' (John 10:18). As a matter of fact, we know that our Lord was crucified about nine o'clock in the morning and that he died about three o' clock in the afternoon of the same day. Mere physical suffering would not acount for this. A person crucified in full health was known sometimes to linger on alive for three days! It is evident therefore that our Lord willed to give up the ghost in the same day that he was crucified, for some wise reason. This reason, we can easily suppose, was to secure the fullest publicity for his atoning death. He died in broad daylight, in the sight of myriads of spectators, and thus the reality of his death could never be denied. This voluntariness and free choice of his death and of the hour of his death, in my judgement, lie at the bottom of the verse before us.

For meditation: *Only God has the power of life and death – Jehovah-Jesus exercised this power.*

Suggested further reading: Isaiah 46:8-13

The 'breaking of the legs' of crucified criminals, in order to despatch them, seems to have been a common accompaniment of this barbarous mode of execution, when it was necessary to make an end of them and get them out of the way. In asking Pilate to allow this breaking of the legs, they did nothing but what was usual. But for anything we can see, the thing would not have been done if the Jews had not asked. The verse supplies a wonderful example of the way in which God can make the wickedest men unconsciously carry out his purposes and promote his glory. If the Jews had not interfered this Friday afternoon, for anything we can see, Pilate would have allowed our Lord's body to hang upon the cross till Sunday or Monday and perhaps to see corruption. The Jews procured our Lord's burial the very day that he died and thus secured the fulfilment of his famous prophecy: 'Destroy this temple of my body, and in three days I will raise it up' (John 2:19). If he had not been buried till Sunday or Monday, he could not have risen again the third day after his death. As it was, the Jews managed things so that our Lord was laid in the grave before the evening of Friday and was thus enabled to fulfil the famous type of Jonah and give the sign he had promised to give of his Messiahship, by lying three days in the earth and then rising again the third day after he died. All this could not have happened if the Jews had not interfered and got him taken from the cross and buried on Friday afternoon! How true it is that the wickedest enemies of God are only axes and saws and hammers in his hands and are ignorantly his instruments for doing his work in the world. The restless, busy meddling of Caiaphas and his companions was actually one of the causes that Christ rose the third day after death and his Messiahship was proved. Pilate was their tool, but they were God's tools! The Romans, in all probability, would have left our Lord's body hanging on the cross till sun and rain had putrefied and consumed it, had such a thing been possible.

For meditation: *Even the enemies of God ultimately fulfil his purpose and assure his victory.*

Suggested further reading: Zechariah 12:10-13:1

We are told that 'One of the soldiers with a spear pierced his side, and forthwith came there out blood and water.' This incident, small as it may seem at first sight, supplies probable proof that the heart of our blessed Lord was pierced and that life was consequently extinct. He did not merely faint, or swoon away, or become insensible, as some have dared to insinuate. His heart actually ceased to beat and he actually died. Great indeed was the importance of this fact. We must all see, on a moment's reflection, that without a real death there could be no real sacrifice, that without a real death there could be no real resurrection and that without a real death and real resurrection, the whole of Christianity is a house built on sand and has no foundation at all. Little indeed did that reckless Roman soldier dream that he was a mighty helper of our holy religion, when he thrust his spear into our Lord's side.

That the 'blood and water' mentioned in this place had a deep spiritual meaning, we can hardly doubt. St John himself seems to refer to them in his First Epistle as highly significant: 'This is he that came by water and blood' (1 John 5:6).

The true meaning of the blood and water is probably to be sought in the famous prophecy of Zechariah, where he says, 'In that day there shall be a fountain opened to the house of David, and to the inhabitants of Jerusalem, for sin and uncleanness' (Zech. 13:1). When was that fountain so truly and really opened as in the hour when Christ died? What emblem of atonement and purification was so well known to the Jews as blood and water? Why then should we hesitate to believe that the flow of 'blood and water' from our Lord's side was a significant declaration to the Jewish nation that the true fountain for sin was at length thrown open and that henceforth sinners might come boldly to Christ for pardon and wash and be clean? Let us make sure that we ourselves are 'washed and made white in the blood of the Lamb' (Rev. 7:14).

For meditation: *The blood of Jesus Christ cleanses us from every sin (1 John 1:7).*

Suggested further reading: Matthew 5:17-20

Three several predictions are specially mentioned, in Exodus, Psalms and Zechariah, which received their accomplishment at the cross. Others, as every well-informed Bible-reader knows, might easily be added. All combine to prove one and the same thing. They prove that the death of our Lord Jesus Christ at Golgotha was a thing foreseen and predetermined by God. Hundreds of years before the crucifixion, every part of the solemn transaction was arranged in the divine counsels and the minutest particulars were revealed to the prophets. From first to last it was a thing foreknown and every portion of it was in accordance with a settled plan and design. In the highest, fullest sense, when Christ died, he 'died according to the Scriptures' (1 Cor. 15:3).

We need not hesitate to regard such fulfilments of prophecy as strong evidence of the divine authority of God's Word. The prophets foretell not only Christ's death, but the particulars of his death. It is impossible to explain so many accomplishments of predicted circumstances upon any other theory. To talk of luck, chance and accidental coincidence as sufficient explanation is preposterous and absurd. The only rational account is the inspiration of God. The prophets who foretold the particulars of the crucifixion were inspired by him who foresees the end from the beginning, and the books they wrote under his inspiration ought not to be read as human compositions, but divine. Great indeed are the difficulties of all who pretend to deny the inspiration of the Bible. It really requires more unreasoning faith to be an infidel than to be a Christian. The man who regards the repeated fulfilments of minute prophecies about Christ's death, such as the prophecies about his dress, his thirst, his pierced side and his bones, as the result of chance and not of design must indeed be a credulous man.

For meditation: *All the promises of God find their confirmation and fulfilment in Christ (2 Cor. 1:20).*

Suggested further reading: *Matthew 13:31-35*

The Greek word rendered 'secretly' is literally 'a concealed' disciple — a past participle. The expression teaches the interesting fact that there were Jews who secretly believed that Jesus was the Messiah and yet had not courage to confess him before his crucifixion. We are distinctly told in John 12:42, that 'Many of the chief rulers believed, but did not confess Christ, because of the Pharisees.' But the character given of them, that 'They loved the praise of men more than the praise of God,' is so condemnatory that we may well doubt whether Joseph was one of these. Want of physical or moral courage was probably the flaw in his character. It is only fair to remember that, as 'a rich man and a counsellor', he had far more to sacrifice and far more opposition to encounter than poor fishermen or publicans would have. His backwardness to confess Christ cannot, of course, be defended. But his case teaches us that there is sometimes more spiritual work going on in men's minds than appears. We must not set down everyone as utterly graceless and godless, who is not bold and outspoken at present. We must charitably hope that there are some secret disciples, who at present hold their tongues and say nothing, and yet, like Joseph, will one day come forward and be courageous witnesses for Christ. All is not gold that glitters and all is not dross that now looks dirty and makes no show. We must be charitable and hope on. His case should also teach us the great power of that mischievous principle, the fear of man. Open sin kills its thousands, but the fear of man its tens of thousands. Let us watch and pray against it. Faith is the grand secret of victory over it. Like Moses, we must ever live as those who 'see him that is invisible' (Heb. 11:27). And to faith must be added the expulsive power of a new principle, the fear of God. 'I fear God,' said holy Col. Gardiner, 'and there is none else that I need fear.'

For meditation: *Just as a little fear can cripple, so a little faith can make us courageous.*

Suggested further reading: 1 Corinthians 1:26-31

There are some true Christians in the world of whom very little is known. The case of Joseph of Arimathæa teaches this very plainly. Here is a man named among the friends of Christ, whose very name we never find elsewhere in the New Testament and whose history, both before and after this crisis, is completely withheld from the church. He comes forward to do honour to Christ when the apostles had forsaken him and fled. He cares for him and delights to do him service even when dead — not because of any miracle which he saw him do, but out of free and gratuitous love. He does not hesitate to confess himself one of Christ's friends at a time when Jews and Romans alike had condemned him as a malefactor and put him to death. Surely the man who could do such things must have had strong faith! Can we wonder that, wherever the gospel is preached, throughout the whole world, this pious action of Joseph is told of as a memorial of him?

Let us hope and believe that there are many Christians in every age who, like Joseph, are the Lord's hidden servants, unknown to the church and the world, but well known to God. Even in Elijah's time there were seven thousand in Israel who had never bowed the knee to Baal, although the desponding prophet knew nothing of it. Perhaps, at this very day, there are saints in the back streets of some of our great towns, or in the lanes of some of our country parishes, who make no noise in the world and yet love Christ and are loved by him. Ill-health, or poverty, or the daily cares of some laborious calling render it impossible for them to come forward in public, and so they live and die comparatively unknown. Yet the last day may show an astonished world that some of these very people, like Joseph, honoured Christ as much as any on earth and that their names were written in heaven. After all, it is special circumstances that bring to the surface special Christians. It is not those who make the greatest show in the church who are always found the fastest friends of Christ.

For meditation: *Most Christians are not famous in this life, but fame matters far less than faithfulness.*

Suggested further reading: Acts 12:25-13:13

There are some servants of Christ whose latter end is better than their beginning. The case of Nicodemus teaches that lesson very plainly. The only man who dared to help Joseph in his holy work of burying our Lord was one who at first 'came to Jesus by night' and was nothing better than an ignorant inquirer after truth. At a later period in our Lord's ministry we find this same Nicodemus coming forward with somewhat more boldness and raising in the council of the Pharisees the question: 'Doth our law judge any man, before it hear him, and know what he doeth?' (John 7:51.) Finally, we see him in the passage before us ministering to our Lord's dead body and not ashamed to take an active part in giving to the despised Nazarene an honourable burial. How great the contrast between the man who timidly crept into the Lord's lodging to ask a question and the man who brought a hundred pounds weight of myrrh and aloes to anoint his dead body! Yet it was the same Nicodemus.

We shall do well to store up these things in our minds and to remember the case of Nicodemus in forming our estimate of other people's religion. We must not condemn others as graceless and godless, because they do not see the whole truth at once and only reach decided Christianity by slow degrees. The Holy Ghost always leads believers to the same foundation truths and into the same highway to heaven. In these there is invariable uniformity. But the Holy Ghost does not always lead believers through the same experience, or at the same rate of speed. In this there is much diversity in his operations. He that says conversion is a needless thing and that an unconverted man may be saved is undoubtedly under a strange delusion, but he that says that no one is converted except he becomes a full-blown and established Christian in a single day is no less under a delusion.

For meditation: *John Mark soon deserted Paul (Acts 13:13), but later proved so useful (2 Tim. 4:11). A bad beginning saw a good ending.*

Suggested further reading: 2 Timothy 4:9-18

The conduct of Joseph deserves our praise and admiration and his name will be held in honour by the church of Christ, in consequence of it, as long as the world stands. Whatever Joseph was at first, he shone brightly at last. 'The last are first' sometimes. Let us see what he did.

a. Joseph honoured Christ when our Lord's own apostles had forsaken him. He showed more faith and courage than his nearest and dearest friends.

b. Joseph honoured Christ when it was a dangerous thing to do him honour. To come forward and avow respect for one condemned as a malefactor, for one cast out by the high priests and leaders of the Jews, to say practically, 'I am Christ's friend,' was bold indeed. St Mark particularly says, 'He went in boldly unto Pilate' (Mark 15:43), showing plainly that it was an act of uncommon courage.

c. Joseph honoured Christ when he was a lifeless corpse and to all appearance could do nothing for him. It was not when Jesus was doing miracles and preaching wonderful sermons, but when there remained nothing of him but a dead body, that he came forward and asked leave to bury him.

Why Joseph's 'fear' departed and he acted with such marvellous boldness now is a question whch we have no means of settling. But reason points out that in all probability he had been an eyewitness of much that had happened this eventful day. He had possibly stood within a short distance of the cross and seen all that took place and heard every one of our Lord's seven sayings. The miraculous darkness for three hours and the earthquake must have arrested his attention. Surely it is not presumptuous to conjecture that all this must have had a mighty effect on Joseph's soul and made him resolve at once to cast fear away and avow himself openly one of Christ's friends.

For meditation: *Even when all men desert us, our Lord stands with us.*

Suggested further reading: 1 Corinthians 15:1-11

Concerning the evidences of Christ's resurrection — the proofs that he actually did rise again from the grave with his body — it is most remarkable to observe how full and various they are. He was seen at least eleven times after he rose again, at different times of day, in different ways and by different witnesses.

The order of Christ' s eleven appearances between his resurrection and ascension, I believe to be as follows: (1) to Mary Magdalene alone (Mark 16:9; John 20:14); (2) to certain women returning from the sepulchre (Matt. 28:9,10); (3) to Simon Peter alone (Luke 24:34); (4) to two disciples going to Emmaus (Luke 24:13); (5) to ten apostles at Jerusalem and some other disciples, Thomas being absent (John 20:19); (6) to eleven apostles at Jerusalem, Thomas being present (John 20:26-29); (7) to seven disciples fishing at the sea of Tiberias (John 21:1); (8) to eleven apostles on a mountain in Galilee and perhaps some others with them (Matt. 28:16); (9) to above five hundred brethren at once (1 Cor. 15:7); (10) to James only (1 Cor. 15:7); (11) to all the apostles and probably some others on Mount Olivet at his ascension.

He was seen first by one woman alone, then by several women together, then by one man, then by two men and each time in the open air. Then he was seen by ten disciples in the evening in a room, then by eleven disciples again in a room and afterwards on five different occasions, at one of which no less than five hundred people were present. Those to whom he appeared touched him, talked with him and saw him eat and drink (Matt. 28:9; John 20:27; Luke 24:42). Nor must it be forgotten that all who saw him were most unwilling at first to believe and most slow to credit the report of his resurrection. Yet they were all finally convinced!

For meditation: *Few historical events are as well documented as the resurrection of our Lord.*

Suggested further reading: 1 Corinthians 15:12-28

Concerning the importance of Jesus Christ's resurrection from
the dead, it would be hard to speak too strongly. It is a cardinal
article of the Christian faith, second to none in value. It is the
grand proof that he was the promised Messiah whom the
prophets had foretold. It is the one great sign which he named
to the Jews when asked to give convincing evidence of his
divine mission — the sign of the prophet Jonas, the rebuilding
of the temple after destruction (Matt. 12:39; John 2:19-21). If
he did not rise again after three days they were not to believe
him. It is the completion of the work of redemption which he
came into the world to accomplish. It proved that the ransom
was accepted and the victory over sin and death obtained.
Christ 'was delivered for our offences, and raised again for our
justification' (Rom. 4:25). 'We are begotten again unto a lively
hope, by the resurrection of Jesus Christ from the dead' (1
Peter 1:3). If he had not risen again, our hope would have been
a huge uncertainty. It is a fact which has the closest connection
with the spiritual life and position before God of all believers.
They are counted by God as 'risen with Christ' and they should
regard themselves as partakers of Christ's resurrection life and
sitting in heavenly places. Not least, it is the pledge and
assurance of our own resurrection at the last day. We need not
fear death and look at the grave with despair, when we remember that Jesus Christ rose again in the body. As surely as the
Head rose, so shall the members be raised. Let these points
never be forgotten. When we think of them we may understand
why the apostles, in their preaching and epistles, dwell so much
upon the resurrection. Well would it be if modern Christians
thought more about it. Myriads seem unable to look at anything in the gospel except the sacrifice and death of Christ and
altogether pass over his resurrection.

For meditation: *The resurrection is God's great statement that
he is satisfied with the penalty our Lord paid for our sin.*

Suggested further reading: Luke 7:36-50

Those who love Christ most are those who have received most
benefit from him. The first whom St John names among those
who came to Christ's sepulchre is Mary Magdalene. The
history of this faithful woman, no doubt, is hidden in much
obscurity. We are distinctly told that she was one out of whom
the Lord had cast 'seven devils' (Mark 16:9; Luke 8:2) — one
who had been subjected in a peculiar way to Satan's possession
— and one whose gratitude to our Lord for deliverance was a
gratitude that knew no bounds. In short, of all our Lord's followers on earth, none seem to have loved him so much as Mary
Magdalene. None felt that they owed so much to Christ. None
felt so strongly that there was nothing too great to do for
Christ. Hence, as Bishop Andrews beautifully puts it, 'She was
last at his cross and first at his grave. She stayed longest *there*
and was soonest *here*. She could not rest till she was up to seek
him. She sought him while it was yet dark, even before she had
light to seek him by.' In a word, having received much, she
loved much, and loving much, she did much, in order to prove
the reality of her love.

How is it that many, whose faith and grace it would be
uncharitable to deny, work so little, give so little, say so little,
take so little pains to promote Christ's cause and bring glory to
Christ in the world? These questions admit of only one answer.
It is a low sense of debt and obligation to Christ which is the
account of the whole matter. Where sin is not felt at all, nothing
is done, and where sin is little felt, little is done. The man who is
deeply conscious of his own guilt and corruption and deeply
convinced that without the blood and intercession of Christ he
would sink deservedly into the lowest hell, this is the man who
will spend and be spent for Jesus and think that he can never do
enough to show forth his praise.

For meditation: *The depth of our self-giving reflects the depth
of our love.*

Suggested further reading: Galatians 3:26-4:7

There are widely different temperaments in different believers. This is a point which is curiously brought out in the conduct of Peter and John, when Mary Magdalene told them that the Lord's body was gone. We are told that they both ran to the sepulchre, but John, the disciple whom Jesus loved, outran Peter and reached the empty grave first. Then comes out the difference between the two men. John, of the two more gentle, quiet, tender, reserved, retiring, deep-feeling, stooped down and looked in, but went no further. Peter, more hot and zealous and impulsive and fervent and forward, cannot be content without going down into the sepulchre and actually seeing with his own eyes. Both, we may be sure, were deeply attached to our Lord. The hearts of both, at this critical juncture, were full of hopes and fears and anxieties and expectations all tangled together. Yet each behaves in his own characteristic fashion. We need not doubt that these things were intentionally written for our learning.

Let us learn from the case before us to make allowances for wide varieties in the inward character of believers. To do so will save us much trouble in the journey of life and prevent many an uncharitable thought. Let us not judge brethren harshly and set them down in a low place, because they do not see or feel things exactly as we see and feel, and because things do not affect or strike them just as they affect and strike us. The flowers in the Lord's garden are not all of one colour and one scent, though they are all planted by one Spirit. The subjects of his kingdom are not all exactly of one tone and temperament, though they all love the same Saviour and are written in the same book of life. The church of Christ has some in its ranks who are like Peter and some who are like John and a place for all and a work for all to do. Let us love all who love Christ in sincerity and thank God that they love him at all. The great thing is to love Jesus.

For meditation: *Variations in ability, background and race are not to overrule our oneness in Christ.*

Suggested further reading: Matthew 28:11-15

Peter found in the empty tomb the clearest evidence of a deliberate, orderly and calmly done transaction. The linen clothes, in which our Lord's body had been wrapped, were lying by themselves. The napkin which had been tied round his head was rolled up by itself in another place, separate from the linen clothes. There were no symptoms of hurry, haste or fear. All had been done decently and in order. Everything that Peter saw contradicted the idea that the body had been stolen. No thief would have taken so much trouble about the clothes and napkin. In fact the person who had removed the body, whoever it was, must have entailed on himself needless labour, if he removed it as a dead corpse, by unwrapping the linen clothes in which the corpse was buried. The easiest plan would have been to carry away the body just as he found it, wrapped up in linen. Why were the linen clothes taken off and left behind? Why were the removers of the body so careful to take away nothing but the body? Questions like these must have sorely perplexed Peter's mind. The body, he saw plainly, was gone. But there was something in the whole appearance of things which he could not understand.

Chrysostom observes, 'The linen cloths lying was a sign of the resurrection. For neither if any person had removed the body, would they, before doing so, have stripped it; nor if any had stolen it, would they have taken the trouble to remove the napkin and roll it up and lay it in a place by itself. They would have taken the body as it was. On this account, John tells us by anticipation that it was buried with much myrrh, which glues linen to the body not less firmly than lead, in order that when thou hearest that the napkin lay apart, thou mayest not endure those who say he was stolen. A thief would not have been so foolish as to spend so much time on a superfluous matter.'

For meditation: *The only armoury the Jewish leaders had against the **fact** of the resurrection was their lies.*

Suggested further reading: Acts 18:24-28

We are taught in these verses that there may be much ignorance even in true believers. This is a point which is brought out here with singular force and distinctness. John himself, the writer of this Gospel, records of himself and his companion Peter, 'As yet they knew not the Scripture, that he must rise again from the dead.' How truly wonderful this seems! For three long years these two leading apostles had heard our Lord speak of his own resurrection as fact and yet they had not understood him. Again and again, he had staked the truth of his Messiahship on his rising from the dead and yet they had never taken in his meaning. We little realize the power over the mind which is exercised by wrong teaching in childhood and by early prejudices imbibed in our youth. Surely the Christian minister has little right to complain of ignorance among his hearers, when he marks the ignorance of Peter and John under the teaching of Christ himself.

After all, we must remember that true grace, and not head knowledge, is the one thing needful. We are in the hands of a merciful and compassionate Saviour, who passes by and pardons much ignorance when he sees 'a heart right in the sight of God'. Some things indeed we must know and without knowing them we cannot be saved. Our own sinfulness and guilt, the office of Christ as a Saviour, the necessity of repentance and faith — such things as these are essential to salvation. But he that knows these things may, in other respects, be a very ignorant man. In fact, the extent to which one man may have grace together with much ignorance, and another may have much knowledge and yet no grace, is one of the greatest mysteries in religion and one which the last day alone will unfold. Let us then seek knowledge and be ashamed of ignorance. But above all let us make sure that, like Peter and John, we have grace and right hearts.

For meditation: *We are to rebuke perversity but to instruct ignorance (Titus 1:9).*

Suggested further reading: Ruth 1:15-18

Those who love Christ most diligently and perseveringly are thoe who receive most privileges from Christ's hand. It is a touching fact, and one to be carefully noted, that Mary Magdalene would not leave the sepulchre when Peter and John went away to their own home. Love to her gracious Master would not let her leave the place where he had been lain. Where he was now she could not tell. What had become of him she did not know. But love made her linger about the empty tomb where Joseph and Nicodemus had lately laid him. Love made her honour the last place where his precious body had been seen by mortal eyes. And her love reaped a rich reward. She saw the angels whom Peter and John had never observed. She actually heard them speak and had soothing words addressed to her. She was the first to see our Lord after he rose from the dead, the first to hear his voice, the first to hold conversation with him. Can anyone doubt that this was written for our learning? Wherever the gospel is preached throughout the world, this little incident testifies that those who honour Christ will be honoured by Christ.

As it was in the morning of the first Easter Day, so will it be as long as the church stands. The great principle contained in the passage before us will hold good until the Lord comes again. All believers have not the same degree of faith, or hope, or knowledge, or courage, or wisdom and it is vain to expect it. But it is a certain fact that those who love Christ most fervently and cleave to him most closely will always enjoy most communion with him and feel most of the witness of the Spirit in their hearts. It is precisely those who wait on the Lord, in the temper of Mary Magdalene, to whom the Lord will reveal himself most fully and make them know and feel more than others. To know Christ is good, but to 'know that we know him' is far better.

For meditation: *True devotion cannot be driven away from the one who is loved.*

Suggested further reading: Isaiah 49:14-23

We see in these verses that the fears and sorrows of believers are often quite needless. We are told that Mary stood at the sepulchre weeping and wept as if nothing could comfort her. She wept when the angels spoke to her: 'Woman,' they said, 'why weepest thou?' She was weeping still when our Lord spoke to her: 'Woman,' he also said, 'why weepest thou?' And the burden of her complaint was always the same: 'They have taken away my Lord, and I know not where they have laid him.' Yet all this time her risen Master was close to her, with 'body, flesh and bones, and all things pertaining to the perfection of man's nature'. Her tears were needless. Her anxiety was unnecessary. Like Hagar in the wilderness, she had a well of water by her side, but she had not eyes to see it.

What thoughtful Christian can fail to see that we have here a faithful picture of many a believer's experience? How often we are anxious when there is no just cause for anxiety! How often we mourn over the absence of things which in reality are within our grasp and even at our right hand! Two-thirds of the things we fear in life never happen at all and two-thirds of the tears we shed are thrown away and shed in vain. Let us pray for more faith and patience and allow more time for the full development of God's purposes. Let us believe that things are often working together for our peace and joy, which seem at one time to contain nothing but bitterness and sorrow. Old Jacob said at one time of his life, 'All these things are against me' (Gen. 42:36), yet he lived to see Joseph again, rich and prosperous, and to thank God for all that had happened. If Mary had found the seal of the tomb unbroken and her Master's body lying cold within, she might well have wept! The very absence of the body, which made her weep, was a token for good and a cause of joy for herself and all mankind.

For meditation: *Most of what we fear will happen never in fact occurs. Much of what does happen is not as terrible as we thought it would be.*

Suggested further reading: Hebrews 1:5-14

Mary saw figures in white sitting inside the grave. They evidently looked like men, but they were in reality angels, two of those mysterious ministering spirits whom the Bible teaches us God is pleased to employ on great occasions. An angel announced the coming birth of John Baptist and of Christ himself. Angels told the shepherds that Christ was born. Angels ministered to our Lord after the temptation and an angel strengthened him in Gethsemane. And now also angels appeared in the day of our Lord's resurrection. They first announced that he was born and they again, after thirty-three years, announced that he was risen.

The whole subject of angels is very deep and mysterious and one about which we must beware of holding anything that is not revealed. But the case before us teaches one or two wonderful things, which we should do well to remember.

It is clear that angels were at the tomb, when the party of women arrived there, after Mary Magdalene had run to tell Peter and John. It is equally clear that they were not to be seen when Peter and John ran to the grave on hearing Mary's report. Not one word do we read of their seeing angels. Yet it is equally clear that when Mary Magdalene looked in, after Peter and John went away, she saw two angels and talked with them. These are very deep things. They prove plainly that the angels of God appear and disappear, are visible or invisible, instantaneously and supernaturally, according as God commissions them. In short, they are beings of a totally different nature to our own and are in all the conditions of their constitution totally unlike us. For anything we know, they were in the tomb when Peter and John inspected it, but at that moment were invisible. For anything we know, they are now very near us every minute of our existence and doing God's will concerning us, though we are utterly unaware of their presence.

For meditation: *The hosts of God encamp around*
The dwellings of the just

(Tate and Brady).

Suggested further reading: Psalm 103:8-18

We are here told how our Lord at last revealed himself to this faithful disciple, after her patience, love and boldness had been fully proved. Little as she had shown herself able to understand the great truth of her Saviour's resurrection, she had at any rate shown that none loved him more, or clung to him more tenaciously, than she did. And she had her reward. One single word was enough to open her eyes, to let the whole truth shine in upon her mind and to reveal the great fact that her Saviour was not dead but alive and that he had won a victory over the grave. Speaking in his usual well-known voice, our Lord addressed her by her name — the name by which, no doubt, he had often addressed her before. That single word touched a spring, as it were, and opened her eyes in a moment. Need we doubt that at once the whole world seemed turned upside down to the astonished woman, and that under the influence of such an amazing revulsion of feeling as that much-loved voice must have caused, her mind could only find expression in one passionate word — 'Rabboni', or Master?

The boundless compassion of our Lord Jesus Christ to his believing people comes out wonderfully in this verse. He can be touched with the feeling of our infirmities. He knows how weak our bodily frame is and how much excessive sorrow can unnerve and stupefy our minds. He can pass over much darkness of understanding, much slowness of comprehension, when he sees real, genuine, hearty, bold , persevering, thorough love to himself and his person. We see this prominently brought out in his dealing with Mary Magdalene, when he revealed himself to her. He graciously pardons her forgetfulness of his oft-repeated declaration that he would rise again after his death, pities her deep sorrow and abundantly rewards her love. These things are written for our learning. Jesus never changes.

For meditation: *The Father and the Son are ever full of pity towards their weak and erring people.*

Suggested further reading: Matthew 17:1-8

What low and earthly thoughts of Christ may creep into the mind of a true believer! It seems impossible to gather any other lesson from the solemn words which our Lord addressed to Mary Magdalene, when he said, 'Touch me not; for I am not yet ascended to my Father.' No doubt the language is somewhat mysterious and ought to be delicately and reverently handled. Yet it is only reasonable to suppose that the first surprise and the reaction from great sorrow to great joy was more than the mind of Mary could bear. She was only a woman, though a holy and faithful woman. It is highly probable that, in the first excess of her joy, she threw herself at our Lord's feet and made greater demonstrations of feeling than were seemly or becoming. Very likely she behaved too much like one who thought all must be right if she had her Lord's bodily presence and all must be wrong in his bodily absence. This was not the highest style of faith. She acted, in short, like one who forgot that her Master was God as well as man. She made too little of his divinity and too much of his humanity. And hence she called forth our Lord's gentle rebuke: 'Touch me not! There is no need of this excessive demonstration of feeling. I am not yet ascending to my Father for forty days; your present duty is not to linger at my feet, but to go and tell my brethren that I have risen. Think of the feelings of others as well as of your own.'

After all, we must confess that the fault of this holy woman was one into which Christians have always been too ready to fall. In every age there has been a tendency in the minds of many to make too much of Christ's bodily presence and to forget that he is not a mere earthly friend, but one who is 'God over all, blessed for ever', as well as man. Let us be content to have Christ dwelling in our hearts by faith and present when two or three are met in his name and to wait for the real presence of Christ's body till he comes again.

For meditation: *We cannot always live in great experiences of the reality of Christ, but we can always know he is with us, however we may feel.*

Suggested further reading:　Hebrews 2:10-13

When our Lord speaks of God as 'My Father and my God', he seems, as usual, to point to the close and intimate union which he always declared to exist between himself and the first person in the Trinity. 'The God and Father of our Lord Jesus Christ' (1 Peter 1:3) is a kindred expression. He does not, we should observe, say, I ascend unto 'our Father', etc., but 'my Father and your Father'. He thus shows that there is a certain distinction between his relation to the Father and ours. Believers are not naturally sons of God; they only become so by grace, by adoption and by virtue of union with Christ. Christ, on the contrary, is in his nature the Son of God.

How kindly and graciously our Lord speaks of his disciples! He bids Mary Magdalene carry a message to them as 'his brethren'. It was but three days before that they had all forsaken him shamefully and fled. Yet this merciful Master speaks as if all was forgiven and forgotten. His first thought is to bring back the wanderers, to bind up the wounds of their consciences, to reanimate their courage, to restore them to their former place. This was indeed a love that passeth knowledge. To trust deserters and to show confidence in backsliders was a compassion which man can hardly understand. So true is that word of David: 'Like as a father pitieth his children, so the Lord pitieth them that fear him. For he knoweth our frame; he remembereth that we are dust' (Psalm 103:13,14).

Let us leave the passage with the comfortable reflection that Jesus Christ never changes. He is the same yesterday, today and for ever. As he dealt with his erring disciples in the morning of his resurrection, so will he deal with all who believe and love him, until he comes again. When we wander out of the way, he will bring us back. When we fall, he will raise us again.

For meditation:
> *Though for good we render ill,*
> *He accounts us brethren still*

(Newton).

Suggested further reading: Romans 5:1-11

Our Lord greeted the apostles when he first met them after his resurrection. Twice over he addressed them with the kindly words: 'Peace be unto you.' We may dismiss as untenable, in all probability, the cold and cautious suggestion that this was nothing better than an unmeaning phrase of courtesy. He who 'spake as never man spake' said nothing without meaning. He spoke, we may be sure, with special reference to the events of the last few days and with special reference to their future ministry. 'Peace' and not blame, 'peace' and not fault-finding, 'peace' and not rebuke was the first word which this little company heard from their Master's lips after he left the tomb.

It was meet and right and fitting that it should be so, and in full harmony with things that had gone before. 'Peace on earth' was the song of the heavenly host when Christ was born. Peace and rest of soul was the general subject that Christ continually preached for three years. Peace, and not riches, had been the great legacy which he had left with the eleven the night before his crucifixion. Surely it was in full keeping with all the tenor of our Lord's dealings that, when he revisited his little company of disciples after his resurrection, his first word should be 'Peace'. It was a word that would soothe and calm their minds.

Peace, we may safely conclude, was intended by our Lord to be the keynote to the Christian ministry. That same peace which was so continually on the lips of the Master was to be the grand subject of the teaching of his disciples. Peace between God and man through the precious blood of atonement, peace between man and man through the infusion of grace and charity — to spread such peace as this was to be the work of the church. Any form of Christianity which burns men at the stake, in order to promote its own success, carries about with it the stamp of an apostasy.

For meditation: *Our Lord Jesus Christ is the Prince of Peace (Isa. 9:6).*

Suggested further reading: *2 Thessalonians 2:9-12*

We should observe in these verses the remarkable evidence which our Lord supplied of his own resurrection. He graciously appealed to the senses of his trembling disciples. He showed them 'his hands and his side'. He bade them see with their own eyes that he had a real material body and that he was not a ghost or a spirit. 'Handle me and see,' were his first words, according to St Luke, 'a spirit hath not flesh and bones, as ye see me have.'

Even in the glory of heaven, according to Revelation, John saw him appear as a 'Lamb that had been slain' (Rev. 5:6). I think we need not doubt that when he ascended up into heaven, those wounds went with him and are a perpetual witness to angels that he has actually suffered for man's sins. When we see his real presence in the day of his appearing, we shall see 'the man Christ Jesus' and see the marks of his crucifixion.

Great indeed was the condescension of our blessed Master in thus coming down to the feeble faith of the eleven apostles! But great also was the principle which he established for the use of his church in every age until he returns. That principle is that our Master requires us to believe nothing that is contrary to our senses. Things *above* our reason we must expect to find in a religion that comes from God, but not things contrary to reason. To require people to believe that men have the quickening power of the Holy Spirit, when our eyes tell us they are living in habitual carelessness and sin, or that the bread and wine in the Lord's Supper are Christ's real body and blood, when our senses tell us they are still bread and wine — this is to require more belief than Christ ever required of his disciples. It is to require that which is flatly contradictory to reason and common sense. Such requisitions Christ never made. Let us not try to be wiser than our Lord.

For meditation: *Belief in the supernatural is conviction as to God's power, not gullibility.*

Suggested further reading: Mark 1:35-39

Our Lord proceeds to tell the disciples the work which he now wished them to do, but in general terms. He meant to send them forth into the world to be his ministers, messengers and witnesses, even as the Father had sent him into the world to be his messenger and witness (Heb. 3:1; John 18:37). As he had gone up and down preaching the gospel, testifying against the evil of the world and proclaiming rest and peace to the heavy laden, so he intended them to go up and down, as soon as he had ascended up into heaven. In short, he at once prepared their minds for the work which was before them. They were to dismiss from their minds the idea that the day of ease and reward had come, now that their Master had risen and was with them once more. So far from that being the case, their real work was now to begin. He himself was about to leave the world and he meant them to take his place. And one purpose for which he appeared among them was to give them their commission.

The repetition of the salutation, 'Peace be unto you,' is very noteworthy. I cannot doubt that it was specially intended to cheer and comfort and animate the disciples. Glad as they doubtless were to see the Lord, we may easily believe that they were frightened and overcome by a mixture of feelings, and the more so when they remembered how they had behaved when they had last seen their Lord. Jesus read the condition of their hearts and mercifully made assurance doubly sure by repeating the gracious words: 'Peace be unto you.' As Joseph said to Pharaoh, 'The thing was doubled,' in order to make it sure and prevent the possibility of mistake.

Augustine says, 'The iteration is confirmation. It is the "peace upon peace" promised by the prophet' (Isa.57:19).

For meditation: *'God only had one Son and he made him a preacher.'*

Suggested further reading: Ezekiel 37:1-14

The action of our Lord, 'He breathed on them,' is one that stands completely alone in the New Testament and the Greek word is nowhere else used. On no occasion but this do we find the Lord 'breathing' on anyone. Of course, it was a symbolical action and the only question is 'What did it symbolize and why was it used?' My own belief is that the true explanation is to be found in the account of man's creation in Genesis. There we read, 'The Lord God formed man of the dust of the ground, and *breathed* into his nostrils the breath of life; and man became a living soul' (Gen. 2:7). Just as there was no life in man until God breathed into him the breath of life, so I believe our Lord taught the disciples, by this action of breathing on them, that the beginning of all ministerial qualification is to have the Holy Spirit breathed into us, and that, until the Holy Ghost is planted in our hearts, we are not rightly commissioned for the work of the ministry.

I do not, however, feel sure that this view completely exhausts the meaning of our Lord when he breathed on the disciples. I cannot forget that they had all forsaken their Master the night that he was taken prisoner, fallen away from their profession and forfeited their title to confidence as apostles. May we not therefore reasonably believe that this breathing pointed to a *revival of life* in the hearts of the apostles and to a restoration of their privileges as trusted and commissioned messengers, notwithstanding their grievous fall? I cannot help suspecting that this lesson was contained in the action of breathing. It not only symbolized the infusion for the first time of special ministerial gifts and graces. It also symbolized the restoration to complete power and confidence in their Master's eyes, even after their faith had so nearly breathed its last and given up the ghost. The first symptom of returning life, when a man is recovered from drowning, is his beginning to breathe again. To set the lungs breathing, in such cases, is the first aim of a skilful doctor.

For meditation: *God's breath gives life to that which is dry and dead – this is revival!*

Suggested further reading: *Ephesians 1:15-23*

The words, 'Receive ye the Holy Ghost,' are almost as deep and mysterious as the action of breathing. They can only signify, 'I bestow on you the Holy Ghost.' But in what sense the Holy Ghost was bestowed is a point that demands attention and we must beware that we do not run into error.

Our Lord, in my opinion, must have meant, 'Receive the Holy Ghost as the Spirit of knowledge and understanding.' He must have meant that he now conferred on them a degree of light and knowledge of divine truth, which hitherto they had not possessed. They had been greatly deficient in light and knowledge up to this time. With all their faith and love towards our Lord's person, they had been sadly ignorant of many things and particularly of the true purpose of his coming and the necessity of his death and resurrection. 'Now,' says our Lord, 'I bestow on you the Spirit of knowledge. Let the time past suffice to have seen through a glass darkly. Receive the Holy Ghost, open your eyes and see all things clearly.' In fact, I believe the words point to the very thing which St Luke says our Lord did on this occasion: 'Then opened he their understanding, that they might understand the Scriptures' (Luke 24:45). Light was the first thing made in the day of creation. Light in the heart is the first beginning of true conversion. And light in the understanding is the first thing required in order to make a man an able minister of the New Testament. Our Lord was commissioning his first ministers and sending them out to carry on his work. He begins by giving them light and knowledge: 'Receive ye the Holy Ghost. I commission you this day, and confer on you the office of ministers. And the first gift I confer on you is spiritual knowledge.' That this is the true view of the words is proved to my own mind by the extraordinary difference in doctrinal knowledge which from this day the apostles exhibited.

For meditation: *Without the Holy Spirit we cannot receive God's truth (1 Cor. 2:14,15).*

Suggested further reading: Acts 13:26-38

Our Lord in this place solemnly commissioned his apostles to go into all the world and preach the gospel as he had preached it. He also conferred on them the power of declaring with peculiar authority whose sins were forgiven and whose sins were not forgiven. That this is precisely what the apostle did is a simple matter of fact, which anyone may verify for himself by reading the book of the Acts. When Peter proclaimed to the Jews, 'Repent ye, and be converted,' and when Paul declared at Antioch of Iconium, 'To you is the word of this salvation sent,' 'Through this man is preached the forgiveness of sins, and by him all that believe are justified,' they were doing what this passage commissioned the apostles to do. They were opening with authority the door of salvation and inviting with authority all sinners to enter in by it and be saved (Acts 3:19; 13:26-28).

Whatever some may please to say, there is not a single instance to be found in the Acts of any apostle granting absolution after confession. Above all, there is not a trace in the two pastoral epistles to Timothy and Titus of such confession and absolution being recommended or thought desirable. In short, whatever men may say about private ministerial absolution, there is not a single precedent for it in God's Word.

Let us leave the whole passage with a deep sense of the importance of the minister's office when that office is duly exercised according to the mind of Christ. No higher honour can be imagined than that of being Christ's ambassadors and proclaiming in Christ's name the forgiveness of sins to a lost world. But let us ever beware of investing the ministerial office with one jot more of power and authority than Christ conferred upon it. To treat ministers as being in any sense mediators between God and man is to rob Christ of his prerogative, to hide saving truth from sinners and to exalt ordained men to a position which they are totally unqualified to fill.

For meditation: *Ministers are neither priests nor prophets, but proclaimers.*

Suggested further reading: *Hebrews 10:19-25*

How much Christians may lose by not regularly attending the assemblies of God's people! Thomas was absent the first time that Jesus appeared to the disciples after his resurrection and consequently Thomas missed a blessing. Of course, we have no certain proof that the absence of the apostle could not admit of explanation. Yet, at such a crisis in the lives of the eleven, it seems highly improbable that he had any good reason for not being with his brethren and it is far more likely that in some way he was to blame. One thing, at any rate, is clear and plain. By being absent he was kept in suspense and unbelief a whole week, while all around him were rejoicing in the thought of a risen Lord. It is difficult to suppose that this would have been the case if there had not been a fault somewhere. It is hard to avoid the suspicion that Thomas was absent when he might have been present.

We shall all do well to remember the charge of the apostle Paul: 'Forsake not the assembling of yourselves together, as the manner of some is' (Heb.10:25). Never to be absent from God's house on Sundays without good reason, never to miss the Lord's Supper when administered in our own congregation, never to let our place be empty when means of grace are going on, this is one way to be a growing and prosperous Christian. The very sermon that we needlessly miss may contain a precious word in season for our souls. The very assembly for prayer and praise from which we stay away may be the very gathering that would have cheered and stablished and quickened our hearts. We little know how dependent our spiritual health is on little, regular, habitual helps and how much we suffer if we miss our medicine. The wretched argument that many attend means of grace and are no better for them should be no argument to a Christian. It may satisfy those who are blind to their own state and destitute of grace, but it should never satisfy a real servant of Christ.

For meditation: *If you have no appetite for God's Word and people **now**, why should things be different later?*

Suggested further reading: 2 Corinthians 5:1-10

The unbelief of Thomas, expressed in this famous sentence, was a sad fault in a good man, which cannot be explained away. He refused to believe the testimony of ten competent witnesses, who had seen Christ in the body with their own eyes. He refused to believe the testimony of ten true friends and brethren, who could have no object in deceiving him. He passionately declares that he will not believe, unless he himself sees and touches our Lord's body. He presumes to prescribe certain conditions which must be fulfilled before he can credit the report of his brethren. He uses singularly emphatic language to express his scepticism: 'Others may believe if they like; but I shall not and will not believe until I see and touch for myself.' All this was very sad and very sinful. Thomas might have remembered that at this rate nothing could ever be proved by witnesses, and that he himself, as a teacher, could never expect men to believe him. His case shows us how foolishly and weakly a believer may speak sometimes and how, under the influence of depression and doubt, he may say things of which afterwards he is heartily ashamed.

After all, the case of Thomas is not an uncommon one. Some people are so strangely constituted that they distrust everybody, regard all men as liars and will believe nothing except they can see it all and work it all out for themselves. They have a rooted dislike to receive anything on trust or from the testimony of others and must always go over the ground for themselves. In people of this kind, though they know it not, there is often a vast amount of latent pride and self-conceit and it is almost ludicrous to observe how entirely they forget that the business of daily life could never go on, if we were always doubting everything which we could not see for ourselves. Nevertheless they exist in the church and always will exist and the case of Thomas shows what trouble they bring on themselves.

For meditation: *There is an arrogance in the demand for personal proof when the evidence is provided by God himself!*

Suggested further reading: *Romans 2:1-4*

Verse 26 describes how Jesus was graciously pleased to appear again to the company of the apostles, for the express purpose of convincing and satisfying the mind of Thomas.

He came when the disciples were 'within'. That means that they were assembled in a room and probably in the same house where they had assembled before. The conviction and reproof of a weak disciple was a thing which was mercifully transacted in private and among friends. We cannot doubt, moreover, that at this period the disciples would hardly dare to assemble in the open air anywhere about Jerusalem. The rumour that they stole the body of our Lord would still be rife in the city and they might well feel the necessity of caution.

He came when 'Thomas was with them'. That means that he timed his visit so that not one of the apostles was missing. He knew exactly who were assembled and where they were assembled and he ordered his appearance accordingly. It should be a great comfort to believers to remember that their Lord's eye is always upon them and that he knows exactly in what place and in what company they are.

He came when the doors were shut. That means that he appeared exactly under the same circumstances under which he appeared a week before, in an evening, when the doors were carefully closed for fear of the Jews. Thus, as on the previous Sunday, he suddenly, without a moment's notice, stood in the midst of the assembled disciples.

He came with the same gracious salutation with which he had appeared before. Once more, the first word that fell from his lips is 'Peace be unto you.' Thomas was there. The disciple who made his emphatic declaration of unbelief might well expect to hear some word of rebuke. But our Lord makes no exception. He saw Thomas and well knew all that Thomas had said, and yet to him, as well as to the other ten, he once more says, 'Peace.'

For meditation: *God is constantly exercising patience towards undeserving men.*

Suggested further reading: 2 Peter 3:8-16

How kind and merciful Christ is to dull and slow believers! It is hard to imagine anything more tiresome and provoking than the conduct of Thomas, when even the testimony of ten faithful brethren had no effect on him and he doggedly declared, 'Except I see with my own eyes and touch with my own hands, I will not believe.' But it is impossible to imagine anything more patient and compassionate than our Lord's treatment of this weak disciple.

He does not reject him, or dismiss him, or excommunicate him. He comes again at the end of a week and apparently for the special benefit of Thomas. He deals with him according to his weakness, like a gentle nurse dealing with a froward child: 'Reach hither thy finger, and behold my hands; reach hither thy hand, and thrust it into my side.' If nothing but the grossest, coarsest, most material evidence could satisfy him, even that evidence was supplied. Surely this was a love that passeth knowledge and a patience that passeth understanding.

A passage of Scripture like this, we need not doubt, was written for the special comfort of all true believers. The Holy Ghost knew well that the dull and the slow and the stupid and the doubting are by far the commonest type of disciples in this evil world. The Holy Ghost has taken care to supply abundant evidence that Jesus is rich in patience as well as compassion and that he bears with the infirmities of all his people. Let us take care that we drink into our Lord's spirit and copy his example. Let us never set down men in a low place, as graceless and godless, because their faith is feeble and their love is cold. Let us remember the case of Thomas and be very pitiful and of tender mercy. Our Lord has many weak children in his family, many dull pupils in his school, many raw soldiers in his army, many lame sheep in his flock. Yet he bears with them all and casts none away.

For meditation: *Although God may chasten his people for their follies, he does so in order not to condemn them with the world (1 Cor. 11:32).*

Suggested further reading: Psalm 8

To come into the world at all, and take a body on him, to allow that body to be scourged, crowned with thorns, nailed to the cross and laid in the grave — all this, beyond doubt, was astonishing condescension. But when the victory over sin and death was won, and he had taken on him his resurrection body, to come to a doubting, sceptical disciple and bid him touch him, put his finger into the nail-prints on his hands and put his hand into the great wound in his side — all this was a condescension which we can never sufficiently admire and adore.

The last sentence of the verse is a rebuke and an exhortation at the same time. It would have been more literally rendered, 'Be not an unbeliever, but a believer.' It is not merely a reproof to Thomas for his scepticism on this particular occasion, but an urgent counsel to be of a more believing turn of mind for time to come: 'Shake off this habit of doubting, questioning and discrediting everyone. Give up thine unbelieving disposition. Become more willing to believe and trust and give credit to testimony for time to come.' No doubt the primary object of the sentence was to correct and chastise Thomas for his sceptical declaration on the preceding Sunday. But I believe our Lord had in view the further object of correcting Thomas's whole character and directing his attention to his besetting sin. How many there are among us who ought to take to themselves our Lord's words! How faithless we often are and how slow to believe!

Let us not fail to observe our Lord's perfect knowledge of all that passed on the previous Sunday, of all that the apostles had said and of the sceptical declaration which Thomas had made.

Let us observe our Lord's thorough acquaintance with the special faults and besetting sins of every one of his people. He saw that Thomas's defect was his unbelief and so he says, 'Be not faithless, but believing.'

For meditation: *Although God is almighty and sovereign, he condescends to meet men at the place of their need.*

Suggested further reading: *Revelation 22:7-9*

Christ was addressed by a disciple as 'God', without prohibition or rebuke on his part. The noble exclamation which burst from the lips of Thomas, when convinced that his Lord had risen indeed — the noble exclamation, 'My Lord and my God' — admits of only one meaning. It was a distinct testimony to our blessed Lord's divinity. It was a clear, unmistakable declaration that Thomas believed him, whom he saw and touched that day, to be not only man, but God. Above all, it was a testimony which our Lord received and did not prohibit and a declaration which he did not say one word to rebuke. When Cornelius fell down at the feet of Peter and would have worshipped him, the apostle refused such honour at once: 'Stand up; I myself also am a man' (Acts 10:26). When the people of Lystra would have done sacrifice to Paul and Barnabas, 'they rent their clothes and ran in among the people . . . saying, Sirs, why do ye these things? We also are men of like passions with you' (Acts 14:14,15). But when Thomas says to Jesus, 'My Lord and my God,' the words do not elicit a syllable of reproof from our holy and truth-loving Master. Can we doubt that these things were written for our learning?

Let us settle it firmly in our minds that the divinity of Christ is one of the grand foundation truths of Christianity and let us be willing to go to the stake rather than let it go. Unless our Lord Jesus is very God of very God, there is an end of his mediation, his atonement, his advocacy, his priesthood, his whole work of redemption. These glorious doctrines are useless blasphemies, unless Christ is divine. For ever let us bless God that the divinity of our Lord is taught everywhere in the Scriptures and stands on evidence that can never be overthrown.

He is God and therefore is 'able to save to the uttermost all who come unto God by him'.

For meditation: *Do you always remember that Jesus is God in your dealings with him?*

Suggested further reading: Job 38:1-18

Nothing is more common nowadays than to hear people say that they decline to believe things above their reason, that they cannot believe what they cannot entirely understand in religion, that they must see everything clearly before they can believe. Such talk as this sounds very fine and is very taking with young persons and superficially educated people, because it supplies a convenient reason for neglecting vital religion altogether. But it is a style of talking which shows a mind either proud, or foolish, or inconsistent.

In matters of science, what sensible man does not know that we must begin by believing much which we do not understand, taking many positions on trust and accepting many things on the testimony of others? Even in the most exact science, the scholar must begin with axioms and postulates. Faith and trust in our teachers is the very first condition of acquiring knowledge. He that begins his studies by saying, 'I shall not believe anything which I do not see clearly demonstrated from the very first,' will make very little progress.

In the daily business of life, what sensible man does not know that we take many important steps on no other ground than the testimony of others? Parents send sons to Australia, New Zealand, China and India, without ever having seen these countries, in faith that the report about them is dependable and true. Probability, in fact, is the only guide of most parts of our life.

In the face of such facts as these, where is the common sense of saying, as many rationalists and sceptics now do, that in such a mysterious matter as the concern of our souls, we ought to believe nothing that we do not see and ought to receive nothing as true which will not admit of mathematical demonstration?

For meditation: *Much (perhaps most) of your knowledge is truth received by you on the basis of the testimony of other witnesses.*

Suggested further reading: Matthew 16:1-4

The would-be wise man of modern times says, 'I dislike any religion which contains any mystery. I must first see and then I will believe.' Christianity replies, 'You cannot avoid mystery, unless you go out of the world. You are only asked to do with religion what you are always doing with science. You must first believe and then you will see.' The cry of the modern sceptic is 'If I could see, I would believe.' The answer of the Christian ought to be 'If you would only believe and humbly ask for divine teaching, you would soon see.'

There are hundreds of people in this latter age of the world who tell us they can believe nothing which is above their reason and that they want stronger evidences of the truth of the doctrine and fact of Christianity than probability. Like Thomas, they must first see before they believe. But what an extraordinary fact it is that the very men who say all this are continually acting all their lives on no better evidence than probability! They are continually doing things on no other ground than the report of others and their own belief that this report is probably true. The very principle on which they are incessantly acting, in the affairs of their bodies, their families and their money, is the principle on which they refuse to act in the affairs of their souls! In the things of this world they believe all sorts of things which they have not seen and only know to be probable and act on their belief. In the things of the eternal world they say they can believe nothing which they do not see and refuse the argument of probability altogether. Never, in fact, was there anything so unreasonable and inconsistent as rationalism, so called! No wonder that our Lord laid down, for the benefit of Thomas and the whole church, that mighty principle: 'Blessed are they that have not seen and yet have believed.'

For meditation: *The world says that 'Seeing is believing.' God says that 'Believing is seeing.'*

Suggested further reading: Hebrews 11:1-6

Have you got this faith? If you have, you will find it possible to refuse seeming good and choose seeming evil. You will think nothing of today's losses, in the hope of tomorrow's gains. You will follow Christ in the dark and stand by him to the very last. If you have not, I warn you, you will never war a good warfare and 'so run as to obtain'. You will soon be offended and turn back to the world.

Above all this, there must be a real abiding faith in the Lord Jesus Christ. The life that you live in the flesh you must live by the faith of the Son of God. There must be a settled habit of continually leaning on Jesus, looking unto Jesus, drawing out of Jesus and using him as the manna of your soul. You must strive to be able to say, 'To me to live is Christ.' 'I can do all things through Christ which strengtheneth me' (Phil. 1:21; 4:13).

This was the faith by which the old saints obtained a good report. This was the weapon by which they overcame the world. This made them what they were.

This was the faith that made Noah go on building his ark, while the world looked on and mocked; and Abraham give the choice of the land to Lot, and dwell on quietly in tents; and Ruth cleave to Naomi, and turn away from her country and her gods; and Daniel continue in prayer, though he knew the lions' den was prepared; and the three children refuse to worship idols, though the fiery furnace was before their eyes; and Moses forsake Egypt, not fearing the wrath of Pharaoh. All these acted as they did because they believed. They saw the difficulties and troubles of this course. But they saw Jesus by faith and above them all, and they pressed on. Well may the apostle Peter speak of faith as 'precious faith' (2 Peter 1:1).

For meditation: *Have you eternal life by faith in Jesus, God's Son?*

Suggested further reading: Acts 4:8-13

We should observe, for one thing, in these verses the poverty of the first disciples of Christ. We find them working with their own hands, in order to supply their temporal wants, and working at one of the humblest of callings — the calling of a fisherman. Silver and gold they had none, lands and revenues they had none and therefore they were not ashamed to return to the business to which they had, most of them, been trained. Striking is the fact that some of the seven here named were fishing when our Lord first called them to be apostles and again fishing when he appeared to them almost the last time. We need not doubt that to the minds of Peter, James and John the coincidence would come home with peculiar power.

The poverty of the apostles goes far to prove the divine origin of Christianity. These very men who toiled all night in a boat, dragging about a cold wet net and taking nothing, these very men who found it necessary to work hard in order that they might eat — these very men were some of the first founders of the mighty church of Christ which has now overspread one-third of the globe. These were they who went forth from an obscure corner of the earth and turned the world upside down. These were the unlearned and ignorant men who boldly confronted the subtle systems of ancient philosophy and silenced its advocates by the preaching of the cross. These were the men who at Ephesus and Athens and Rome emptied the heathen temples of their worshippers and turned away multitudes to a new and better faith. He that can explain these facts, except by admitting that Christianity came down from God, must be a strangely incredulous man. Reason and common sense lead us to only one conclusion in the matter. Nothing can account for the rise and progress of Christianity but the direct interposition of God.

For meditation: *Is the most striking thing about you that you have 'been with Jesus'?*

Suggested further reading: 1 Corinthians 12:12-26

Once more, on this deeply interesting occasion, we see Peter and John side by side in the same boat, and once more, as at the sepulchre, we see these two good men behaving in different ways. When Jesus stood on the shore, in the dim twilight of the morning, John was the first to perceive who it was and to say, 'It is the Lord,' but Peter was the first to spring into the water and to struggle to get close to his Master. In a word, John was the first to see, but Peter was the first to act. John's gentle loving spirit was quickest to discern, but Peter's fiery, impulsive nature was quickest to stir and move. And yet both were believers, both were true-hearted disciples, both loved the Lord in life and were faithful to him unto death. But their natural temperaments were not the same.

Let us never forget the practical lessons before us. As long as we live, let us diligently use it in forming our estimate of believers. Let us not condemn others as graceless and unconverted, because they do not see the path of duty from our standpoint, or feel things exactly as we feel them. 'There are diversities of gifts, but the same Spirit' (1 Cor. 12:4). The gifts of God's children are not bestowed precisely in the same measure and degree. Some have more of one gift and some have more of another. Some have gifts which shine more in public and some which shine more in private. Some are more bright in a passive life and some are more bright in an active one. Yet each and all the members of God's family, in their own way and in their own season, bring glory to God. Martha was 'careful and troubled about much serving,' when Mary 'sat at the feet of Jesus and heard his word' (Luke 10:39,40). Yet there came a day at Bethany when Mary was crushed and prostrated by overmuch sorrow and Martha's faith shone more brightly than her sister's (John 11:20-28). Nevertheless both were loved by our Lord.

For meditation: *What application does Luke 9:49-50 have to your attitudes to fellow Christians?*

Suggested further reading: *1 Corinthians 15:35-49*

Here, as in other places, we find an unanswerable proof that our Lord rose again with a real material body and a proof seen by seven grown-up men with their own eyes at one and the same time. We see him sitting, talking, eating, drinking on the shore of the lake of Galilee and to all appearance for a considerable time. The morning sun of spring shines down on the little party. They are alone by the well-known Galilean lake, far away from the crowd and noise of Jerusalem. In the midst sits the Master, with the nail-prints in his hands — the very Master whom they had all followed for three years and one of them, at least, had seen hanging on the cross. They could not be deceived. Will anyone pretend to say that stronger proof could be given that Jesus rose from the dead? Can anyone imagine better evidence of a fact? That Peter was convinced and satisfied we know. He says himself to Cornelius, '[We] did eat and drink with him after he rose from the dead' (Acts 10:41). Those who in modern times say they are not convinced may as well say that they are determined not to believe any evidence at all.

Let us all thank God that we have such a cloud of witnesses to prove that our Lord rose again. The resurrection of Christ is the grand proof of Christ's divine mission. He told the Jews they need not believe he was the Messiah, if he did not rise again the third day. The resurrection of Christ is the top-stone of the work of redemption. It proved that he finished the work he came to do and, as our Substitute, had overcome the grave. The resurrection of Christ is a miracle that no infidel can explain away. Men may carp and cavil at Balaam's ass and Jonah in the whale's belly, if they please, but till they can prove that Christ did not rise again we need not be moved. Above all, the resurrection of Christ is the pledge of our own. As the grave could not detain the Head, so it shall not detain the members.

For meditation: *What does Luke 16:31 teach about the nature of unbelief?*

Suggested further reading: *Philippians 3:3-11*

A true Christian is not a mere baptized man or woman. He is
something more. He is not a person who only goes, as a matter
of form, to a church or chapel on Sundays and lives all the rest
of the week as if there was no God. Formality is not Christianity. Ignorant lip-worship is not true religion. The Scripture
speaketh expressly: 'They are not all Israel which are of Israel'
(Rom. 9:6). The practical lesson of those words is clear and
plain. All are not true Christians who are members of the
visible church of Christ.

The true Christian is one whose religion is in his heart and
life. It is felt by himself in his heart. It is seen by others in his
conduct and life. He feels his sinfulness, guilt and badness, and
repents. He sees Jesus Christ to be that divine Saviour whom
his soul needs and commits himself to him. He puts off the old
man, with his corrupt and carnal habits, and puts on the new
man. He lives a new and holy life, fighting habitually against
the world, the flesh and the devil. Christ himself is the corner-
stone of his Christianity. Ask him in what he trusts for the forgiveness of his many sins, and he will tell you — in the death of
Christ. Ask him in what righteousness he hopes to stand innocent at the judgement day, and he will tell you it is the
righteousness of Christ. Ask him by what pattern he tries to
frame his life and he will tell you that it is the example of Christ.

But, beside all this, there is one thing in a true Christian
which is eminently peculiar to him. That thing is love to Christ.
Knowledge, faith, hope, reverence, obedience are all marked
features in a true Christian's character. But his picture would
be very imperfect if you omitted his 'love' to his divine Master.
He not only knows, trusts and obeys. He goes further than this
— he loves.

For meditation: *Is 'love' the word that most adequately sums up
your attitude to Christ?*

Suggested further reading: 1 Corinthians 16:19-24

'Faith towards our Lord Jesus Christ' is an expression which
many Christians are familiar with. Let it never be forgotten
that love is mentioned by the Holy Ghost in almost as strong
terms as faith. Great as the danger is of him 'that believeth not',
the danger of him that 'loveth not' is equally great. Not believing and not loving are both steps to everlasting ruin.

Hear what St Paul says to the Corinthians:'If any man love
not the Lord Jesus Christ, let him be Anathema Maran-atha'
(1 Cor. 16:22). St Paul allows no way of escape to the man who
does not love Christ. He leaves him no loophole or excuse. A
man may lack clear head-knowledge and yet be saved. He may
fail in courage and be overcome by the fear of man, like Peter.
He may fall tremendously, like David, and yet rise again. But if
a man does not love Christ, he is not in the way of life. The
curse is yet upon him. He is on the broad road that leadeth to
destruction.

Hear what St Paul says to the Ephesians: 'Grace be with all
them that love our Lord Jesus Christ in sincerity' (Eph 6:24).
The apostle is here sending his good wishes and declaring his
good will to all true Christians. Many of them, no doubt, he
had never seen. Many of them in the early churches, we may be
very sure, were weak in faith and knowledge and self-denial.
How, then, shall he describe them in sending his message?
What words can he use which will not discourage the weaker
brethren? He chooses a sweeping expression which exactly describes all true Christians under one common name. All had not
attained to the same degree, whether in doctrine or practice.
But all loved Christ in sincerity.

Hear what our Lord Jesus Christ himself says to the Jews: 'If
God were your Father, ye would love me' (John 8:42). No love
to Christ — then no sonship to God!

For meditation: *What do you think of Christ? This remains for
all eternity the crucial question.*

Suggested further reading: *Galatians 2:20-3:14*

A true Christian loves Christ for all he has done for him. He has suffered in his stead and died for him on the cross. He has redeemed him from the guilt, the power and the consequences of sin by his blood. He has called him by his Spirit to self-knowledge, repentance, faith, hope and holiness. He has forgiven all his many sins and blotted them out. He has freed him from the captivity of the world, the flesh and the devil. He has taken him from the brink of hell, placed him in the narrow way and set his face towards heaven. He has given him light instead of darkness, peace of conscience instead of uneasiness, hope instead of uncertainty, life instead of death. Can you wonder that the true Christian loves Christ?

And he loves him, besides, for all that he is still doing. He feels that he is daily washing away his many shortcomings and infirmities and pleading his soul's cause before God. He is daily supplying all the needs of his soul and providing him with an hourly provision of mercy and grace. He is daily leading him by his Spirit to a city of habitation, bearing with him when he is weak and ignorant, raising him up when he stumbles and falls, protecting him against his many enemies, preparing an eternal home for him in heaven. Can you wonder that the true Christian loves Christ?

Does the debtor in jail love the friend who unexpectedly and undeservedly pays all his debts, supplies him with fresh capital and takes him into partnership with himself? Does the prisoner in war love the man who, at the risk of his own life, breaks through the enemies' lines, rescues him and sets him free? Does the drowning sailor love the man who plunges into the sea, dives after him, catches him by the hair of his head and by a mighty effort saves him from a watery grave? In the same way, and upon the same principles, a true Christian loves Jesus Christ.

For meditation: *There is no love or self-giving greater than that of God in Christ (Rom. 5:6-8).*

Suggested further reading: 1 Samuel 20:1-17

This love to Christ is the inseparable companion of saving faith. A faith of devils, a mere intellectual faith, a man may have without love, but not that faith which saves. Love cannot usurp the office of faith. It cannot justify. It does not join the soul to Christ. It cannot bring peace to the conscience. But where there is real justifying faith in Christ there will always be heart love to Christ. He that is really forgiven is the man who will really love (Luke 7:47). If a man has no love to Christ, you may be sure he has no faith.

Love to Christ is the mainspring of work for Christ. There is little done for his cause on earth from sense of duty, or from knowledge of what is right and proper. The heart must be interested before the hands will move and continue moving. Excitement may galvanize the Christian's hands into a fitful and spasmodic activity. But there will be no patient continuance in well-doing, no unwearied labour in missionary work at home or abroad, without love. The nurse in a hospital may do her duty properly and well, may give the sick man his medicine at the right time, may feed him, minister to him and attend to all his wants. But there is a vast difference between that nurse and a wife tending the sick-bed of a beloved husband, or a mother watching over a dying child. The one acts from a sense of duty; the other from affection and love. The one does her duty because she is paid for it; the other is what she is because of her heart. It is just the same in the matter of the service of Christ. The great workers of the church, the men who have led forlorn hopes in the mission-field and turned the world upside down have all been eminently lovers of Christ.

Many great Christians have left a mark on the world. And what was the common feature of their characters? They all loved Christ. They not only held a creed. They loved a person, even the Lord Jesus Christ.

For meditation: *If Jonathan could work for David even though he was the heir to the throne and David a mere soldier, shall not we, mere sinners, work for our Master out of love?*

Suggested further reading: Revelation 5

Love to Christ is the point which we ought specially to dwell upon, in teaching religion to children. That he loved them even to his death and that they ought to love him in return is a creed which meets the span of their minds.

Love to Christ is the common meeting-point of believers of every branch of Christ's church on earth. Whether Episcopalian or Presbyterian, Baptist or Independent, Calvinist or Arminian, Methodist or Moravian, Lutheran or Reformed, Established or Free — here at least they are agreed. About forms and ceremonies, about church government and modes of worship, they often differ widely. But on one point, at any rate, they are united. They have all one common feeling towards him on whom they build their hope of salvation. They love the Lord Jesus Christ in sincerity (Eph. 6:24). Many of them, perhaps, are ignorant of systematic divinity and could argue but feebly in defence of their creed. But they all know what they feel towards him who died for their sins. 'I cannot speak much for Christ, sir,' said an old uneducated Christian woman to Dr Chalmers, 'but if I cannot speak for him, I could die for him!'

Love to Christ will be the distinguishing mark of all saved souls in heaven. The multitude which no man can number will all be of one mind. Old differences will be merged in one common feeling. Old doctrinal peculiarities, fiercely wrangled for upon earth, will be covered over by one common sense of debt to Christ. Luther and Zwingli will no longer dispute. Wesley and Toplady will no longer waste time in controversy. Churchmen and dissenters will no longer bite and devour one another. All will find themselves joining with one heart and voice in that hymn of praise: 'Unto him that loved us, and washed us from our sins in his own blood, and hath made us kings and priests unto God and his Father; to him be glory and dominion for ever and ever. Amen' (Rev. 1:5,6).

For meditation: *Names and sects and parties fall:*
Thou, O Christ, art all in all
(Wesley).

Suggested further reading: Psalm 116

Three times we find the apostle saying, 'Thou knowest that I love thee.' Once we are told that he said, 'Thou knowest all things.' Once we have the touching remark made that he was 'grieved to be asked the third time'. We need not doubt that our Lord, like a skilful physician, stirred up this grief intentionally. He intended to prick the apostle's conscience and to teach him a solemn lesson. If it was grievous to the disciple to be questioned, how much more grievous must it have been to the Master to be denied!

The answer that the humbled apostle gave is the one account that the true servant of Christ in every age can give of his religion. Such a one may be weak and fearful and ignorant and unstable and failing in many things, but at any rate he is real and sincere. Ask him whether he is converted, whether he is a believer, whether he has grace, whether he is justified, whether he is sanctified, whether he is elect, whether he is a child of God — ask him any one of these questions and he may perhaps reply that he really does not know! But ask him whether he loves Christ and he will reply, 'I do.' He may add that he does not love him as much as he ought to do, but he will not say that he does not love him at all. The rule will be found true with very few exceptions. Wherever there is true grace, there will be a consciousness of love towards Christ.

What, after all, is the great secret of loving Christ? It is an inward sense of having received from him pardon and forgiveness of sins. Those love much who feel much forgiven. He that has come to Christ with his sins and tasted the blessedness of free and full absolution, he is the man whose heart will be full of love towards his Saviour. The more we realize that Christ has suffered for us and paid our debt to God and that we are washed and justified through his blood, the more we shall love him for having loved us and given himself for us.

For meditation: *What would you add to David's statement: 'I love the Lord because...'?*

Suggested further reading: *Matthew 20:20-28*

We should notice in these verses Christ's command to Peter. Three times we find him saying, 'Feed' my flock: once, 'Feed my lambs,' and twice 'my sheep'. Can we doubt for a moment that this thrice-repeated charge was full of deep meaning? It was meant to commission Peter once more to do the work of an apostle, notwithstanding his recent fall. But this was only a small part of the meaning. It was meant to teach Peter and the whole church the mighty lesson that usefulness to others is the grand test of love and working for Christ the great proof of really loving Christ. It is not loud talk and high profession; it is not even impetuous, spasmodic zeal and readiness to draw the sword and fight — it is steady, patient, laborious effort to do good to Christ's sheep scattered throughout this sinful world, which is the best evidence of being a true-hearted disciple. This is the real secret of Christian greatness. It is written in another place: 'Whosoever will be great among you, let him be your minister; and whosoever will be chief among you, let him be your servant: even as the Son of man came not to be ministered unto, but to minister' (Matt. 20:26-28).

Forever let the parting charge of our blessed Master abide in our consciences and come up in the practice of our daily lives. It is not for nothing, we may be sure, that we find these things recorded for our learning, just before he left the world. Let us aim at a loving, doing, useful, hard-working, unselfish, kind, unpretentious religion. Let it be our daily desire to think of others, care for others, do good to others and to lessen the sorrow and increase the joy of this sinful world. This is to realize the great principle which our Lord's command to Peter was intended to teach. So living and so labouring to order our ways, we shall find it abundantly true that 'It is more blessed to give than to receive' (Acts 20:35).

For meditation: *The desire to be useful to God should far exceed the desire to be important before men.*

Suggested further reading: Psalm 139:1-6

The future history of Christians, both in life and death, is fore-known by Christ. The Lord tells Simon Peter, 'When thou art old, thou shalt stretch forth thy hands, and another shall gird thee, and carry thee whither thou wouldest not.' These words, without controversy, were a prediction of the manner of the apostle's death. They were fulfilled in after days, it is commonly supposed, when Peter was crucified as a martyr for Christ's sake. The time, the place, the manner, the painfulness to flesh and blood of the disciple's death were all matters foreseen by the Master.

The truth before us is eminently full of comfort to a true believer. To obtain foreknowledge of things to come would, in most cases, be a sorrowful possession. To know what was going to befall us, and yet not to be able to prevent it, would make us simply miserable. But it is an unspeakable consolation to remember that our whole future is known and forearranged by Christ. There is no such thing as luck, chance, or accident, in the journey of our life. Everything from beginning to end is foreseen — arranged by one who is too wise to err and too loving to do us harm.

Let us store up this truth in our minds and use it diligently in all the days of darkness through which we may yet have to pass. In such days we should lean back on the thought: 'Christ knows this, and knew it when he called me to be his disciple.' It is foolish to repine and murmur over the troubles of those whom we love. We should rather fall back on the thought that all is well done. It is useless to fret and be rebellious, when we ourselves have bitter cups to drink. We should rather say, 'This also is from the Lord: he foresaw it, and would have prevented it, if it had not been for my good.' Happy are those who can enter into the spirit of that old saint, who said, 'I have made a covenant with my Lord, that I will never take amiss anything that he does to me.'

For meditation: *The future that is hidden to us is an open book before a sovereign God.*

Suggested further reading: Philippians 1:20-27

A believer's death is intended to glorify God. The Holy Ghost
tells us this truth in plain language. He graciously interprets the
dark saying, which fell from our Lord's lips about Peter's end.
He tells us that Jesus spake this, 'signifying by what death he
should glorify God'.

The thing before us is probably not considered as much as it
ought to be. We are so apt to regard life as the only season for
honouring Christ, and action as the only mode of showing our
religion, that we overlook death, except as a painful termi-
nation of usefulness. Yet surely this ought not so to be. We may
die to the Lord as well as live to the Lord; we may be patient
sufferers as well as active workers. Like Samson, we may do
more for God in our death than we ever did in our life. It is
probable that the patient deaths of our martyred Reformers
had more effect on the minds of Englishmen than all the
sermons they preached and all the books they wrote. One
thing, at all events, is certain — the blood of the English
martyrs was the seed of the English church.

We may glorify God in death, by being ready for it whenever
it comes. The Christian who is found like a sentinel at his post,
like a servant with his loins girded and his lamp burning, with a
heart packed up and ready to go, the man to whom sudden
death, by the common consent of all who knew him, is sudden
glory — this, this is a man whose end brings glory to God. We
may glorify God in death, by patiently enduring its pains. The
Christian whose spirit has complete victory over the flesh, who
quietly feels the pins of his earthly tabernacle plucked up with
great bodily agonies and yet never murmurs or complains, but
silently enjoys inward peace — this, this again, is a man whose
end brings glory to God. We may glorify God in death, by
testifying to others the comfort and support that we find in the
grace of Christ.

For meditation: *If God would be more glorified by your death
than your life should you not be willing to die?*

Suggested further reading: *1 Corinthians 9:24-27*

Whatever we may think about the condition of other people, we should think first about our own. When Peter inquired curiously and anxiously about the future of the apostle John, he received from our Lord an answer of deep meaning: 'If I will that he tarry till I come, what is that to thee? Follow thou me.' Hard to understand as some part of that sentence may be, it contains a practical lesson which cannot be mistaken. It commands every Christian to remember his own heart first and to look at home.

Of course, our blessed Lord does not wish us to neglect the souls of others, or to take no interest in their condition. Such a state of mind would be nothing less than uncharitable selfishness and would prove plainly that we had not the grace of God. The servant of Christ will have a wide, broad heart, like his Master, and will desire the present and eternal happiness of all around him. He will long and labour to lessen the sorrows and to increase the joys of everyone within his reach and, as he has opportunity, to do good to all men. But, in all his doing, the servant of Christ must never forget his own soul. Charity and true religion must both begin at home.

It is vain to deny that our Lord's solemn caution to his impetuous disciple is greatly needed in the present day. Such is the weakness of human nature that even true Christians are continually liable to run into extremes. Some are so entirely absorbed in their own inward experience and their own heart's conflict that they forget the world outside. Others are so busy about doing good to the world that they neglect to cultivate their own souls. Both are wrong and both need to see a more excellent way, but none perhaps do so much harm to religion as those who are busy-bodies about others' salvation and at the same time neglecters of their own. From such a snare as this may the ringing words of our Lord deliver us!

For meditation: *How often the unbelievers show a deep concern for 'those who have never heard' as an excuse by which they direct attention away from their own need!*

Suggested further reading: 2 Timothy 3:10-17

St John concludes his Gospel with these remarkable words: 'There are many other things which Jesus did, the which, if they should be written every one, I suppose the world itself could not contain the books that should be written.' To suppose that the evangelist meant the world could not hold the material volumes which would be written is evidently unreasonable and absurd. The only sensible interpretation must be a spiritual and figurative one.

As much of Christ's sayings and doings is recorded as the mind of man can take in. It would not be good for the world to have more. The human mind, like the body, can only digest a certain quantity. The world could not contain more, because it would not. As many miracles, as many parables, as many sermons, as many conversions, as many words of kindness, as many deeds of mercy, as many journeys, as many prayers, as many warnings, as many promises are recorded as the world can possibly require. If more had been recorded, they would have been only thrown away. There is enough to make every unbeliever without excuse, enough to show every inquirer the way to heaven, enough to satisfy the heart of every honest believer, enough to condemn man if he does not repent and believe, enough to glorify God. The largest vessel can only contain a certain quantity of liquid. The mind of all mankind would not appreciate more about Christ, if more had been written. There is enough and to spare. This witness is true. Let us deny it if we can.

We may well be humble when we think how ignorant we are and how little we comprehend of the treasures which this Gospel contains.But we may well be thankful when we reflect how clear and plain is the instruction which it gives us about the way of salvation. The man who reads this Gospel profitably is he who 'believes that Jesus is the Christ and, believing, has life through his name'. Do we so believe?

For meditation: *There is much about our Lord's ministry that we do not know, but all that is necessary is recorded.*

Suggested further reading: John 20:30-31

I have now completed my notes on St John's Gospel. I have given my last explanation. I have gathered my last collection of the opinions of commentators. I have offered for the last time my judgement upon doubtful and disputed points. I lay down my pen with humbled, thankful and solemnized feelings. The closing words of holy Bullinger's *Commentary on the Gospels*, condensed and abridged, will perhaps not be considered an inappropriate conclusion to my *Expository Thoughts on St John*.

'Reader, I have now set before thee thy Saviour the Lord Jesus Christ, that very Son of God, who was begotten by the Father by an eternal and ineffable generation, consubstantial and coequal with the Father in all things . . . but in these last times, according to prophetical oracles, was incarnate for us, suffered, died, rose again from the dead and was made King and Lord of all things . . . This is he who is appointed and given to us by God the Father, as the fulness of all grace and truth, as the Lamb of God who taketh away the sins of the world, as the ladder and door of heaven, as the serpent lifted up to render the poison of sin harmless, as the water which refreshes the thirsty, as the bread of life, as the light of the world, as the redeemer of God's children, as the shepherd and door of the sheep, as the resurrection and the life, as the corn of wheat which springs up into much fruit, as the conqueror of the prince of this world, as the way, the truth and the life, as the true vine and, finally, as the redemption, salvation, satisfaction and righteousness of all the faithful in all the world, throughout all ages. Let us therefore pray God the Father, that, being taught by his gospel, we may know him that is true and believe in him in whom alone is salvation, and that, believing, we may feel God living in us in this world and in the world to come may enjoy his eternal and most blessed fellowship.' Amen and Amen.

For meditation: *John wrote his Gospel so that you might believe and have everlasting life. Have you?*

Other titles by

J.C.Ryle

published by Evangelical Press

HOLINESS

This book is one of the classics of evangelical literature.
In his foreword Dr. D. M. Lloyd-Jones writes:

*'The characteristics of Bishop Ryle's method and style are
obvious. He is pre-eminently and always scriptural and
expository. He never starts with a theory into which he
tries to fit various scriptures. He always starts with the
Word and expounds it. It is exposition at its very best and
highest. It is always clear and logical and invariably leads
to a clear enunciation of doctrine. It is strong and virile
and entirely free from the sentimentality that is often
described as "devotional".*

*Ryle, like his great masters, has no easy way to holiness to
offer us, and no 'patent' method by which it can be
attained; but he invariably produces that 'hunger and thirst
after righteousness' which is the only indispensable
condition to being "filled".'*

Large paperback, 324 pages

LIGHT FROM OLD TIMES

This book is both historical and biographical. It is about facts and men.

The author was an Anglican. The first Bishop of Liverpool, who made no secret of his strong evangelical convictions. His writings are well known and are considered today as classics of the evangelical faith.

Of the thirteen chapters in this book, six are biographies of some leading champions of the English Reformation: John Rogers, John Hooper, Rowland Taylor, Hugh Latimer, John Bradford, and Nicholas Ridley, along with a chapter on the reasons why many Reformers were burned; one is a study of Archbishop Laud and his times; three trace the lives of great Puritans of the 17th century: Samuel Ward, Richard Baxter, and William Gurnall; the remaining two dealing with the life of John Wycliffe and some events during the reign of James II.

This book makes enthralling reading, and its challenging message is timely for our own generation.

Casebound, 462 pages

THE TRUE CHRISTIAN

J. C. Ryle is famous for his writings on *Holiness,* his
expositions of the Gospels, and for his inspiring essays
on his spiritual ancestors in the Reformation and Puritan
era and the eighteenth-century evangelical Awakening.

The True Christian is a selection of his best sermons, by
no means so well known, but displaying all the qualities
which have caused his writings to be treasured by
Christians of all denominations.

From his early days in a country parish to his last years
as the first Bishop of Liverpool he was an earnest herald
of the gospel of Christ, both in sermons and tracts.

While this collection covers many subjects, it is
especially clear and forceful on the question of the true
and false Christian. Bishop Ryle's wisdom and
discernment are as necessary and helpful as they have
ever been.

Casebound, 312 pages